WRITING: ADVICE AND DEVICES

OTHER BOOKS BY THE SAME AUTHOR

BOOKS ON WRITING: WRITING: ADVICE AND DEVICES • WRITING NON-FICTION
PROFESSIONAL WRITING • WRITING MAGAZINE FICTION

BIOGRAPHIES: KIT CARSON • SITTING BULL • WARPATH • KING OF THE FUR
TRADERS • BIGFOOT WALLACE • JIM BRIDGER

HISTORIES: THE OLD SANTA FE TRAIL • NEW SOURCES OF INDIAN HISTORY
MOUNTAIN MEN • WARPATH AND COUNCIL FIRE

REGIONAL BOOKS: SHORT GRASS COUNTRY • THE MISSOURI

VERSE: FANDANGO, BALLADS OF THE OLD WEST

NOVELS: 'DOBE WALLS • REVOLT ON THE BORDER • THE WINE ROOM MURDER

JUVENILE: HAPPY HUNTING GROUNDS

Writing: Advice and Devices

BY WALTER S. CAMPBELL (STANLEY VESTAL), DIRECTOR,

COURSES IN PROFESSIONAL WRITING, UNIVERSITY OF OKLAHOMA

808
V583

DOUBLEDAY AND COMPANY, INC., GARDEN CITY, NEW YORK, 1950

24286

COPYRIGHT, 1950, BY WALTER STANLEY CAMPBELL
ALL RIGHTS RESERVED
PRINTED IN THE UNITED STATES
AT THE COUNTRY LIFE PRESS, GARDEN CITY, N. Y.

DEDICATED TO ANNE MALORY

ACKNOWLEDGMENTS

I wish to express my gratitude to the following for permission to quote from their publications:

To Longmans, Green and Company, Inc., for the passage quoted from *The Present Position of History*, by G. M. Trevelyan, New York, 1927.

To Mr. Christopher Morley for the couplet quoted.

To *The Writer*, for passages incorporated in this book, from two articles of mine, published in *The Writer*, November and December 1934.

To Doubleday and Company, Inc., for passages quoted from my *Writing Magazine Fiction*, New York, 1940.

To Miss Naomi John White for the short story "A Very Valuable Quality," published in *Collier's*, February 2, 1946.

To the *Reader's Digest* and the author for the article "A Formula for Presence of Mind," by Fulton Oursler, published in the *Reader's Digest*, January 1949.

To Allan Vaughan Elston for the novelette "Eva? Caroline?" published in the *Woman's Home Companion*, April 1949.

To Dr. Ian Stevenson for his article "Why Medicine Is Not a Science," published in *Harper's Magazine*, April 1949.

To Mr. W. L. Heath for the short short story "Bargain Hunters," published in *Collier's*, June 18, 1949.

To the editors of the *Southwest Review* for the story "Dakotah Courtship," by Stanley Vestal, from the January 1939 issue.

PREFACE

This book is a manual for writers—that is, for all who not merely wish to write, but wish to learn how to write.

We learn by doing. Every writer, whether he takes a course of training or not, must have certain experiences before he understands what he is about. Without a guide he may lose a dozen years in gaining these experiences; with guidance he may acquire them and the resulting understanding of his art within a few months.

This book is intended as such a guide. Its earlier chapters give advice on writing as an art, which Webster defines as "the general principles of any developed craft"; the later chapters are devoted to the craft of writing—the particular devices and specific techniques commonly used. Hence our title, *Writing: Advice and Devices.*

Professional writers as well as amateurs and beginners may hope to profit by submitting to the discipline offered here. Sound education, in John Milton's phrase, "fits a man to perform."

At one time I was badly in need of a secretary. An intelligent young woman applied for the job. She was the product of one of those progressive high schools. What projects she had taken up there I cannot tell, but they did not include anything useful.

She could not type because she could not spell. She could not file letters because she had never learned her ABCs. She could not keep books, for she had never heard of the multiplication table. She explained why she could not write a decent sentence or frame a paragraph—because at her school they had ignored grammar and "just studied English"! She knew no shorthand; she said that at school she had always been *too busy with her projects to learn anything.*

Occasionally I meet a would-be writer who reminds me of that would-be secretary.

For self-expression is not equivalent to creation. Spontaneity is the end, not the beginning, of training; we have to learn to walk before we can dance—and even then we have to learn the dance steps. A polo player is never any better than his horse, nor is an artist any better than his craftsmanship. We may all thank heaven that Shakespeare never attended a progressive school.

For there is abundant proof in his own works that he, like other masters in the art of writing, was thoroughly familiar with grammar, rhetoric, and all the literary devices known to ancient and modern authors. Like Shakespeare, those great writers knew what they were doing and could therefore do it well. We shall be wise to follow their example. Ignorance is not incurable. And groping is no hallmark of intelligence.

Fortunately, there is no secret about the craft of writing. All its magical effects are achieved with words on paper. And so every device a writer ever used lies there under your nose plainly set down in black and white.

All you need do is learn to *see* what is there, *what goes on there.* This book is intended to help you acquire that simple trick—of opening your eyes. It is one well worth acquiring.

The advice and devices offered you here have helped others who are now successful in almost every field of authorship. The method has been thoroughly tested and proven for years past in the Courses in Professional Writing offered at the University of Oklahoma, both in residence and by correspondence.

Here, if you are willing to *work,* you may be made aware of the actual problems faced by writers everywhere, you will be shown devices commonly used to solve such problems, and you will be given some practice in using them. Thus you may come to understand and to cope with literary problems, as thousands have done before you.

The methods used here are the fruits of experience on the part of the author. He has been an editor, free-lance writer, critic, reviewer, and long-time teacher of Professional Writing. He has published work including a variety of kinds, both of fiction and non-fiction: verse, novels, biographies, histories, articles, criticism, essays, reviews, novelettes, short stories, short short stories, scientific papers, juveniles, lectures, and feature stories. His work has appeared in quality magazines, little magazines, popular magazines, literary reviews, juvenile magazines, scientific journals, and newspapers. He has published twenty-one books, edited three, acted as scout and reader for publishers, and served on the editorial staff of a literary quarterly. This experience is placed at your service here.

The Table of Contents outlines our method; it is one of precept, example, and practice.

Walter S. Campbell

(STANLEY VESTAL)

THE UNIVERSITY OF OKLAHOMA
NORMAN, OKLAHOMA

CONTENTS

CHAPTER 1 THE QUALIFICATIONS OF A WRITER

The act of writing consists simply of arranging words in rows on paper. Anyone can do that because, as Mark Twain wittily remarks, the words are all in the dictionary.

But the art of writing is not so simple. For words have meanings, most of them several meanings, and these meanings vary and are qualified by the context or arrangement in which they are placed. Thus an almost infinite series of possible combinations offers itself to the writer.

It is this vast range of opportunity, this inexhaustible challenge, which makes writing so fascinating, a pursuit which can never grow stale. And since success in writing consists in taking advantage of this opportunity and in meeting this challenge, a primary qualification of a writer is a love of words and a delight in exploring and exhibiting their possibilities.

It is no accident that the greatest English writer used more words than any other and used them more variously. Shakespeare reveled in verbal feats. There is probably no rhetorical figure, scarcely any literary device, which he did not attempt. He frankly delighted in his dexterity and in the sheer fun of word-juggling. No wonder he outdid all others in mastery of our language.

Therefore, if you love words, if you delight in a witty phrase, a euphonious sentence, a precise pattern; if you enjoy the flow of nar-

1

rative, the sparkle of dialogue, the snap of a pun, the jingle of a couplet, the sonorous march of epic verse, or the subtle harmony of prose, you have the first qualification of a writer.

But a love for words and their ways is not enough; with that only you may remain a mere punster or phrasemonger all your days. You must also find pleasure in patterns, delight in design; you must acquire a love of longer units of expression—the paragraph, the sequence, and the whole composition—and so come not only to understand and appreciate but also to choose for yourself that pattern —whether story, novel, biography, article, novelette, play, or what not—through which your talent may best function. And to do this you must learn to recognize and use the many technical devices employed to make up such creative units of expression.

Of course you must have other qualifications:

> You must be interested in something about which you wish to write, otherwise you cannot hope to interest others.
>
> You must be a communicative person, eager to tell others about what interests you.
>
> You must be one who seeks a response from readers and who likes appreciation.
>
> *Above all, you must have an earnest desire to write well.*

Without such a desire to write well you can never succeed, simply because you will never take the trouble to do so. You will never develop that infinite capacity for taking pains which is called genius. But if you really love words and their possibilities, it is certain that, if you write, you will wish to write *well*.

And that is most important. For nobody can make you write, nor can you force yourself to write well by a mere act of will, by gritting your teeth and clenching your fists. A writer has no boss, no hours of work he must keep, and no pay at first; therefore, unless he really desires to write well, he will never buckle down and do it.

John Keats declared in one of his letters that fine writing, next to fine doing, is the top thing in this world. His idea was sound, for life must come before art, if only because experience provides the materials of literature. Yet his statement implies a fallacy.

In *Cleon* Robert Browning makes the old Greek poet complain:

> Because in my great epos I display
> How divers men young, strong, fair, wise, can act—
> Is this as though I acted?

2

Yet Browning knew well enough, as every writer knows, that writing *is* doing. Writing is work, and good writing is hard work.

When I first undertook to train writers I was under the illusion that talent would be rare and fortitude plentiful, but I found that talent was fairly common, while character was rare. Many who imagined they wished to be writers did not really wish to write. When they discovered that they could not sit down and dash off a masterpiece they went looking for something easier to do.

Such conduct still fills me with astonishment. It seems incredible that anyone capable of writing should refuse to do it, the rewards of a writer are so many and so great.

To begin with: prestige. As Dr. Samuel Johnson declared, "The chief glory of every people arises from its authors."

Yet the writer's greatest reward is not fame (a somewhat doubtful advantage), nor money (always a by-product in the arts), but rather the great satisfaction of trying to contribute something of value, of sharing experience, the joy of expressing oneself and having one's work appreciated.

Of course the writer enjoys other advantages—most of them quite beyond the reach of other men.

To begin with, people actually pay a writer for doing what he likes to do. Moreover, he is master of his own time, able to arrange his own schedule of working hours. Also, in his home town he is largely free from interference, since his pay for his writing comes from afar. He can live wherever he likes, since he can carry on his work wherever he can find a post office.

His travels, adventures, even his mishaps, may all be of service to the writer. Everything that happens to him brings fresh material, teaching him something more about human life and human nature. Even illness may benefit him, for ideas swarm and burgeon in an idle brain.

And more than any other, his art is democratic. Any qualified person may establish himself as a writer. He requires no license, no capital, no union card—only a piece of paper and a pencil. And if what he writes is readable, no one can prevent him from publishing.

There is no age at which a writer must retire. If readers like what he writes, he may go on publishing to the end of his days. What is even more cheering is the fact that his work will never grow stale, since his problems are never quite the same. Each piece he undertakes makes new demands upon his skill and imagination. Each project is a fresh expression of his own interests and his own tastes.

And surely never in the history of the world have writers faced such glorious opportunities. Never were there so many readers of English, so many markets for the written word, so many publishing houses, magazines, newspapers, radio stations, theaters, motion-picture and television companies. When a writer confronts a newsstand he knows that month after month every one of those serried magazines has to be filled with readable copy paid for in hard cash.

To share such glittering rewards and privileges you must have a real desire to write well, the character to make yourself work hard, and courage.

You must not be afraid to try—and keep on trying. Every writer will do well to remember the words of Cardinal Newman: "Egotism is true modesty . . . each of us can speak only for himself."

After all, what is there to be afraid of? There is no penalty for failure in literature. If what you write is unreadable, nobody will read it! It will soon be forgotten. Lawyers lose cases; doctors lose patients: why should a writer expect everything he does to be a success?

If you wish to write well, two things are required of you:

> *first,* that you learn to see and understand the problems every writer must solve, and
> *second,* that you learn how the best masters have solved such problems.

This book is intended to help you acquire these qualifications.

With them, you can lack only one thing: the ready mastery of technique which comes of *practice.*

Without this study and practice of technique your talent is smothered, useless. You must reject the amateurish notion that self-expression is creation. It is no accident that our greatest poets were also our greatest masters of technique. Without mastery of technique they could not have displayed their genius.

For as Ben Jonson said of Shakespeare, "A good poet's made as well as born."

WORK PROGRAM 1

1. Name the qualifications of a writer mentioned in the first chapter.
2. How many of these qualifications do you feel that you possess?
3. If you lack any of these qualifications, is there any reason why you cannot develop it?

CHAPTER 2   TWO PARTS OF TECHNIQUE

The technique of writing has two parts: that which takes place in the mind of the writer and that which is set down on paper. Because the first is not visible, some thoughtless people imagine that technique consists entirely of the choice and arrangement of words. Far from it.

By the part of technique which happens in the mind I do not refer to the motive which leads a man to write. Beginners often waste a good deal of time and nervous energy worrying about whether they have the right motive or not. The history of literature shows quite clearly that the motive which leads a man to sit down and write has nothing whatever to do with the quality and value of what he puts on paper. Good books have been written from almost every conceivable motive, good and bad, while many a dull and futile sermon has been penned from the very noblest motives.[1]

Good books have been written from such motives as spite, anger, vanity, rivalry, hatred, envy, malice, jealousy, lust for power, love of social position, the desire to influence somebody or win a woman's love, from patriotism, indignation, or mere love of prestige. You may agree with Dr. Samuel Johnson that the man who writes for anything but money is a blockhead, and may recall that he himself wrote *Rasselas,* one of our classics, in order to earn the money to pay for his mother's funeral.

---

[1] "Let us dismiss, as irrelevant to the poem, *per se,* the circumstance—or say the necessity—which, in the first place, gave rise to the intention of composing a poem that should suit at once the popular and the critical taste."—Edgar Allan Poe, *The Philosophy of Composition.*

5

You may therefore dismiss from your mind any concern as to the correctness of your motive for writing. For it is not why you act but *what* you do and *how* you do it that matters.

Moreover, since what you write will inevitably grow out of your own experience of living, the chances are that each piece you produce will be written from a different motive. In fact, whatever the motive that sets you writing may be, you will promptly forget all about it once you have really warmed to your work.

To begin with, then, you must have something to say.

By "having something to say" I mean that *you must have a very strong interest in your subject.*

Though rather fantastic, it is nevertheless theoretically possible that with a sufficient battery of mechanical brains or calculating machines, plenty of time, and several billion dollars you might take all the words in the unabridged dictionary and put them into every possible combination. The flood of books resulting would cover the earth, and most of them, of course, would be sheer nonsense. But somewhere in those innumerable volumes would be every novel, poem, or play that has ever been written or can ever be written in our language. In that vast library would lie all future literature and the lost works of writers dead and gone. That love letter you burned last week would be there, along with your unpaid bills—and your obituary. Every possible literary experiment would be on the record, along with your own—as yet unwritten—works.

But since this fantastic enterprise will never be undertaken—since words must be selected and arranged by men and not by machines— it follows that what goes on in the mind of a man before he selects and arranges his words is at least half the battle.

In fact, the quality of a writer's work holds an exact ratio to the quality or intensity of imagination which he puts into it. For unless the writer's imagination is intense, unless his interest in his subject is keen, it will not seem real or vivid to him, and therefore he can never make it seem so to his readers.

"Having something to say," therefore, means that you think about your subject with emotion, pleasant or unpleasant, as the case may be, and that you have thought of it and felt strongly about it, not just once, not just yesterday, but for a long time and in various moods and circumstances.

In this way your particular subject becomes enriched by rubbing up against other ideas, moods, and experiences in your mind until, like the hub of a wheel, though central, it is related to other matters on all sides. For the meaning of a thing lies in its relation to other things, and since a brand-new subject that has only just come to your notice cannot have rubbed up against all your other interests, you can hardly hope to treat it significantly. You have not had time to feel the relationships of your new subject to others.

Every fact is far more significant than anything you or I can possibly say about it.

For example, a landscape. When a farmer looks at it he sees it in terms of fields, crops, cattle; that is the meaning of the landscape to him. An architect sees it as offering building sites. A soldier automatically thinks of gun emplacements, fox holes, and cover for troops.

A real estate man thinks of that same landscape in terms of building lots and the appeal of the site to buyers. An artist sees the landscape as form and color, while a geologist is concerned with structures, outcrops, and horizons. Thus the same landscape means something different to everyone who beholds it. Only our Creator can see that landscape in all its rich significance, in all its many meanings, in all its relationships to the rest of the universe.

Thus the interests of each writer are narrow. But as writers we try to make up for the narrowness of our interest by its intensity. For if our interest is *intense*, so that our emotions and imagination are aroused, we are enabled to discover constantly deeper and more varied meanings. Thus the subject which we have at heart becomes rich and various, and we find we "have something to say."

This means that a writer cannot afford to be bored. For boredom means inattention to the life around us—and such lack of interest in life is suicide to the writer's imagination.

Without a well-developed active imagination we cannot write well, and it is too little considered that the imagination, like a muscle, can be developed by exercise. Unless we have imagination which enables us to put ourselves in the shoes of other people and so understand and sympathize with them, we cannot help or serve them, and our good will is futile. As Shelley pointed out, the development of the imagination is the great social function of the arts.

Without imagination to bring your subject matter to life, no amount of skill with words can make your story the story it might have been.

7

Once you have something of your own to say, something vital and *fully imagined,* you have only to find and arrange the words that will convey it to your reader. And this is the part of technique which we can most readily explain and illustrate.

From Aristotle down there have been many critics and authors who have discovered and pointed out methods, rhetorical figures, and literary devices which serve the writer's purpose. They tell us how to construct and style our work.

Other critics, impatient of such matters, insist that the reaction of the reader is the test of good writing. They demand of the poet that ecstasy which magically transports us out of the world of everyday life to some far more glorious region. The fragmentary essay *On the Sublime,*[2] attributed to Longinus, is the best early statement of this point of view.

As writers we cannot afford to neglect either of these demands. For without skillful handling of the language we cannot say what we have in mind, and without a lively imagination we shall have nothing worth saying. We require both means and ends.

Aristotle declared poetry a higher and more philosophical thing than history, because poetry expresses universal truth, whereas history merely states particular facts. History, according to Aristotle, shows merely what one man in particular circumstances actually did and suffered, while poetry shows us what generally happens to such a man. And of course it is the general truth or law we need for understanding and guidance in life.

But I fear that modern historians will no longer patiently accept the position Aristotle gave them on his lower shelf. They argue that in his day facilities for writing history were in their infancy—that the vast array of modern libraries, catalogues, reference works, records, and files did not then exist. Historians, however brilliant, were then few, and few of them lived long enough to have coped with modern facilities, even if these had then existed.

In fact, no comprehensive view of world history was possible to the ancients; they turned to the poets for truth simply because adequate materials for general history were not at hand. A modern scholar's life expectancy may encourage him to hope that he may see enough and comprehend enough to arrive at truths as universal as those offered by the poets. . . .

[2]*De Sublimitate.*

8

At any rate, there is no doubt that the modern historian is no mere chronicler, memoirist, or reporter. He, too, employs imagination.

George M. Trevelyan has well stated the modern historian's view of this matter: "The appeal of History to us all is in the last analysis poetic. But the poetry of History does not consist of imagination roaming at large, but of imagination pursuing the fact and fastening upon it. That which compels the historian to 'scorn delights and live laborious days' is the ardour of his own curiosity to know what really happened long ago in that land of mystery which we call the past. To peer into that magic mirror and see fresh figures there every day is a burning desire that consumes and satisfies him all his life, that carries him each morning, eager as a lover, to the library and muniment room. It haunts him like a passion of almost terrible potency, because it is poetic. The dead were and are not. Their place knows them no more and is ours today. Yet they were once as real as we, and we shall tomorrow be shadows like them. In men's first astonishment over that unchanging mystery lay the origins of poetry, philosophy, and religion. From it, too, is derived in more modern times this peculiar call of the spirit, the type of intellectual curiosity that we name the historical sense. Unlike most forms of imaginative life it cannot be satisfied save by facts. In the realm of History, the moment we have reason to think that we are being given fiction instead of fact, be the fiction ever so brilliant, our interest collapses like a pricked balloon. To hold our interest you must tell us something we believe to be true about the men who once walked the earth. It is the fact about the past that is poetic; just because it really happened, it gathers round it all the inscrutable mystery of life and death and time. Let the science and research of the historian find the fact, and let his imagination and art make clear its significance."[3]

Let it be clear then that *every* writer must cultivate, develop, and use his imagination, whether he writes poetry or history, fiction or non-fiction. . . .

Dr. Samuel Johnson has given a description (in his *Lives of the Poets*) of his friend Savage, a description which,[4] as Raleigh says,

[3]"The Present Position of History" in *The Modern Historian*, edited by Professor Charles H. Williams of the University of London (Thomas Nelson and Sons, 1938), p. 72. Quoted by permission of Longmans, Green and Company, Inc.

[4]Walter Raleigh, *Shakespeare* (English Men of Letters Series, the Macmillan Company, London, 1907), pp. 11–12.

9

applies as well to Shakespeare: "His mind was in an uncommon degree vigorous and active. His judgment was accurate, his apprehension quick, and his memory so tenacious, that he was frequently observed to know what he had learned from others, in a short time, better than those by whom he was informed; and could frequently recollect incidents, with all their combination of circumstances, which few would have regarded at the present time, but which the quickness of his apprehension impressed upon him. He had the art of escaping from his own reflections, and accommodating himself to every new scene. To this quality is to be imputed the extent of his knowledge, compared with the small time which he spent in visible endeavours to acquire it. He mingled in cursory conversation with the same steadiness of attention as others apply to a lecture; and amidst the appearance of thoughtless gaiety lost no new idea that was started, nor any hint that could be improved. He had therefore made in coffee-houses the same proficiency as others in their closets; and it is remarkable, that the writings of a man of little education and little reading have an air of learning scarcely to be found in any other performances."

It is just so that you may cultivate your imagination and knowledge of men and the world—by exercising it on everything that passes around you. That is, by being thoroughly *alive*.

The happy man—and the successful writer—is he whose creative power is active, who knows how to apply his imagination, to get ideas. He may sit down to write because he has to eat, but he writes because creation is a joy forever, because it is fun. Often he enjoys his writing most when it is done under pressure.

Thank heaven, then, for *any* pressure which makes you creative. For you must have drive in you to write well, and if the drive is already provided by external forces, that makes the writing all the easier.

How can you get ideas? There are certain questions which every newshawk asks himself when on a story: What? Who? When? Where? Why? How?

Answer those, and you will have six ideas you can use.

Again, in Shakespeare's day, writers had a series of queries which they often used, called Topics of Invention. Shakespeare himself used these and indeed frequently refers to them in his sonnets and plays; they enabled him to find matter for composition.

Ben Jonson lists these topics in his *Cynthia's Revels:*

10

A thing done.
Who did it?
With what was it done?
Where was it done?
When was it done?
For what cause was it done?
What followed upon the doing of it?
Who would have done it better?

You will not have many ideas in an ivory tower. Do not hide from life, get out among things and men, and you will find them. Daydreaming will not do it. Worry will not do it. You must drive and guide your imagination.

That is, you must *search* for the ideas you want, and when you get them, *shape* them. That is, find truth, find facts, find reality firsthand; then work these over into something you can use. Take it to pieces and put it together again.

Do not just read, listen to the radio, watch a movie or a ball game. Take part in real life, be interested—and then do something about it.

Get to work. Begin! And then keep going.

There is no escaping the fact that words not only have explicit and recognized meanings to be found in the dictionary—that is to say, denotations; words also have connotations, suggestive significances, implications, emotional overtones, so that no one can use words without suggesting some kind of feeling or arousing some degree of imagination, however slight.

Thus the dictionary gives the denotation of the word "mother" as "female parent." But who ever thought of his mother in any such terms? When he utters the word "mother," it connotes far more.

Dryden said of Shakespeare, "When he describes anything, you more than see it, you feel it too."

And *every* writer, if he is to be effective, must write imaginatively. He must convey what he feels as well as what he knows.

And this is done through language—the choice and arrangement of words.

WORK PROGRAM 2

1. Why must a successful writer have a strong interest in his subject?
2. What are the two parts or steps of technique?
3. How may you develop your imagination?
4. Define (a) denotation, (b) connotation.

5. List twenty common words, and write after each one (a) its denotation and (b) the connotation which it has for you. *E.g.*, home (a) denotation—habitul abode; (b) connotation—safety, comfort.

CHAPTER 3 A WORLD OF WORDS

In one of his critical papers John Dryden remarks, "The employment of a poet is like that of a curious gunsmith, or watchmaker: the iron or silver is not his own; but they are the least part of that which gives the value: the price lies wholly in the workmanship." We who write in the English language are fortunate; it offers unequaled opportunities for curious workmanship.

By a poet, of course, Dryden meant any creative writer, whether in fiction or non-fiction. So did Dante—and after him Cervantes— when they declared that a poet must write in the language learned at his mother's knee. And others have declared that no man can write poetry—that is to say, write creatively—in a foreign tongue. The reason given is that only one acquainted with the language from childhood can possibly be aware of all the connotations of his words.

No language offers greater opportunities to writers than English. In the first place, it comprises far more words than any other. English-speaking people have ever been quick to borrow words from other tongues, and this habit has vastly enriched our vocabulary. He who writes in English has a wide choice of words.

Our habit of borrowing words from other languages also gives English a greater variety of sounds, single and in combination. It is hardly surprising, therefore, that our literature excels in poetry, where word music plays so great a part.

At the end of the Middle Ages our ancestors dropped the endings from a multitude of English words. This change has brought it about that an English word may begin or end in any vowel or consonant in the alphabet. This gives our speech incomparable variety. If, then, we fail as writers, it will not be for lack of words or sound effects.

The dropping of endings (by destroying those indications of the syntactical relations between words) also imposed a stricter word order on our speech, thus providing certain definite patterns which writers must follow.

It is obviously easier to follow a pattern already existing than to create one from scratch. This can be demonstrated by considering how many thousand persons have written correct rhymed verse, in which the length of the line, the beat of the accent, and the form of the stanza are already laid down. By comparison there are few poets who excel in blank verse, even though the length of the line and the beat of the accent are predetermined, simply because the absence of rhyme immediately betrays the least failure in the music of the verse, just as the absence of traps in an orchestra betrays incompetent musicians.

But, if blank verse be difficult, consider the appalling problem of the poet who attempts free verse and so has to create his whole pattern from beginning to end. No wonder really good poems in free verse are so rare!

We may be thankful for the word order required by our speech, both in prose and verse.

The two great glories of the English-speaking peoples are their liberty and their literature, and these have interacted to the great advantage of both. It is no accident that our literature excels in the essay and lyric poetry—the frank expression of personal feeling—and in portraiture of individual characters. We find more living characters in Shakespeare's works alone than in the entire literature of any other people, and our lyric poets have excelled all others in modern times.

The reason is plain. Only a free man dares express himself freely in his writing; and only under a free government do men dare to be eccentric and individual enough to provide authors with a wide range of characters to portray.

This liberty of ours has also had a strong effect upon the freedom with which we use our common speech. Even in France, one of the more democratic countries, the control of the French Academy over the teaching of French in the schools and its great influence upon authors and critics have somewhat discouraged the free and easy experimentation characteristic of English-speaking countries—both among writers and among the people generally. . . .

Follow the methods of the masters. And of these masters prefer the best. Whenever you are in doubt as to what to do in your writing, you may ask yourself, "What did Shakespeare do?"

In this matter of vocabulary and freedom of speech we find that he not only used more words than any other poet in our language, but employed them more variously, consistently using every part of speech to do the work of every other part of speech.[1]

Freedom of speech means far more than political liberty to say what one likes. For an author, freedom of speech means freedom to use the language in every possible effective way. A man who writes English may say what he likes in any way he likes, provided he makes sense—or good nonsense! And this is both a cause and an effect of our long tradition of personal liberty.

There was a time, before philology became a science, when the theory was held that a language is not a growing thing, but can be standardized, established, and fixed—that it should be fixed. It was believed that every civilized language must have a polite usage forever distinct from common usage, that language should be exclusive rather than comprehensive.

Fortunately this mistaken theory has been exploded by modern philology, and today whatever helpful usage or useful word (however strange) comes along we therefore, as a stranger, give it welcome. Since the time of Shakespeare our writers have never enjoyed such linguistic freedom as now, such a world of words.

This is a matter for profound congratulation, a matter for pride, as it was in Elizabethan times, when Richard Carew in his *The Excellency of the English Tongue* declared: "The copiousness of our language, appeareth in the diversity of our dialects; for we have court, and we have country English, we have Northern and Southern, gross and ordinary, which differ each from other, not only in the terminations, but also in many words, terms, and phrases, and express the same things in divers sorts, yet all right English alike."

Again he says: "The *Italian* is pleasant but without sinews, as too stilly fleeting water; the *French* delicate but over nice, as a woman scarce daring to open her lips for fear of marring her countenance; the *Spanish* majestical, but fulsome, running too much on the o, and terrible like the devil in a play; the *Dutch* manlike, but withal very harsh, as one ready at every word to pick a quarrel. Now we in borrowing from them give the strength of consonants to the *Italian*, the full sound of words to the *French*, the variety of terminations to

[1] E. A. Abbot, *Shakespearian Grammar*, London, 1909.

14

the *Spanish*, and the mollifying of more vowels to the *Dutch;* and so, like bees, gather the honey of their good properties and leave the dregs to themselves. And thus, when substantialness combineth with delightfulness, fullness with fineness, seemliness with portliness, and courrantness with staidness, how can the language which consisteth of all these sound other than most full of sweetness?

"Again, the long words that we borrow, being intermingled with the short of our own store, make up a perfect harmony, by culling from out which mixture (with judgement) you may frame your speech according to the matter you must work on, majestical, pleasant, delicate, or manly, more or less, in what sort you please. Add hereunto, that whatsoever grace any other language carrieth, in verse or prose, in tropes or metaphors, in echoes or agnominations, they may all be lively and exactly represented in ours."

Another characteristic of English which has had a powerful effect in maintaining our freedom and advancing our literature is its stress accent. Of course, by a stress accent we mean that a speaker emits more breath when uttering an accented syllable than he emits when uttering an unaccented one. If there are several unaccented syllables in a word, each of them gets so little breath that, as time passes, speakers slur, diminish, and finally drop one or more of the unaccented syllables. Thus, sooner or later the unaccented syllables are no longer pronounced and the word is shortened. And naturally those words most commonly used are first to suffer this abbreviation. This means that the oldest and commonest words in the language are usually the shortest. Many of them have only one or two syllables. Such words make up the vocabulary which we call Plain English.

It is obvious that the words most commonly used—the words learned at Mother's knee—are also those most closely associated with the experience and life of the people. These are the words most saturated with emotion, warm with connotations—just the words a writer who wishes to produce a powerful emotional effect would choose.

And so it comes about that, in our literature, the most powerful passages are usually written in our simplest and commonest words, the vocabulary of Everyman. This fact not only makes for a more democratic culture. It also provides the fortunate author with a far larger public than he would be likely to find among the readers of some other literatures.

Yet at the same time we have any number of long words suited to the expression of the most intricate and elaborate matters. Every one of those words—long or short, charged with emotion or cold as mathematics—stands ready to serve your turn.

WORK PROGRAM 3

1. List the advantages offered to the writer by the English language.
2. How have the following characteristics affected the English language?

   a. stress accent
   b. freedom
   c. fixed word order

3. Here follow a list of dictionaries. Record the titles of any (whether on this list or not) which (a) you own or to which (b) you have access.

   The Oxford English Dictionary (13 vols.).
   The Concise Oxford English Dictionary (1 vol.).
   Roget's Thesaurus. Pocket Books, Inc., New York, 1946.
   A Dictionary of Modern English Usage, by H. W. Fowler. Oxford University Press.
   A Dictionary of Slang and Unconventional English, by Eric Partridge. The Macmillan Co.
   A Dictionary of Modern American Usage, by H. W. Horwill. Oxford University Press, 1935.
   The American College Dictionary. Harper & Brothers, New York, 1947.
   Webster's New International Dictionary (Unabridged). G. & C. Merriam Co., Springfield, Massachusetts.
   Words: The New Dictionary. Grosset & Dunlap, New York, 1947.

CHAPTER 4   THREE GUIDING PRINCIPLES

It is scarcely surprising that, with such an arsenal of words and the freedom which English-speaking people have enjoyed so long, literature in our language should provide so many masterpieces from which you can learn the art of writing.

And now for some guiding principles.

The great experiences of life are shared experiences. The four greatest experiences of human life—love, war, religion, and art—are all of this kind. In each a man gives himself freely and does his best and so may hope for appreciation. As Robert Louis Stevenson remarked, there must always be two to a satisfactory kiss. In war the soldier exercises his valor and combative instincts and finds himself to that degree a hero in the eyes of those he defends. And so with the others. In all of them selfishness is always a mistake.

Certainly in writing, when a man thinks of himself first, he blunders and bungles his work. People talk about "prostituting one's art" by writing for money, but the real prostitution of an artist or writer is a different thing. It consists in the lack of an artistic conscience, in the failure to give one's best, in the sparing of oneself in the effort to please one's reader. Such an attitude, such a failure to follow through, invariably shows in the finished—or rather unfinished —work.

Our first principle, then, must be to avoid this fault, and this means first of all that you must feel a genuine enthusiasm for your project. If you have that and give it rein, you will have obeyed the first law, which is: *Love your subject.*

So far so good. The second law is not unlike the first: *Love your reader.*

This also requires imagination, an ability to put yourself in the shoes of the reader you have chosen. If you understand his thoughts and feelings, then you can say what you have to say in a way that he can understand and enjoy.

An illustration may be helpful here. Among your correspondents, if you are fortunate, there is at least one to whose letters you look forward with keen anticipation. He knows just how to appeal to you, what gossip to relate, what news to include, and how to phrase and arrange his message so as to give you most satisfaction.

Your correspondent can do this because he knows you well, what you like, what you had rather not hear, and the style to which you are accustomed. No wonder you look forward to that correspondent's letters.

On the other hand, you get letters from some dull or selfish fellow who takes no thought for your comfort or pleasure but only unloads whatever happens to be uppermost in his own mind in the way most convenient for himself. You do not look forward to his letters. In fact, you had rather not get them. That relationship is a chore and a bore.

It is just so with writers and readers.

Did you ever try to write a letter to Nobody? I am afraid such an assignment would stymie Shakespeare himself. With no reader in mind, you would not know what to say or how to say it.

Therefore, when you write, you must write for Somebody, a person or type of person whom you know well, whose prejudices, opinions, and attitude toward life are familiar to you.

When you know your reader, you can learn how to reach him, what to say to him, and how to say it.

If, then, you know and love your subject so that your imagination is aroused, you can always create something worth saying. But you must also know and love your reader if you ever expect to take the pains to please him.

Of course every writer loves the reader who appreciates what he has written. So, since you are going to love your reader sooner or later, I suggest that you begin at once.

Moreover, by loving your subject and loving your reader you get emotion into your work, and without this emotion you can never succeed either in fiction or non-fiction, for the reader cannot be deceived in such matters. You may persuade a reader that the moon is made of green cheese, for you can sometimes deceive him in matters of fact. But you can never fool him with regard to your feeling for your subject and your feeling toward him.

Therefore, you should do your best to please your reader. By pleasing your reader I do *not* mean that you should throw overboard your own convictions or falsify your own presentation. Quite the contrary. I mean that you should wish earnestly to *share* with him your own enthusiasm for your subject, wish earnestly to present it in such a way and in such terms as will make him enjoy it as you do.

In non-fiction, where as a rule you deal with facts more than with people, you will have to take particular pains that your enthusiasm for your subject and your friendly feeling toward your reader get into your style, so that every sentence is convincing evidence of your attitude. In a word, you must combine fact with strong emotion.

And so it is in fiction, the subject of which is human relations. Here your task is perhaps somewhat easier because there are people in your story and the reader likes to be with people. It is for this reason that non-fiction in our time goes in so heavily for fictional technique; since, of course, fictional technique simply means that people and their relationships are brought in.

There are two great sources of interest in literature: the familiar and the strange.

That subject will therefore be the best subject which provides the maximum of both. Since we are human beings ourselves, it is obvious that there will be more of the familiar in human beings than in any other subject. We cannot know why a rabbit runs from a dog. We can only assume that, if the rabbit were human, his motive must be fear. But we have no assurance of that fact because we are not rabbits and do not know how rabbits think or feel.

The only way we can make the average reader take the slightest interest in a rabbit is to put into the rabbit's nervous system human motives and reactions. And this, of course, is nature faking.

I do not mean to imply that such stories are necessarily bad or improper. Of course such stories have their place. They show, in effect, people masquerading as animals. And any story about people, however you disguise them, can be a good story.

You sometimes hear people sneer at certain types of reading as "escape literature." But the nature of "escape" is not always clearly understood. When a reader finds himself alone in some dull spot waiting for a train or snowbound in his room, he picks up a book and, as they say, "escapes." But actually the reader is not escaping *from* life, but escaping *into* a more abundant life. A man does not die when he begins to read, and what he reads may present him with more life than he can find without it. If it does not, he is foolish to go on reading. And in all likelihood he is the best judge of what, for him, is the more abundant life.

A man may, in fact, prefer to read a good book even in the company of other people for a very good reason: namely, that he can never get inside the minds of living people, nor can he ever be quite sure he shares or understands their thoughts and feelings. Even your best friend will sometimes do or say something which astounds you.

But in a good novel or short story the reader is under the illusion —created by the author—of getting into the minds and hearts of the characters, or at least one of them, and thus sometimes may live a richer life than he can even among real people whom he knows well.

19

This is the great trade secret of the fiction writer: that he knows how to create this illusion and take his reader into the minds and hearts of his imaginary creatures, the characters in his book or story.

This handling of viewpoint (VP) is a matter too little considered by beginning writers of fiction. It is very important, if you wish to please your reader. In fact, misuse of viewpoint often makes publication impossible.

I reiterate: every story is *Somebody's* story—it is not just *a* story. Of course the reader reads in order to share the emotion of the character, to be moved and stirred; as one of them put it, "I want to suffer intelligently." Obviously, the reader cannot so "suffer," sharing the emotions of the character, unless the story is so told that the reader gets into that character's mind and heart and feels the same emotions as the character. In fact, the chief reason why people read fiction and find fictional characters so fascinating is that the writer takes the reader into the mind and heart of his character and so gives the reader an experience which he cannot have with people in real life. If you do *not* take your reader into the mind and heart of your character, you are not writing fiction at all. What is more, nobody will read what you write.

Of course whenever anything happens to two or three people, that story *might* be told as any one of them sees, feels, and knows it. But in every case, some *one* of the characters feels the experience more deeply than the others, and since the writer wishes to interest and excite the reader as much as he can, the wise writer naturally chooses the character who suffers most for his viewpoint character. He takes the reader into the mind and heart of that character and shows the story as from the point of view of the "chief sufferer."

Remember, a story is *not* the facts—it is how someone *feels* those facts. A story is not motion, but emotion; the character's thoughts and feelings make the story, and the facts are mentioned *only* to make the reader believe in those thoughts and feelings. Facts are all very well for history or science, but they count for very little in fiction; they are just the coins which represent the real, *emotional* values. Every reader hates facts, unless these are saturated with the character's emotions.

You will have to decide which of your characters is the chief sufferer. It may be that a man who falls down the well and hits his head on the side of it as he falls is knocked out and does not suffer at all; his wife, looking on unhurt, may go through emotional torment over the accident. In that case, she would be the chief sufferer. In short, the suffering we refer to is not physical breakage but *emotional agony*. Bear this firmly in mind. Always choose that character for your viewpoint character who has to endure the most emotional suffering.

Once you have chosen a viewpoint, stick to it. If your story is to be seen through the feelings and thoughts of one character, then you must *not*, must *never*, leave that character's mind to tell what some other character is thinking or feeling. Of course you can indicate these through action, speech, and by other means, so that the reader gets them. *But you must not mention anything which your viewpoint character does not see, sense, know, or feel emotionally.* The easiest way to be sure of this is to write the story in the first person, as if the chief sufferer (the viewpoint character) were telling it to the reader. Afterward you can put it in the third person, if that seems advisable.

After you have learned how to stay in one character's mind and heart you will learn how to shift into the viewpoint of another character on the rare occasions when this is necessary. But until you know when you *are* in viewpoint, *how* can you know when you have shifted it? You cannot. Remember, every time you shift the viewpoint from one character to another you lose all the emotion you have built up in the first viewpoint. Unless you take care, this will ruin your story.

Thus, three great principles of writing successfully are: (1) know and love your subject; (2) know and love your reader; and (3) take the reader into the mind and heart of the character. These three principles, faithfully followed, will solve most of your problems of technique.

WORK PROGRAM 4

1. Name three great principles of writing mentioned in the preceding chapter.
2. What will be your advantage if you know and love your subject?
3. What will be your advantage if you know and love your reader?
4. What advantage will you reap if you take your reader into the heart and mind of your character?

PART *2* PATTERNS

CHAPTER 5   THE METHODS OF THE MASTERS

In an earlier chapter we discovered that the motive which leads you to sit down and write has nothing to do with the quality of the work you produce. But this does not mean that the attitude you take toward your work while doing it is unimportant. Therefore, we had best now consider the characteristic approach of the great master writers.

They all wrote in different styles, on different subjects, and for different publics; but we find on examination that there are certain attitudes and procedures characteristic of these masters which we shall do well to emulate. For convenience we may choose Shakespeare as the archetype.

To begin with, he was interested in people—and people of all kinds. Dr. Samuel Johnson declares in his Preface to Shakespeare: "This therefore is the praise of *Shakespeare*, that his drama is the mirrour of life; that he who has mazed his imagination, in following the phantoms which other writers raise up before him, may here be cured of his delirious extasies, by reading human sentiments in human language, by scenes from which a hermit may estimate the transactions of the world, and a confessor predict the progress of the passions."

It is obvious that in order to acquire such an understanding of people an author must be a man of wide sympathies, a man who delights in social contacts. No man who put people on guard when he appeared could possibly have observed humanity in all its rich variety as he did. You may be sure that when he walked down the street the old folks went on gossiping, the young folks went on making love, the children went on playing. They saw that it was only Master Shakespeare passing by: nobody was shy or ashamed. They felt even on brief acquaintance that he liked them, that he was no stern and critical superior being looking down his nose at them. They sensed his zest for life.

He turned as naturally toward happiness and joy as a sunflower turns to the sun. He looked outward and liked what he saw. Indeed his close friend Ben Jonson describes him as "honest, and of an open and free nature," and repeatedly he was described by his contemporaries as "the gentle Shakespeare."

The late Sir Walter Raleigh remarked, "Everyone was more himself for being in the company of Shakespeare." He added, "Shakespeare's villains and evil characters are all self-absorbed and miserable and retrospective . . . Jealousy, born of deprivation is a passion as common as mud; to Shakespeare's thinking it is the core of all uttermost evil."[1]

It was this universal sympathy that made him able to make friends with, and so portray, his rogues and vagabonds, who would never have revealed themselves to a man of less sunny and genial a nature. He suffered fools gladly; his fools are among the most lifelike of his characters.

Such a temperament enabled him to understand and experience almost the whole range of human motivation.

Yet Shakespeare saw life steadily and saw it whole. He knew the worst as well as the best, yet kept his balance. He was free from that inverted idealism which vitiates some of the writing of our time —that stupid, partial view of life which mistakes sentimentality, crudity, and toughness for honesty and understanding.

Like Dante, who began his *Divine Comedy* in hell, Shakespeare was never content to stop there. Sir Gilbert Murray has said of Homer: "Is it not a marvel of sympathetic imagination which makes us feel with the flying Hector, the cruel Achilles, the adulterous Helen, without for an instant losing hold of the ideals of courage, mercifulness, and chastity?"

The ideal here so well stated is just as true of Shakespeare as of other great masters.

[1]*Shakespeare,* pp. 14–15.

23

He lived like other people of his time: went to school, fell in love, married, raised a family, made a fortune, was acquainted with men in all walks of life, acquired—not without a struggle—the status of a gentleman, and at last retired to his small home town, bought the largest house there, and set himself up as the local boy who had made good.

We also find that Shakespeare, like most other master writers, was not only a better writer than his competitors, but was more prolific. The notion that facility—that is, the knowledge of what to do next and the ability to do it quickly—is an undesirable quality for a writer simply will not hold water when confronted with the history of literature. Practice makes perfect. Moreover, since even Shakespeare's work was uneven, it is clear that with all writers only a portion of their work can possibly be their best work. If, therefore, we are to have any great quantity of "best," it is obvious that we, too, must produce a good deal.

We also find that Shakespeare pleased both the critics and the public of his time. As a young man he deliberately set out to please men of taste and critical training. His early poems, *Venus and Adonis, The Rape of Lucrece,* and the *Sonnets,* were not addressed to Tom, Dick, and Harry, but were definitely and artfully created to please a critical audience. Those poems show that he took most exacting pains to perfect his technique and please that audience.

But he was not content with that. He also pleased the public and filled the pit of his theater with groundlings, many of them illiterate and ignorant spectators, who flocked to his plays no less eagerly than the gallants who sat in the rooms or on stools upon his stage.

This is a great merit in an author, not merely because he may receive a greater reward by appealing to a large public, but because the more different kinds of people he pleases, the richer his work necessarily becomes. The reader who strives only to please a clique may be compelled to do so because of lack of talent or skill, but he is not thereby a better writer. Nothing was ever so well written that only a few could appreciate it. On the contrary, the best works are known to millions. A great master will reach the heart as well as the head of his public.

It is noteworthy also that Shakespeare competed with his rival poets and playwrights. He was thoroughly professional and adapted his work to the taste of his contemporaries, perfecting and completing what his rivals only groped for.

Thus when John Lyly was writing for the court delicate comedies in rhymed verse with only a slight love interest, Shakespeare perceived at once that the love interest should be the principal interest in such comedies and straightway outdid Lyly with his own plays of that type. Ever since, the theater has followed his lead in this matter.

Again, when Christopher Marlowe charmed London with his ranting heroes and his "mighty line," Shakespeare promptly adopted the blank verse and tragedy which Marlowe had naturalized in England, and outdid Marlowe with his *Richard III*.

Whatever his rivals made popular he took up, surpassing them, not merely with superior genius, but also superior technique. Some of them were bitter enough about it, and Greene described him as "an upstart crow beautified with our feathers."

Again we find that Shakespeare was never content with his work, as is shown in various editions and revisions he made in *Hamlet* and certain other plays. Though, like other playwrights, he necessarily used again and again similar characters and similar scenes, he steadily perfected his skill in presenting these as time passed.[2]

The same is true of Chaucer. He began by imitating the French poets, then, by the study of the Italians, learned the true structure of a story and wrote our first great English romance, *Troilus and Criseyde,* afterward going even beyond this into his English period and the rich and native expression of the *Canterbury Tales*. And so with many another great writer.

We know, too, that Shakespeare was never content to go it blind and write by guess. Though "his mind and hand went together," he was thoroughly familiar with the art of rhetoric as taught in the schools of his time and frequently referred to figures of speech and literary devices even as he used them.[3]

He was much praised for being the poet of Nature. But Ben Jonson, who consorted with him in the London taverns, knew better and declared:

> Thy Art,
> My gentle Shakespeare, must enjoy a part.

[2]George Pierce Baker, *The Development of Shakespeare as a Dramatic Artist,* New York, 1907.

[3]Sister Miriam Joseph, C.S.C., *Shakespeare's Use of the Arts of Language,* New York, 1947.

24286

However "copious and happy" his writing was, Shakespeare understood the art that conceals art so highly recommended by Horace.

It is characteristic also of great masters that they generally do their best. Sometimes Shakespeare wrote passages which were dull, flat, and insipid because the particular subject matter offered little opportunity for the expression of his talent. But John Dryden declared: "He is always great when some great occasion is presented to him; no man can say he ever had a fit subject for his wit, and did not then raise himself . . . high above the rest of poets."

Such procedures and approaches are characteristic of the great masters. You and I may well consider them and strive to emulate them in so far as our gifts and character permit.

For it is not our task to imitate the works of great writers of the past; they wrote for readers now dead and gone. Few of us would care to write tragedies in blank verse for the contemporary public. And indeed the imitation of the work of great writers is a bookish, "literary," secondhand, and uncreative enterprise. No, it is not their *works* that we should imitate, but their *methods* which we must follow.

These methods, of course, are not confined to such general principles and procedures as I have just described. They include a great range of particular and detailed devices and rhetorical figures which are the units of literary expression. Each of these small units is a step onward in the whole work, a tool useful for some small purpose necessary to the whole.

We must study these small tangible techniques, these devices and figures of rhetoric, and learn how to use them, discover what they are good for, until we, too, may hope to apply the great principles intelligently and so become not only creative artists but creative craftsmen.

Whatever success you achieve will rest not merely upon intangibles, not merely upon imagination, not merely upon your conception of the whole work, but also upon your ability to work out each detail and use each tool in the proper way at the proper time to carry the whole forward.

For the over-all pattern consists of parts arranged in an effective series. If, then, you have all the necessary parts, all properly constructed and proportioned and all arranged in the right order, you have achieved the whole.

And now let us consider the over-all pattern, its parts, propor-
tions, and arrangement.

WORK PROGRAM 5

1. What is the difference between imitating the works of a writer and following his methods?
2. Enumerate the methods of the master writers discussed in the preceding chapter.
3. In your own writing how many of these methods have you followed in the past?

CHAPTER 6   THE OVER-ALL PATTERN

Every well-written piece has an over-all pattern which, as Aristotle tells us, must have a Beginning, a Middle, and an End. Each of these three portions of the over-all pattern should have a certain quality and arouse a certain kind of interest. Each also has its own specific problems.

1. The Beginning must be *clear* and should arouse *curiosity* in the reader.

2. The Middle should be *coherent* and should arouse *suspense* in the reader.

3. The End must be *brief* and inspire the reader with *satisfaction.*

If the Beginning is not clear, the reader will be puzzled, since he is turning from other thoughts and other matters to what you have to say, and unless you arouse curiosity in him at the start he will never follow through and read the rest of your piece.

The Middle must be coherent so that each item in it follows from and leads to another. Otherwise there can be no feeling of continuity and no suspense.

The End must be brief, because by the time the reader reaches the beginning of the End he already foresees it.

The End must give him satisfaction, or he will feel that he has made a mistake in reading what you have written.

27

Since literature is an art which exists in time, since one word or phrase follows another into the reader's mind, continuity of thought or feeling is of the utmost importance. Without continuity you lose your reader. And the reader who has once been disappointed by an author is usually reluctant to read anything else by him.

If this be true, it is obvious that the writer must know what the End is to be before he begins. Otherwise his Beginning will not point to the End, nor his Middle lead to it.[1]

Thus the problem of the over-all pattern is essentially a problem of *structure*. We must decide just what we wish to do, do that, and then stop.

Of course, as all critics agree, you never begin your story or article at the beginning or, as Horace puts it, "from the egg," but rather with the full-grown rooster about to be attacked in the cockpit; you always begin in the midst of things, preferably as near the End as may be.

Perhaps you will have to go back, after you are sure the reader is thoroughly interested in your story or article, and give him the story behind the story, the events leading up to your first situation in so far as they are necessary to his understanding of that. But in any case, you begin with the chicken, not the egg.

Otherwise your structure suffers and you will write like the farmer who built his house haphazardly and *then* sent to town for an "architect to put the architecture on it"!

The architecture of your piece is fundamental. Without that planned in advance, you cannot be said to have written at all. What you produce without a plan in mind is merely the raw material of your story. In planning your piece you have to consider three things:

1. What is my subject?
2. Who is my reader?
3. What effect do I wish to produce upon that reader—what mood, what kind of pleasure, what conviction, and to what result?

Thus you may wish to tell a fairy story to a child. Your subject is the adventures of Jack with his beanstalk. Your reader is a five-

[1] "Nothing is more clear than that every plot, worth the name, must be elaborated to its *denouement* before anything be attempted with the pen. It is only with the *denouement* constantly in view that we can give a plot its indispensable air of consequence, or causation, by making the incidents, and especially the tone of all points, tend to the development of the intention."—Edgar Allan Poe, *The Philosophy of Composition.*

28

year-old and you strive to produce the effect of wonder, suspense, and eventual satisfaction.

Again you may have a reader whom you wish to make laugh, or weep, or accept some idea new to him. In each case you will have to plan your piece accordingly.

The first thing to ask yourself is: "How long should my story or article be?" This will be determined not merely by what you have to say and by the patience of your reader but also by the space required to present effectively what you have to say—to produce the effect you desire upon the reader. Thus there are poems which are effective only if read at one sitting. Again there are books like the *Iliad* or the Bible of which the general drift is already familiar to the reader and of which he will endure at one time only the reading of a single chapter or passage.

Your choice of a length may be influenced also by your desire to have your piece published, with the knowledge that the magazine at which you aim has certain limits of length for a piece of the kind you are planning.

Having determined the approximate length of your piece, you may then consider how you may hope to get it read. Since language is intended for communication, there seems little point in writing without a reader in view. It takes two persons at least to produce anything readable: the writer and the reader. These two form a team of collaborators, and neither can have any fun or much success without the other. As John Milton pointed out, the reader should bring as much to the reading of the book as the author did to the writing of it. Without that, the reading is a pretty one-sided affair, for an author cannot express himself well or effectively unless he knows what he and the reader both take for granted and how far he may count upon the reader's co-operation.

It is the lack of this co-operation which makes some classes so dull. The teacher feels that the student will not willingly co-operate. The teacher therefore puts upon himself the whole burden and lectures the student instead of merely enabling him to discover the meaning for himself. Then the student, feeling that he is being *told* and that the teacher is doing everything that can be done, feels completely left out; he is bored and indifferent, and the class becomes a failure.

Just so it is with writers and readers. Each must contribute his part if the undertaking is to be worth while.

WORK PROGRAM 6

1. State the characteristic quality and kind of interest proper to (a) the Beginning, (b) the Middle, (c) the End.
2. Why must you have a definite type of reader in mind when you write?

PART 3   PRACTICE

CHAPTER 7   TECHNICAL DEVICES

The same general principles apply to the over-all pattern whether you write fiction or non-fiction.

In each case you must first of all catch the reader's *attention;* then make him feel that what you have to say is of *interest to him.* Having thus got him started in the Beginning to read your piece, you then go on with the Middle, *getting down to cases* and narrating your story or presenting your ideas in the most effective sequence. Finally, in the End, you wind up your story or reach the conclusion of your article briefly and to the reader's *satisfaction.*

These steps are found in every good piece of writing, whether fiction or non-fiction. But the technical devices used in carrying out this program vary somewhat as between fiction and non-fiction because the subject matter of each is different. It will therefore be convenient here to take up fiction and non-fiction separately.

Before we consider the story and the article, however, let us discuss, define, and illustrate what is meant by a technical device.

A technical device may be defined as a choice and arrangement of words which solve a particular problem for the author by producing a desired effect upon the reader.[1]

An effect has been defined as "an impression intended by the

[1] This matter of effects is discussed at greater length in *Professional Writing,* by W. S. Campbell, Chapter IV, "The Choice of an Effect." Published by the Macmillan Company, New York, 1938.

author and produced upon the reader." It may be intellectual or emotional, or both.

A good story, a good article or book, is simply a series of such small effects carefully planned and executed with a view to the effect of the whole.

In order to master the devices which produce these effects it is necessary to (1) isolate them, (2) analyze them, and (3) practice them.

Your first step, then, is to clip out a passage from a story or article which embodies such a device. Paste it upon a sheet of paper in a loose-leaf notebook—paper of typewriter size, 8½ × 11 inches. Above the clipping place a heading which indicates the nature of the device. Below the clipping state first the problem of the author—that problem which he was faced with in writing that particular passage. *The author's problem always has reference to his reader.*

Then state the solution used by the author to solve his problem.

Following that, describe the effect produced upon the reader by the device.

Finally add a note of comment of your own in which you criticize the comparative success or failure of the device.

In this book we shall give samples of many of the standard devices used in solving typical problems in both fiction and non-fiction.

It is desirable that you should not rest content merely with the standard devices given in this book but also collect other devices and file them for yourself. Besides studying those in this book and collecting others for your file, you must also practice all these devices, following the same pattern and structure and seeking the same effect, but using *different subject matter* and *different words*.

In that way you will soon become master of the usual devices and so eventually work out patterns of your own to serve every purpose. For, once you have isolated, mastered, and practiced the standard devices used in a story or article, you will be qualified to write the whole piece.

Writing is like playing football. When a man joins the football squad he does not go out and play football right away, even though he may know the rules and purpose of the game. No, he first learns to block, to tackle, to pass, to kick. Then, having mastered each of these tricks, he is qualified to learn the teamwork necessary to make him an efficient player. Just so it is with writers.

I shall present these devices as Problems of the Beginning, Problems of the Middle, and Problems of the End. Some of them will be useful both in fiction and non-fiction. Others are particularly adapted to one or the other of these forms.

And now for a few examples of technical devices which will familiarize you with their form. Let us consider a technical device described by the eminent American novelist Edith Wharton, which, because of the illustration she uses, is generally called the Wave Formula.

This is a device often used for characterization. It consists of three steps: *first,* the motive of the character; *second,* the gesture or action of the character; *third,* the dialogue or speech of the character. These occur in that order.

The Wave Formula is frequently used. The motive is given first because, if it is not indicated at once, the reader will probably dream up a motive of his own which differs from that the author had in mind. So if you give the character's action first of all, the reader may misinterpret the action, and if the writer then gives the motive, the reader will refuse to believe it. Depend upon it—in any argument between author and reader, the reader is always right!

Again, if the author makes his character speak before the motive is indicated, the reader is by no means sure that the character is telling the truth as to his motive. It is therefore necessary as a rule to give the motive first, the action or gesture second, and the character's speech or dialogue last of all.

Mrs. Wharton compared this formula with a wave of the sea making toward the shore. The power of the winds behind the wave is the motive, the rising of the wave as it rolls up the beach is the action or gesture, and the foam on the crest as the wave breaks is the dialogue or speech.

Now let us consider an example of this technical device, the Wave Formula.

Heading · CHARACTERIZATION

Clipping

1. Joe was weary. 2. He slumped in his chair. 3. "I'm exhausted," he gasped.

Problem of the Author   To display the motive of a character convincingly.

Solution by the Author The Wave Formula is used. The author gives (1) the motive of the character; then (2) the action which illustrates the motive; following these by (3) the actual words of the character which corroborate the motive and the action.

Effect upon the Reader This triple presentation of the character's motive is convincing and therefore may arouse the sympathy of the reader for the character.

Student's Comment This device is standard and frequently used. Here all three steps are given in full. Sometimes the motive may be implied or omitted if it has already been established in a previous passage.

This is the form in which technical devices are best isolated, displayed, and explained. You will find numerous examples in the later chapters of this book—examples of most of the standard devices commonly used. They are put there for your careful study and imitation.

Having thus isolated and analyzed a device, you can memorize it by writing what one may call Finger Exercises, following the same pattern but using *different subject matter* and *different words*. For example, the Finger Exercise of your Wave Formula as you write it up may run as follows:

Clipping

Mary was happy. Her eyes danced. "Oh, I am having fun," she laughed.

Or, using other subject matter, you might say:

The prisoner was furious. He struggled to free himself. "Let me go," he growled.

Or again you might write:

Toby, the cat, was impatient to be fed. He clawed at the screen door, trying to get in. "Meow," he screamed.

No doubt you have heard that the way to add a new word to your vocabulary is to use it three times the day you learn it. After that it sticks in your memory. Just so a technical device such as the Wave Formula, if imitated three times, will become a permanent part of your arsenal of technical devices.

You should therefore make it a practice, whenever you find a well-written passage that embodies a good device, to write it up three

34

times—each time with *different words* and *different subject matter*—until you have fixed the pattern of the device in your mind. In each case you should give it a proper Heading, state the Problem of the Author, state his Solution, then describe the Effect upon the Reader, and finally add your own Comment as to the effectiveness of your solution.

You must take care always in stating the Problem, Solution, and Effect to exclude references to the character's name or to the particular facts of the subject matter. For your object is *not* to memorize the subject matter of the passage but to memorize the *pattern* of the device. It is therefore absolutely necessary that you use general terms, such as "character," and never mention the character's name, "Joe." In like manner when describing an emotion, you do not use the word "jealousy" but some more general term, such as "passion" or "emotion." In this way you keep the pattern clear so that you can memorize it and use it again with different subject matter of your own.

If you follow the advice given in this book, you will collect devices and practice Finger Exercises based upon them until you are master of all the standard devices necessary to the kind of work you wish to do.

One caution: Though in this book we take up first fiction and afterward non-fiction, it is not intended that you should neglect one in favor of the other. You should master both, for every writer nowadays who hopes for any great success finds it necessary to use techniques of fiction in non-fiction articles and to use non-fiction techniques in stories. Today a writer may expect to write both fiction and non-fiction and to mix the techniques of both in either case.

If we are to be writers, we might as well be all-around writers, commanding a whole arsenal of technical devices. Then only can we truly follow the methods of the masters.

As you progress in your mastery of these techniques you will be prompted by your study of devices to invent patterns and tricks of your own, thus perfecting your technique and outdoing your rivals in the art. For creation is by no means limited to imagining the materials of your work. *Imagination may work just as freely and forcefully in the field of verbal technique.* One fine phrase inspires another.

Consider Samuel Taylor Coleridge's description of Shakespeare's habit of work:

"Shakespeare goes on creating, and evolving B out of A, and C out of B, and so on, just as a serpent moves, which makes a fulcrum of its own body, and seems forever twisting and untwisting its own strength. . . . In Shakespeare one sentence begets the next naturally; the meaning is all inwoven. He goes on kindling like a meteor through the dark atmosphere."[2]

Obviously, when you know how to do all the things that must be done in the Beginning, the Middle, and the End of a story or article, you can then readily put these devices end to end and so create your over-all pattern, your whole composition, your article or your story or your poem.

Remember that the passage embodying a technical device is an *experience* for the reader. Each passage he reads, each device he follows through, gives him a *kind* of experience, and it is for this that he reads. Experience consists of stimuli and reactions, or you may say discoveries and reversals—or, what is much the same thing, sensations and emotions.

Always remember that the reader has only a certain amount of attention to give you and that his attention continually waxes and wanes. If you make a firefly crawl along a line of printed words, you will see that the little creature glows and fades, alternately lighting some words brilliantly and others dimly. Just so the reader's attention waxes and wanes. You have to take account of this in your writing.

Reading requires effort—first of all in a recognition of the letters, words, and marks of punctuation; this uses up a certain amount of the reader's energy and attention. Of what remains he must devote a part to calling up in imagination the meanings and images which the words suggest to him; this takes still more of his attention, his nervous energy. What is left of these he can devote to experiencing the effect which you intend, whether this effect be thought, feeling, or both.

Obviously, if the reader's energy is all taken up by recognizing the letters and words and by calling up the images suggested by them, he will have none left with which to realize the emotions and thoughts—the effects which you desire.

Your reader will read your work only if he finds the *experience* rewarding.

Therefore, hard as it may be for you, you *must* take care to make

[2]*Table Talk.*

it easy for the reader; for as Ben Jonson well said, "Easy writing's curst hard reading."

WORK PROGRAM 7

1. You will find some further remarks on the over-all pattern later in this book, both as regards its use in fiction and non-fiction. Hereafter we must concern ourselves for the most part with those technical devices found in all kinds of writing. For further instructions as to the larger patterns, I must refer you to my book *Writing Magazine Fiction*, published by Doubleday and Company, New York, and to my book *Writing Non-Fiction*, published by The Writer, Inc., Boston. In these you will find all the standard types discussed at length. And now for the questions of this Work Program.
   What are the four steps or parts of the over-all pattern?
2. Define an effect.
3. Prepare a notebook for your technical devices, as suggested in Chapter 7.
4. What is the Wave Formula?
5. Write three Finger Exercises embodying the Wave Formula, like those given in this chapter, but using in each one different subject matter and different words of your own.
6. Finally, before proceeding to the next chapter, turn to the Appendix and read Section A-1, including the first of the Pieces for Analysis, the story *Dakotah Courtship*, from which many of the fictional devices given in this book have been taken.

CHAPTER 8   FICTION • DEVICES OF THE BEGINNING

THE SHORT STORY

In any short piece of writing the Beginning is by far the most important part, for the reader of a short story will never read the rest of your yarn unless you can catch and hold his attention with your Beginning. Readers will sometimes wade through a confused or dull first chapter of a novel or biography, but a short story or short article must *immediately* catch the attention and seize the interest of the reader.

Unfortunately, the Beginning of a short story is not only the most important part but much the most difficult to write.

That is because when the reader picks up your story his mind is taken up with other matters, and in all likelihood he is not in the mood of your story. Moreover, you have not only to catch his attention and seize his interest without delay, but you are confronted with an even more difficult problem—that of conveying to him the information necessary for his understanding of what follows.

The reader of a short story is on holiday and temperamentally averse to being instructed and informed. He wants to read fiction, not fact, and if the facts you must convey are numerous or complex, you will have all you can do to make them clear and interesting.

The Beginning of a story extends up to that point where the reader becomes fully aware of the main problem confronting your "hero"— that is to say, your principal or viewpoint character. By viewpoint character we mean that character from whose point of view the events of the story are seen and expressed, that character with whom the reader sympathizes—in other words, the chief sufferer.

In this Beginning, which may fill one or two and (more rarely) three or even four pages, there are certain things which you *must* do:

- a. Catch the attention of your reader.
- b. Introduce all your important characters—at least by name or some unmistakable suggestion, so that the reader knows they exist even though not all of them appear in person immediately.
- c. Set your stage plainly so that the reader knows what the setting is—the time, the place, and the social atmosphere in which the story takes place.
- d. State the main problem with which your hero is confronted.
- e. Suggest the main complication which is to follow.
- f. Hint, however vaguely, at the solution.
- g. Set the emotional tone so that the reader quickly becomes aware whether your story is to be comic, tragic, farcical, satirical, sentimental, or what not.
- h. Indicate the type of story you are writing, whether a story of atmosphere, action, character, or idea.

i. Plant the essential facts.

j. Point, however vaguely, to important events to follow.

k. Tell, if necessary, the story behind the story—that is, the events preceding the actual Beginning of the yarn in so far as these are necessary to make the reader understand and believe in the situation in which the hero finds himself. This is the flashback.

l. Suggest unmistakably the two conflicting emotions in the hero's mind, those emotions out of which the plot will grow.

m. Offer a promise of conflict.

n. Characterize all your persons in the story so that the reader readily identifies one as the protagonist (hero or heroine), another as the antagonist (opponent of the hero, or villain), as well as each of the minor characters.

All these things have to be done in the Beginning. They have to be done quickly, effectively, and in an interesting manner. They need not be done in the order given here. *But until these things are done in some effective way, the Beginning of your story is not complete.*

Here follow examples of technical devices commonly used to accomplish these ends:

A. Devices of Attention · Bait

Since the reader will judge whether he wishes to read your story or not by his reaction to the first sentence or paragraph, the first thing to do is to make sure that the very first sentences catch his attention and arouse his interest. This is done by a device commonly called Bait.

In an atmospheric story you may be able to catch the reader's attention with an interesting setting; in an action story, by an arresting incident; in a story of character, by presenting your hero or the narrator of the story in a fresh or exciting way; in an idea story, by stating the theme or idea to be illustrated.

Since as a rule the reader tends to sympathize with and even identify himself with the first character he meets in your yarn, the character introduced first is usually the hero, the viewpoint character.

But since Conflict rivals Character as the chief source of interest, Bait may consist of a statement of the hero's predicament, his problem, or at least a predicament leading into and relevant to his main problem in the story. Sometimes Bait may even consist of an indication of the emotional tone defined above, but generally it will have reference to the hero and his problem. It is obviously better, if possible, to bring in both these main sources of interest at once and so make sure that the reader's interest is immediately caught. Obviously, the quicker you can catch the reader's interest, the better, and this interest should be based upon and related to the main interest of the story as a whole.

And now for some examples of Bait:

Heading · DEVICES OF THE BEGINNING · BAIT

Clipping From *The Cask of Amontillado,* by Edgar Allan Poe
1. The thousand injuries of Fortunato I had borne as best I could, but when he ventured upon insult I vowed revenge.

Problem of the Author To catch the reader's attention.

Solution by the Author The hero is introduced as resolute, though faced by an intolerable situation and an antagonist, which promise dangerous conflict.

Effect upon the Reader This excites interest in the situation, the two antagonists, and also arouses curiosity as to how the hero's problem will be solved.

Student's Comment This is a splendid example of plunging into the midst of the action (*in medias res*). It also introduces two characters and presents the flashback in the first clause, sets forth the situation in the second clause, and points to the solution in the third clause.

Here are three samples of this device set up as Finger Exercises:

1. I put up with Laura's nagging as patiently as possible, but when she dared to lock me out, I decided to quit.

2. I tolerated Tommy's abuse with patience until he double-crossed me. Then I struck him.

3. Joe endured the bee's buzzing with fatalism. But when it stung him, Joe went berserk.

Clipping From *A Very Valuable Quality*—in Appendix

1. Until the day that my sister Suzie was jilted, I didn't know how smart she was. 2. Up until then I had thought of my sister Suzie as being a pretty brunette whose clothes I might be able to wear next year. 3. I, Laurie, am fifteen and large for my age. 4. But the day that Henry Brown jilted Suzie, I learned that she had brains, too. 5. Brains are a very valuable quality for a woman to have.

Problem of the Author To catch the reader's attention.

Solution by the Author The heroine is introduced, faced with an apparently unsolvable problem but with a weapon which may solve it.

Effect upon the Reader Immediate interest and curiosity.

Student's Comment The sympathetic narrator wins our sympathy for heroine.

Clipping From *Dakotah Courtship*—in Appendix

1. Joe Lone Bear was a confident young man with a long reach and a steady eye, and plenty proud of his battered, stripped-down car, daubed all over with what Joe believed were the latest collegiate mottoes: MEN AT WORK, CHICKEN COOP, THAT MAN IS HERE AGAIN, SOCKO, SO LONG, EXCUSE MY DUST. 2. But as Joe gradually approached the gate of Chief Hardtack's allotment, his young heart missed almost as often as his chugging engine. 3. Lillie Fineweather lived there.

Problem of the Author To catch the reader's attention.

Solution by the Author Three characters are introduced: two of them lovers, the other an obstacle to love.

Effect upon the Reader The hero is presented sympathetically, being both admirable and with a natural weakness and a problem to face. The names of all three characters suggest unusual color.

41

The hero is presented first and is given most space in the passage, thus focusing the sympathies of the reader upon him.

Note that in offering these devices the object is to provide you with samples from which you may write Finger Exercises of your own, following the same pattern, but using different words and different subject matter of your own.

In stating these devices I have, for your convenience, numbered each sentence (1, 2, 3, etc.) to correspond to the numbered sentence in the story in the Appendix.

Sometimes (where a longer passage is required to make the device clear to you) I have underscored the essential words which embody the device in the clipping.

B. The Introduction of Characters

It is not always possible and necessary that all the characters should appear in person on page one, but the existence of each should be indicated in some interesting way without delay.

Here follow some devices illustrating the Introduction of One or More Characters:

Heading · DEVICES OF THE BEGINNING · INTRODUCTION OF CHARACTERS

Clipping From *Dakotah Courtship*—in Appendix

1. Joe Lone Bear was a confident young man with a long reach and a steady eye, and plenty proud of his battered, stripped-down car, daubed all over with what Joe believed were the latest collegiate mottoes: MEN AT WORK, CHICKEN COOP, THAT MAN IS HERE AGAIN, SOCKO, SO LONG, EXCUSE MY DUST. 2. But as Joe gradually approached the gate of Chief Hardtack's allotment, his young heart missed almost as often as his chugging engine. 3. Lillie Fineweather lived there.

Problem of the Author To introduce our hero at the very beginning of the story with characteristic behavior and motivation.

Solution by the Author Our hero is first described by the author, who notes his temperament, his capacity, a physical trait implying a moral quality (steady eye), and a sympathetic motive, pride of possession of a typical young man of his sort. In sentence 2 his age is suggested and his reaction to others in 2 and 3.

Effect upon the Reader The hero is presented as admirable and sympathetic in his pride, his love, and his fears.

Student's Comment Since the reader tends to make friends with the first character he meets in the story, it is well to introduce the hero first. He can most readily be made sympathetic by showing him to be likable, with human weaknesses and troubles, but at the same time able to look out for himself. The reader wishes to identify himself with the hero.

Heading · DEVICES OF THE BEGINNING · INTRODUCTION OF CHARACTERS

Clipping From *Dakotah Courtship*—in Appendix
1. Joe Lone Bear was a confident young man with a long reach and a steady eye, and plenty proud of his battered, stripped-down car, daubed all over with what Joe believed were the latest collegiate mottoes: MEN AT WORK, CHICKEN COOP, THAT MAN IS HERE AGAIN, SOCKO, SO LONG, EXCUSE MY DUST. 2. But as Joe gradually approached the gate of Chief Hardtack's allotment, his young heart missed almost as often as his chugging engine. 3. Lillie Fineweather lived there. . . . 11. But now he had to face old Mrs. Hardtack and her stuffy old man, and hurdle their objections. . . . 16. So Joe had brought along his own grandparents to make the match in the old-time way. . . . 18. Anxiously, he shouted to caution the aged warrior at his elbow. 19. Chief Lone Bear sat braced against the gale clutching his splintered stiff straw hat with gnarled fingers, staring fiercely through the windshield. . . . 40. Old Mrs. Lone Bear, after a moment's silent dismay at the distance to be covered afoot, heaved her two hundred pounds up from the rumble-seat and slowly clambered to the ground. . . . 534. The driver was a big red-faced bruiser, thick in the neck and wide in the shoulders.

Problem of the Author In these scattered passages to introduce all the characters in the story briefly but unmistakably.

Solution by the Author The hero is introduced by description (1). Chief Hardtack is indicated by name and status (2). Lillie Fineweather is indicated by name, relationship to the hero, and place of residence. Mrs. Hardtack and her husband are introduced by name, age, and reaction of the hero to them (11). The hero's grandparents are introduced by their relationship to him and their function in the story (16). Chief Lone Bear (18, 19) is introduced by age, status, gesture, and mood. Mrs. Lone Bear (40) is introduced through motivation, appearance, and action. The driver of the truck (534) is introduced by description.

Effect upon the Reader The effect intended by the author was to bring these characters in swiftly, briefly, but unmistakably.

Student's Comment All but one of these characters is brought in within the first forty sentences. All but two are brought in within the first twenty. The driver had to be brought in late, as the hero, being a fighter, had to have somebody to knock down and could scarcely attack any of the other characters in the story.

Heading · DEVICES OF THE BEGINNING · INTRODUCTION OF CHARACTERS

Clipping From *Dakotah Courtship*—in Appendix
16. So Joe had brought along his own grandparents to make the match in the old-time way. 17. But now, as he rolled in through Hardtack's gate, Joe began to get cold feet about that.

18. Anxiously, he shouted to caution the aged warrior at his elbow. 19. Chief Lone Bear sat braced against the gale, clutching his splintered stiff straw hat with gnarled fingers, staring fiercely through the windshield. 20. "Grandfather," Joe yelled, "the wars are over. 21. We are friends with these people now. 22. Remember that!"

23. The old Dakotah shifted his moccasins to a firmer position upon the hot floorboards, turned red-rimmed eyes upon his grandson, and showed his yellow teeth in a grin of pleasurable anticipation. 24. "Make your heart strong, my grandson," he quavered. 25. "I know how to handle the Crows. 26. I have killed plenty of them in my day, and made them run like rabbits. 27. *He-han!* 28. Who is this Hardtack? 29. He has seen only seventy-six winters. 30. I have nothing to fear from that boy!"

31. The old man's words upset Joe. 32. Then and there he killed his engine. 33. The car jolted to a stop.

44

Problem of the Author To introduce a principal character as quickly and vividly as possible.

Solution by the Author On page 2 of the typed script the author brings in the character Chief Lone Bear and indicates his motivation. Chief Lone Bear's existence is indicated in sentence 16. He is characterized as follows: by description (18, 19, 23); by action (19, 23); by speech (24–30); by reaction of others (16–22, 31–33); by reaction to others (23–30).

Effect upon the Reader The characterization should be effective here, as it uses four of the strongest methods.

Student's Comment Chief Lone Bear is characterized even more elaborately than Mrs. Hardtack in this yarn but not so fully as the hero and heroine, who are somewhat more complex.

C. Setting the Stage · Time, Place, Social Atmosphere

The *time* may be indicated as a time of day, a time of year, a period of history; the *place* as a country, a region, a town, or the very spot where the action begins. Generally speaking, the more you can narrow this down, the better. The more specific you can be, as a rule, the more the reader can see and feel your setting. By indicating the *social atmosphere* we mean that you let the reader know what kind of society the hero moves in, whether café society, military life, or Western range life. Sometimes all three—time, place, and social atmosphere—can be indicated briefly, as in this sentence of dialogue: "Wake up, Dad," the boy whispered, "there's a burglar downstairs."

Here you know the time, night; the place, an upstairs room; the social atmosphere, family life.

In describing setting there are three methods:

1. *Factual* description, which *names* the facts, as: "The room was square, badly lighted, and contained a table and a battered chair." Such factual description is sometimes called "Solid."
2. *Sensory* description, which consists in telling in terms of one or more of the five senses what can be seen, smelled, heard, felt, or tasted, as: "The room was brightly lighted by the red rays of the setting sun and had a faintly musty odor." Such sensory description of a setting is sometimes called "Liquid."

3. Presenting the setting in terms of the *emotion* which the character felt with regard to it, with only a minimum of factual or sensory description, as: "What a dismal room it was! I was eager to escape from it." Such emotional description has been dubbed "Gaseous."

Nowadays, what with television, motion pictures, illustrated magazines, and easy travel, most readers have seen settings of all kinds and are able to imagine one suggested with a minimum of description.

Here follow devices for Setting the Stage:

Heading · DEVICES OF THE BEGINNING · SETTING THE STAGE—THE TIME

Clipping From *Dakotah Courtship*—in Appendix
34. It was a good long hundred yards across the blistering prairie to Hardtack's unpainted shack and the brush arbor alongside. 82. The sun beat down on it with all the steady purpose of an August afternoon.

Problem of the Author To indicate the time at which his story takes place.

Solution by the Author In two sentences, widely spaced, the weather, the month, and the time of day are mentioned.

Effect upon the Reader The time is well indicated: (1) by a sensation (heat), and (2) by a picture of the sun beating down one August afternoon.

Student's Comment Sensations and emotions are an immediate means of convincing the reader.

Heading · DEVICES OF THE BEGINNING · SETTING THE STAGE—THE PLACE

Clipping From *Dakotah Courtship*—in Appendix
2. But as Joe gradually approached the gate of Chief Hardtack's allotment, his young heart missed almost as often as his chugging engine. . . . 17. But now, as he rolled in through Hardtack's gate, Joe began to get cold feet about that. . . . 34. It was a good long hundred yards across the blistering prairie to Hardtack's unpainted shack and the brush arbor alongside. . . . 81. Chief Hardtack's allot-

46

ment was a flat, uncompromising square of short Montana grass surrounded by a sagging fence of rusty barbed wire.

Problem of the Author   To locate the setting for his story at a definite place in an unmistakable manner.

Solution by the Author   In these four sentences, widely spaced, he repeatedly refers to the scene of the story, each time adding significant details.

Effect upon the Reader   These four sentences, each giving no more than is needed by the reader at the time, together present an adequate picture of the place where the story is laid.

Student's Comment   All these details could have been given at once at the beginning of the story, but nothing would have been gained by lumping them all together. This is an example of how incremental repetition may do good service.

Heading · DEVICES OF THE BEGINNING · SETTING THE STAGE—SOCIAL ATMOSPHERE

Clipping   From *Dakotah Courtship*—in Appendix

1. Joe Lone Bear was a confident young man with a long reach and a steady eye, and plenty proud of his battered, stripped-down car, daubed all over with what Joe believed were the latest collegiate mottoes: MEN AT WORK, CHICKEN COOP, THAT MAN IS HERE AGAIN, SOCKO, SO LONG, EXCUSE MY DUST. 2. But as Joe gradually approached the gate of Chief Hardtack's allotment, his young heart missed almost as often as his chugging engine. 3. Lillie Fineweather lived there.

4. That motor trouble in Joe's fighting heart was not entirely due to Lillie's near presence, however. 5. Lillie and Joe had mostly got along fine—at the Indian Boarding School. 6. The pocket of his blue shirt contained a well-thumbed letter in her firm Spencerian hand, assuring him, in a curious mixture of school slang and Indian poetry, that she loved him: "Hurry up, Big Boy. 7. I'm crazy about you. 8. All time you way off in South Dakota, my lips are still on your lips."

9. Lillie was okay. 10. One in a million. 11. But now he had to face old Mrs. Hardtack and her stuffy old man, and hurdle their objections. 12. Dakotah and Crow had been enemies from away back.

13. When a Dakotah boy came courting a Crow girl, there was likely to be trouble.

14. Lillie had warned Joe that her grandma was terrible old-fashioned. 15. Lillie said Joe couldn't wrangle the old lady single-handed. 16. So Joe had brought along his own grandparents to make the match in the old-time way.

Problem of the Author   To indicate as promptly as possible the social atmosphere or the kind of life represented in his story.

Solution by the Author   The social atmosphere: Contemporary Plains Indian life; here indicated by contrast between the young lovers facing the future and their grandparents loyal to the past.

Effect upon the Reader   The reader is readily interested in social contrasts if these are presented amusingly.

Student's Comment   Of course all the color of the social atmosphere cannot be presented in one page in a story of this kind. There are a good many other such passages. The social atmosphere is most important and perhaps the chief interest of the reader.

D. Stating the Problem

The problem faced by the hero should preferably be one which, being the kind of man he is, he cannot solve.

For if you give the hero an easy problem, the reader will take no interest. You can arrange this either by making the problem so tough that it seems no one could solve it, or by handicapping the hero in some way so that he, at any rate, is not prepared to solve it. A problem is essentially a predicament, a situation, a dilemma in which the hero is torn by two emotions pulling in opposite directions, a conflict between love and duty, or some other pair of strong emotions.

Here follow devices for Stating the Problem:

Heading · DEVICES OF THE BEGINNING · STATING THE HERO'S MAIN PROBLEM

Clipping   From *Dakotah Courtship*—in Appendix

11. But now he had to face old Mrs. Hardtack and her stuffy old man, and hurdle their objections. 12. Dakotah and Crow had been

enemies from away back. 13. <u>When a Dakotah boy came courting a Crow girl, there was likely to be trouble.</u>

14. Lillie had warned Joe that her grandma was terrible old-fashioned. 15. Lillie said Joe couldn't wrangle the old lady single-handed.

Problem of the Author   To make the reader thoroughly aware of the problem confronting the hero.

Solution by the Author   The problem is presented briefly in terms of the hero's own thoughts.

Effect upon the Reader   Staying in the viewpoint of the hero enables the reader to identify himself with the hero and thus feel his problem more keenly.

Student's Comment   The author here states his problem on page one where it belongs, though it is hinted at as early as sentence 2. As a rule, the sooner the reader can be made aware of the hero's problem, the better. Sentence 13 gives the nub of the matter. Hence the under-scoring.

I suggested earlier that, when necessary for clarity to include in your Clipping more than the actual number of words devoted to the particular advice under consideration, you will find it useful (as was done in the device just preceding) to underscore the words embodying the device, thus setting them off from the rest of the passage.

E. Suggesting the Complication

By the complication we mean the difficulty (sometimes there are a series of complications) into which the hero will fall in his efforts to solve his original problem. Of course in order to build up the suspense of your yarn the complication must be—or at any rate seem—far worse than the original problem. Otherwise you have an anti-climax, which is fatal to interest.

Since your hero's character is established as being thus and so, you cannot change that without disappointing the reader. There is neither time nor space in a short story to develop character, and the reader will not tolerate a sudden change of character just to enable the hero to solve his problem.

It follows that the only thing you can change to save your hero is the original problem itself, and this you do by changing it as much as possible—by having the hero jump out of the frying pan into the fire. The reader thinks only of the dangers of the fire and does not realize that the fire is only a device to get the hero out of the frying pan. Thus *the complication is always the worst thing that can happen to the hero under the circumstances of his original problem.* Think up the worst thing that could happen—then you have your complication. Thus, if your hero is bound hand and foot and left to die in the lonely cabin, the worst thing that could happen to him would be for the cabin to catch fire. But actually the fire provides the means of burning his bonds and setting him free.

Of course you do not come right out and tell the reader in plain words that the hero is going to be saved by burning his bonds, but you may suggest that the cabin is dry as tinder or have someone remark that there is a forest fire or that the stove in the cabin is a flimsy affair, easily kicked over.

In this way you prepare the reader to accept the complication when it arrives.

Here follow some devices for Suggesting the Complication:

Heading · DEVICES OF THE BEGINNING · SUGGESTING THE MAIN COMPLICATION

Clipping From *Dakotah Courtship*—in Appendix

44. Just as they started, Joe saw Lillie leave the arbor and hurry into the shack. . . . 102. "You don't have to," she countered. . . . 229. "But don't pull any fast ones about my folks. 230. I can't take it." . . . 283. "I'm going to marry you." 284. "Maybe," she said, her eyes brimming with angry tears. . . . 497. Stung by the shame of having him touch her in the presence of her relatives, Lillie struggled to wrench herself free. 498. "Let go of me," she raged. . . . 503. She whirled and ran. . . . 523. "Nowhere with you," she replied. 524. "And don't you follow me neither—if you ever do get that thing started. 525. You damn Dakotah, I'm through." . . . 529. Lillie raised her thumb and waggled it in the air above her head.

Problem of the Author To suggest the main complication so that the reader will keep it in mind and fear for the hero.

Solution by the Author The author suggests in these passages that the heroine may walk out on the hero and leave him flat.

Effect upon the Reader The reader is convinced by the heroine's quick temper and the repeated references to the possibility of her leaving the hero that there is a real danger here.

Student's Comment The main complication is by definition the worst thing that can happen to the hero under the circumstances of his original problem. Since the hero desires to marry the girl, the worst thing that can happen is to have her leave him flat. It is necessary in a short story to keep this disaster in the reader's mind.

Of course there are a number of other complications in this story. A main one is the wrangling of the old folks whom the hero had brought together with the purpose of making the match. A complication is brought on by the hero's attempt to solve his problem.

F. Hinting at the Solution

The solution may also be prepared for, so that when it comes the reader will not be utterly surprised. He may be surprised, but on looking back on your story he may find that you had prepared him for it surreptitiously. Naturally, since it is the solution for which the reader reads the story, it must not be given away but only hinted at.

Here follow devices for Hinting at the Solution:

Heading · DEVICES OF THE BEGINNING · HINTING AT THE SOLUTION

Clipping From *Dakotah Courtship*—in Appendix

4. That motor trouble in Joe's fighting heart was not entirely due to Lillie's near presence, however. 5. Lillie and Joe had mostly got along fine—at the Indian Boarding School. 6. The pocket of his blue shirt contained a well-thumbed letter in her firm Spencerian hand, assuring him, in a curious mixture of school slang and Indian poetry, that she loved him: "Hurry up, Big Boy. 7. I'm crazy about you. 8. All time you way off in South Dakota, my lips are still on your lips."

Problem of the Author To hint at the possible solution of the hero's problem.

51

Solution by the Author This is done by a flashback giving the hero's thoughts and stating the relationship of hero and heroine and quoting her cherished letter then in his pocket.

Effect upon the Reader The reader is now convinced that the hero and heroine are in love with each other.

Student's Comment The quotation from the letter, being both slangy and poetical in the Indian manner, suggests to the reader that there will be a reconciliation between the old tribal loyalties represented by the older Indians and the future purposes of the hero and heroine. Other hints at a happy solution to the hero's problem may be found in sentences 67, 110, 225, 372–74, 409, and 504.

G. Setting the Emotional Tone

Letting the reader know what kind of mood dominates your story is one of the chief means of inducing interest. It is one of the things a reader looks for first of all in a yarn and should be indicated quite early, if possible in the first sentence or paragraph, though of course the mood will be developed further as the story progresses. But the reader wants to know at once whether he may expect to laugh or to sob, whether the story is to be sentimental or comic, or whatever the mood is to be.

The emotional tone may be set by a choice of words, by an incident, a bit of dialogue, a characterization, or indeed anything that serves the purpose.

Here follow devices which serve this purpose:

Heading · DEVICES OF THE BEGINNING · SETTING THE EMOTIONAL TONE

Clipping From *Dakotah Courtship*—in Appendix

1. Joe Lone Bear was a confident young man with a long reach and a steady eye, and plenty proud of his battered, stripped-down car, daubed all over with what Joe believed were the latest collegiate mottoes: MEN AT WORK, CHICKEN COOP, THAT MAN IS HERE AGAIN, SOCKO, SO LONG, EXCUSE MY DUST. 2. But as Joe gradually approached the gate of Chief Hardtack's allotment, his young heart missed almost as often as his chugging engine. 3. Lillie Fineweather lived there.

4. That motor trouble in Joe's fighting heart was not entirely due to Lillie's near presence, however. 5. Lillie and Joe had mostly got along fine—at the Indian Boarding School. 6. The pocket of his blue shirt contained a well-thumbed letter in her firm Spencerian hand, assuring him, in a curious mixture of school slang and Indian poetry, that she loved him: "Hurry up, Big Boy. 7. I'm crazy about you. 8. All time you way off in South Dakota, my lips are still on your lips."

Problem of the Author   To indicate to the reader what kind of emotion his story is intended to provoke, whether comic, satirical, or what not. Here his purpose is to indicate that the story is humorous.

Solution by the Author   The contrast between the hero's Indian past and American future is so phrased as to suggest a humorous story and a happy ending. His eccentricities are not treated satirically, nor his love sentimentally.

Effect upon the Reader   The combination of slang and poetry, the past and the future, gives the reader a feeling that the story is intended to be humorous.

Student's Comment   From sentence 2 on, the passage is in viewpoint. It is sometimes possible and indeed not unusual to begin a story describing the character from outside, but such passages should be brief. Getting into viewpoint and staying there are essential to the reader's happiness, for the only thing a fiction writer can offer the reader which he does not and cannot find in real life is the privilege of getting inside the mind of somebody else.

H. Indicating the Type of Story

Some readers like action stories with a great deal happening. Some prefer atmospheric yarns in which the setting sets the mood. Still others are interested primarily in character and want to know at once whether character is to be the main interest, while others prefer to see an idea or theme worked out. Each of these readers expects to be tipped off promptly so that he can the better choose or refuse to read.

As indicated earlier in this chapter, the story usually begins with atmosphere, action, character, or idea, according to its type.

Here follow some devices which illustrate Indicating the Type of Story:

Clipping   From *The Fall of the House of Usher,* by Edgar Allan Poe

1. During the whole of a dull, dark, and soundless day in the autumn of the year, when the clouds hung oppressively low in the heavens, I had been passing alone, on horseback, through a singularly dreary tract of country; and at length found myself, as the shades of the evening drew on, within view of the melancholy House of Usher. 2. I know not how it was—but, with the first glimpse of the building, a sense of insufferable gloom pervaded my spirit. 3. I say insufferable . . .

Problem of the Author   To indicate the type of story he is writing.

Solution by the Author   Deliberate description by a lone narrator of the country, weather, season, time of day, and one building, leading up to an ominous state of mind in the narrator. All the adjectives used are carefully chosen to suggest the tone desired.

Effect upon the Reader   The unrelieved consistency of the words, images, ideas, reaction of the narrator, and pace of the passage produces a strong and definite effect upon the reader, preparing him for the story which is to follow. The effect grows upon the reader line by line.

Student's Comment   The author has overlooked nothing that would contribute to a strong and unified impression. He continues in this mood for a full page before he introduces a second character. Today, as a rule, readers expect a briefer Beginning.

Clipping

1. Peter was the kind of man everybody liked—until they got to know him. 2. He always meant well, but had not the vitality to follow through. 3. He soon wearied of well-doing. 4. Then his manner grew irritable, his voice shrill—and he lost a pal.

Problem of the Author   To indicate that he is writing a character story.

Solution by the Author   He opens the story with a characterization consisting of exposition involving contrast between the character's

54

intentions and behavior in sentence 1. This is followed by psychological analysis in sentences 2 and 3, ending with an account of his behavior illustrating his traits in sentence 4.

Effect upon the Reader The reader anticipates incidents further developing and illustrating the character's traits.

Student's Comment It is usually wise to introduce a character doing the sort of thing he is to do at the climax of the story.

Heading · DEVICES OF THE BEGINNING · INDICATING THE KIND OF STORY

Clipping
1. As a rule, a wise man gets an idea in his head, while a fool gets it in the neck. 2. But Tommy still had his idea coming—and had no notion as yet where it would hit him.

Problem of the Author To indicate that he is offering the reader an idea story.

Solution by the Author He opens the story by the statement of his theme.

Effect upon the Reader From such a beginning the reader will understand that he is to look for the illustration of the theme.

Student's Comment The proper phrasing of the theme to please the reader is half the battle in such a beginning.

Heading · DEVICES OF THE BEGINNING · INDICATING THE KIND OF STORY

Clipping
1. Lefty ducked into the nearest doorway and sucked the blood from his wounded hand. 2. "They almost got me that time," he gasped.

Problem of the Author To indicate that he is writing an action story.

Solution by the Author He opens the story with action.

Effect upon the Reader The effect of such dramatic action of a hero in difficulties is calculated to arouse the reader's interest in the story.

I. Planting the Essential Facts

It has been said that you can tell a Harvard man, but you can't tell him much. Readers appear all to have been educated at Harvard. *They will not believe anything you tell them.* Therefore, the art of making fiction plausible consists in *showing* the reader how things might happen and, in order to do this, preparing his mind *before-hand* so that he will believe that they are possible when they do happen. The more impossible a thing is, as a rule, the more preparation of the reader's mind there must be.

This preparation comprises these devices:

1. "Plants"
2. Pointers

The technical term "Plant" means that the author lets the reader know that certain things or conditions exist which it is necessary that the reader know in order to understand and follow the story. Thus, if the hero is to defend himself with a loaded gun, it will never do to have him suddenly produce the gun when need arises. The author must "plant" the gun, letting the reader know beforehand that the hero has such a weapon and that it is loaded.

The Beginning of a story is full of Plants; a skillful writer weaves his Plants into almost every sentence in the Beginning. Thus, in the Beginning of *Hamlet,* Shakespeare plants the fact that Hamlet's father is dead, that his ghost has been seen.

Here follow devices serving the purpose of Planting:

Heading · DEVICES OF THE BEGINNING · PLANTS

Clipping   From *Dakotah Courtship*—in Appendix
    1. Joe Lone Bear was a confident young man with a long reach and a steady eye, and plenty proud of his battered, stripped-down car, daubed all over with what Joe believed were the latest collegiate mottoes: MEN AT WORK, CHICKEN COOP, THAT MAN IS HERE AGAIN, SOCKO, SO LONG, EXCUSE MY DUST. 2. But as Joe gradually approached the gate of Chief Hardtack's allot-

56

ment, his young heart missed almost as often as his chugging engine. 3. Lillie Fineweather lived there.

4. That motor trouble in Joe's fighting heart was not entirely due to Lillie's near presence, however. 5. Lillie and Joe had mostly got along fine—at the Indian Boarding School. 6. The pocket of his blue shirt contained a well-thumbed letter in her firm Spencerian hand, assuring him, in a curious mixture of school slang and Indian poetry, that she loved him: "Hurry up, Big Boy. 7. I'm crazy about you. 8. All time you way off in South Dakota, my lips are still on your lips."

9. Lillie was okay. 10. One in a million. 11. But now he had to face old Mrs. Hardtack and her stuffy old man, and hurdle their objections. 12. Dakotah and Crow had been enemies from away back. 13. When a Dakotah boy came courting a Crow girl, there was likely to be trouble.

Problem of the Author To plant information in the mind of the reader necessary to the understanding of the story.

Solution by the Author. As early as possible the following facts are planted on page one. In sentence 1 the hero's name is planted. We also learn that he is an aggressive fighter, proud of his car, has been to an Indian school, and is trying to be up-to-date. In sentence 2 we learn that he is driving the car, approaching Chief Hardtack's allotment, and in an unsettled state of mind, like his engine. In sentence 3 we learn the name of the heroine, where she lives, and that the hero loves her. In sentence 4 the hero's problem is hinted at and we are again reminded that he is a fighter and in love. In sentence 5 we learn the name of the school to which the hero and heroine went and that they "got along fine." In sentence 6 we learn that the hero's shirt is blue, that it has a pocket and a letter in the pocket written in a Spencerian hand, that the heroine loved him, that she used both slang and Indian poetry and was firm. From the dialogue quoted we learn her pet name for the hero, her own word that she loves him, and learn that his home is in South Dakota. In sentences 9 and 10 the author plants the hero's approval of the heroine. And in 11 he introduces a new character (Mrs. Hardtack), characterizes her husband more fully, and states the problem more clearly. In sentence 12 we learn the names of the two tribes to whom the characters belong and that they have long been hostile. In sentence 13 we learn that the hero is a Dakotah and the heroine is a Crow, and that trouble is in the wind.

Effect upon the Reader The author's purpose was to present all this information as briefly and interestingly as possible.

Student's Comment The beginning of a story is compact of plants. The handling of these so that there is a steady development or increase of the reader's information about each thing planted is well worth study.

Other plants in *Dakotah Courtship* will be found in the following passages: 14, 15, 16, 18, 23, 30, 31, 32, 44, 45, 50, 59, 60, 64, 73, 80, 81, 82, 86, 97–99, 123, 128, 129, 134, 161, 163, 174, 176–81, 190–96, 204–07, 217, 234, 235, 237, 240, 255, 328, 364, 483, 577, 578.

J. Pointing to Events to Follow

By a Pointer we mean any indication that a certain thing might, could, or will happen later on in the story. A Pointer differs from a Plant in that it suggest an *event* to follow. Thus, in *Hamlet,* after the Prince has seen his father's ghost, the poet plants the idea that Hamlet is going to pretend to be mad. This is done dramatically by having Hamlet make his friends swear that they will keep the appearance of the ghost a secret and never let on that Hamlet's madness is feigned. This Pointer prepares us for the scenes in which Hamlet behaves like a madman.

Here follow devices called Pointers:

Heading · DEVICES OF THE BEGINNING · POINTERS

Clipping From *Dakotah Courtship*—in Appendix
2. But as Joe gradually approached the gate of Chief Hardtack's allotment, his young heart missed almost as often as his chugging engine. . . . 32. Then and there he killed his engine. 33. The car jolted to a stop. . . . 35. But Joe was too disheartened to try to start the car again. 36. Chances were it wouldn't start, anyhow, and he did not want the visit to begin by Lillie's folks having the laugh on him. . . . 516. He was still trying to start it when Lillie Fineweather passed by on her way to the gate. . . . 524. "And don't you follow me neither—if you ever do get that thing started." . . . 526. Joe stamped on the starter furiously, and held his foot down. . . . 589

58

Joe got in and fiddled with things on the dash, while Lillie waited to see whether it would go or not. 590. At last, by some method which Joe pretended to understand, but did not, he managed to start the engine.

Problem of the Author   To prepare the reader in the beginning for events occurring later in the story.

Solution by the Author   Repeated references to the difficulty of starting the car prepare the reader for the fact that the car will start eventually.

Effect upon the Reader   There is something amusing in a machine that will not work and relief if it finally does.

Student's Comment   The final starting of the car objectifies and symbolizes the solution of our hero's difficulties.

Heading · DEVICES OF THE BEGINNING · POINTERS

Clipping   From *Dakotah Courtship*—in Appendix

1. Joe Lone Bear was a confident young man with a long reach and a steady eye . . . 4. That motor trouble in Joe's fighting heart was not entirely due to Lillie's near presence, however. . . . 161. "Moreover, he learned to fight with fists like white men, wearing mittens of leather, in a rope corral. 162. I saw him. 163. He knocked down every young man his size in the school, and four white boys." . . . 534. The driver was a big red-faced bruiser, thick in the neck and wide in the shoulders. 535. Fat, though. 536. Automatically, Joe judged the man outweighed him twenty pounds. 543. "Get going, you big ape," Joe commanded, "or I'll knock you cold."

Problem of the Author   To prepare the reader in the beginning for events occurring later in the story.

Solution by the Author   The author indicates that our hero is a boxer in the first sentence and by incremental repetition reminds the reader again and again until the hero actually strikes his opponent.

Effect upon the Reader   Convincing.

Student's Comment   The idea is repeated, but in different words.

59

Clipping　From *Dakotah Courtship*—in Appendix

13. When a Dakotah boy came courting a Crow girl, there was likely to be trouble.

14. Lillie had warned Joe that her grandma was terrible old-fashioned. 15. Lillie said Joe couldn't wrangle the old lady single-handed. 16. So Joe had brought along his own grandparents to make the match in the old-time way.

Problem of the Author　To prepare the reader in the beginning for events occurring later in the story.

Solution by the Author　The author inserts passages in the beginning which will lead the reader to expect certain events later on in the story.

Effect upon the Reader　The reader delights in feeling that he is in the know, that he sees farther into the future than the hero can.

Student's Comment　The art of fiction is the art of preparation. The reader prefers recognition to surprise, and the wise author never gives the reader anything until the reader has been led to want it.

Pointers are to be found in *Dakotah Courtship* in the following passages: 116, 161, 217, 225, 255, 269–73, 283, 284, 399–403, 468–75, 483, 494, 503, 504, 510, 526, 543.

List these sentences one by one and indicate what event each one points to. Thus, the Pointer in 98 points to 517.

K. The Flashback

Since, as we have already discovered, a story never begins at the beginning, but always when the hero is faced with his great problem, it is usually necessary to go back and present to the reader what has gone before so that he will know how the hero fell into his predicament. Thus Shakespeare's *Hamlet* does not begin with the murder of his father, but only with Hamlet meeting with his father's ghost and the ghost's charge that Hamlet avenge him. It is only when the ghost appears and talks with Hamlet that we learn of the murder and his mother's conduct.

The flashback is thus no part of the story, but history. The reader of fiction abhors history, which he can read at the public library for nothing, and it is absolutely *fatal* to the reader's interest if the writer brings in the flashback before the reader has become thoroughly interested in the hero and his problem. Even then there is grave danger of repelling the reader and killing his interest in the story unless you can somehow make the flashback exciting, and this poses one of the stiffest problems the writer of fiction has to face.

The reader does not wish to be instructed or informed; he demands to be amused, and the writer who fails to keep him amused while reading the flashback runs a grave risk of losing his reader.

"Flashbacks are parts of the story which inform the reader what has happened before the story proper begins, that tell 'the story behind the story.' Handling these is one of the major problems of making the Beginning of a story readable. There are several methods to be considered here:

> presenting the flashback as a part of the emotional experience of one (usually the chief) character; as a sort of emotional reminiscence;
>
> presenting the flashback in rapid, running narrative, thus relying upon the movement of the form of discourse to keep the reader reading;
>
> presenting the flashback as the answer to a question previously propounded, so that the reader wades through it in order to get the answer;
>
> presenting the flashback as the solution to a puzzle presented at the beginning of the story—for example, the reader is given some surprising set of circumstances, which demand explanation;
>
> by presenting the flashback in a series of dramatic scenes;
>
> by breaking it up into little bits and then scattering these through the main narrative of your story;
>
> by presenting the flashback in a delightful style, dialect or fresh phrasing, interesting in itself;
>
> by presenting the flashback in dialogue, or with successive passages of dialogue, thus bringing it into the present;
>
> by presenting, within the flashback, a letter, document—not too long—or other paper quoted or recalled so as to get away from the 'historical' narrative;
>
> by combining dramatic action and dialogue;
>
> by combining dramatic action, dialogue, and emotional reminiscence.

"Any or all of these methods are serviceable. You will make sure to use the one that suits your purpose in the given instance. In case you are not sure, you had better try them all and find out."[1]

Here follow examples of some of the devices just listed in presenting flashbacks in an interesting manner:

Heading · DEVICES OF THE BEGINNING · FLASHBACK

Clipping From *Dakotah Courtship*—in Appendix

4. That motor trouble in Joe's fighting heart was not entirely due to Lillie's near presence, however. 5. Lillie and Joe had mostly got along fine—at the Indian Boarding School. 6. The pocket of his blue shirt contained a well-thumbed letter in her firm Spencerian hand, assuring him, in a curious mixture of school slang and Indian poetry, that she loved him: "Hurry up, Big Boy. 7. I'm crazy about you. 8. All time you way off in South Dakota, my lips are still on your lips."

Problem of the Author To inform the reader of circumstances leading to the immediate situation.

Solution by the Author An expository statement of fact (sentence 5), a quotation from a document attesting to the relationship of the two characters, hero and heroine (sentences 6, 7, 8).

Effect upon the Reader The author's problem here of first telling and then showing and the use of a passage in quotation marks is convincing.

Student's Comment The word "firm" also characterizes the heroine and carries a threat of conflict between her and her sweetheart.

Heading · DEVICES OF THE BEGINNING · FLASHBACK

Clipping From *Dakotah Courtship*—in Appendix

14. Lillie had warned Joe that her grandma was terrible old-fashioned. 15. Lillie said Joe couldn't wrangle the old lady single-handed.

Problem of the Author Further to inform the reader of the dangers faced by our hero.

[1]Walter S. Campbell, *Writing Magazine Fiction* (Doubleday & Co., Inc., New York, 1940), pp. 119–20.

Solution by the Author Here the hero recalls warnings given by another character.

Effect upon the Reader A character witness is always more effective than anything the author can say.

Student's Comment The flashback may be used for a great variety of purposes.

Heading · DEVICES OF THE BEGINNING · FLASHBACK

Clipping From *Dakotah Courtship*—in Appendix
91. She turned towards him, shamefaced. 92. "Believe it or not," she said defiantly. 93. "Go on and laugh. 94. I know I look awful. 95. Grandma made me do it."
96. She hardly looked the bobbed-haired beauty Joe had dated and dragged to the movies at school.

Problem of the Author To explain extraordinary appearance of the heroine.

Solution by the Author By a brief flashback in one sentence (95) spoken by the heroine.

Effect upon the Reader The emotion of this statement (95), borne out by the appearance of the character, is quite convincing.

Student's Comment The brevity of this flashback makes it all the more effective.

Heading · DEVICES OF THE BEGINNING · FLASHBACK

Clipping From *Dakotah Courtship*—in Appendix
161. "Moreover, he learned to fight with fists like white men, wearing mittens of leather, in a rope corral. 162. I saw him. 163. He knocked down every young man his size in the school, and four white boys."

Problem of the Author To present more fully facts already hinted at in sentence 1.

Solution by the Author One character makes a statement concerning our hero before witnesses.

Effect upon the Reader A statement presented in quotation from the mouth of one of the characters is always more convincing than anything the author can say. The earnestness of the speaker also counts, and her quaint expression makes for interest.

Student's Comment This flashback, being in character and also characterizing our hero, is a standard device. Flashbacks with dialogue usually seem more emphatic and convincing.

Heading · DEVICES OF THE BEGINNING · FLASHBACK

Clipping From *Dakotah Courtship*—in Appendix
189. "Look at my husband. 190. He got his name stealing bread from the soldiers at the fort. 191. He was the meanest boy we ever had. 192. When he was little he used to steal his mother's butcher knife and slash holes in the tent. 193. She could not stop him. 194. He was bad. 195. Heap bad. 196. Always making trouble." 197. She beamed.

Problem of the Author To characterize one of the opponents of our hero.

Solution by the Author A third character is made to describe the actions of one of the hero's opponents in his youth, thus accounting for his present motivation.

Effect upon the Reader A flashback in dialogue is always more emphatic. The character of the speaker is also emphasized here, and her enthusiasm may be conveyed to the reader.

Student's Comment A flashback in dialogue uttered enthusiastically by a creditable witness is generally convincing.

Heading · DEVICES OF THE BEGINNING · FLASHBACK

Clipping From *Dakotah Courtship*—in Appendix
205. "You Crows all remember him. 206. He stole plenty horses from you—every winter, they say. 207. But he was never mean to women—not even Crow women."
208. Mrs. Hardtack laughed unpleasantly. 209. "He never had a chance to be."

210. Mrs. Lone Bear replied with emphatic gestures. 211. "I was told his warriors gave him a Crow woman. 212. They captured her. 213. Sitting Bull gave her a good horse and sent her home."

214. "No Crow woman would have married him," Mrs. Hardtack snapped back. 215. "She would die first." 216. Her black eyes shone fiercely. 217. "That is the way when Dakotah and Crow marry. 218. They are never happy."

219. Mrs. Lone Bear could not resist that opening. 220. With gusto she signaled, "That was what Sitting Bull said."

Problem of the Author   To use the past to motivate the characters in the story in the present and advance the plot.

Solution by the Author   Two characters are made to argue about controversial past events.

Effect upon the Reader   The dramatic conflict is interesting to the reader, particularly because most of it is in dialogue.

Student's Comment   A heated argument is always effective if no actual violence can be afforded the reader.

Heading · DEVICES OF THE BEGINNING · FLASHBACK

Clipping   From *Dakotah Courtship*—in Appendix

256. Lone Bear smacked his lips again and grinned. 257. "The Dakotahs killed Long Hair and hundreds of his soldiers. 258. Their bodies covered the hills like a big blue blanket. 259. I saw it. 260. I was in the fight. 261. You were only a boy then, too young to fight. 262. That was your good luck. 263. But we did not kill many Crows that day. 264. They ran away."

Problem of the Author   To keep the plot rolling.

Solution by the Author   A flashback is introduced consisting of a statement uttered by one of the characters about the past extremely annoying to another.

Effect upon the Reader   The reader anticipates further conflict.

Student's Comment   Flashbacks may be used all through a story to advance the plot by keeping up tension in the characters by references to matters about which they were at odds in the past.

65

Clipping From *Dakotah Courtship*—in Appendix

23. The old Dakotah shifted his moccasins to a firmer position upon the hot floorboards, turned red-rimmed eyes upon his grandson, and showed his yellow teeth in a grin of pleasurable anticipation. 24. "Make your heart strong, my grandson," he quavered. 25. "I know how to handle the Crows. 26. I have killed plenty of them in my day, and made them run like rabbits.

Problem of the Author To make the reader aware of the past history of the hero's relative, thus establishing the old man's motives.

Solution by the Author The character is shown shifting his position, anticipating trouble with pleasure, and making a confident statement by word of mouth. The author uses what is in effect the Wave Formula.

Effect upon the Reader The Wave Formula is always convincing.

Student's Comment This flashback is doubly convincing because it characterizes.

Clipping From *Dakotah Courtship*—in Appendix

271. "Them soldiers came looking for trouble, and found it. 272. They died fighting—with guns in their hands and cartridges in their belts. 273. That was a fair fight, and no massacre."

274. "That's what *you* think," Lillie snapped. 275. "I know. 276. Some of my relatives were there."

277. Joe swayed with restless irritation. 278. "They did not stay long," he countered.

Problem of the Author To keep the quarrel between two lovers boiling when they have nothing to quarrel about in the present.

Solution by the Author The lovers are made to argue about matters of history in which their family loyalties are involved.

Effect upon the Reader The reader enjoys this, as it is always fun to see those near and dear to each other at odds. He is perhaps also pleased to get some free information about American history.

Student's Comment   The historical incident referred to is controversial and widely known to persons interested in the kind of life portrayed in this story. It amuses the reader to see people fighting a war over again three quarters of a century later.

Heading · DEVICES OF THE BEGINNING · FLASHBACK

Clipping   From *Dakotah Courtship*—in Appendix
293. "The soldiers shot fast that day. 294. But we made them run, we killed them. 295. It was a great day. 296. Every little while I picked up a feather for my cap. 297. I cannot remember how many I killed that day."

298. "My relatives told me it was a hard fight to the end," the Crow objected.

299. Lone Bear ignored the interruption. 300. "I was there. 301. I saw. 302. We Dakotahs made the Crows who came with the white men run for their lives. 303. I have heard that they did not stop running for three days. 304. Some of them are running still, maybe." 305. Lone Bear laughed.

306. Hardtack threw up his head. 307. His eyes glittered. 308. "There are too many tongues. 309. That day the Crows fought well. 310. They captured the ponies of your people. 311. Long Hair told them to do that. 312. The Crows charged ahead of the soldiers, and ran off the ponies. 313. But they were not told to stand and die. 314. When they saw that the soldiers could not win, they ran away. 315. If the soldiers had been smart, they would have run away too. 316. A good warrior knows when to charge and when to retreat. 317. The Crows did both better than the white soldiers."

318. Lone Bear gave a hearty gesture of assent. 319. "The Crows ran well that day." 320. He laughed. 321. "I chased them."

Problem of the Author   To aggravate the quarrel between those whose alliance is necessary for the hero's welfare.

Solution by the Author   This is done by prolonging a heated argument in dialogue.

Effect upon the Reader   The reader enjoys a scene and, knowing the motivation of the characters well by this time, can enjoy their argument to the full.

67

American readers love scenes, particularly those which characterize. It is noteworthy that in this story each argument about the past is prolonged and made more violent. This applies also to the flashbacks in sentences 356–64, 371, 386, 579, and 585.

L. Suggesting the Conflict in the Hero's Mind

Every story is somebody's story, and that somebody is the chief sufferer, the hero, or viewpoint character, and the story really takes place in his mind, his heart, his soul. It is the story of two conflicting emotions: cowardice and duty; love and honor, and so on. These conflicts are always between the self and the not-self in the hero's mind. For every story is a conflict and an adjustment, more or less complete, of the hero's selfish desires or impulses and his unselfish duty to others. He has to choose between what he wishes to do and what he ought to do, between right and wrong, or between what he wants and what society expects of him.

A story is a parable based upon the old text, "He that loseth his life shall save it," upon the idea that two heads are better than one— that is to say, that the standards of mankind should take precedence over the selfish desires of the individual. Without this moral struggle there could be no problem, no decision, no sacrifice, and therefore no plot. And without plot you have only a character sketch, a mood, an atmosphere, an idea. Writing such fragments is not story writing, and there are few publishers who will print them.

This conflict in the hero's mind had better be presented early, at the time when his problem is made plain.

Here follow devices which present emotional conflict of the hero:

Heading · DEVICES OF THE BEGINNING · SUGGESTING UNMISTAKABLY THE CONFLICTING EMOTIONS IN THE HERO'S MIND

Clipping From *Dakotah Courtship*—in Appendix
2. But as Joe gradually approached the gate of Chief Hardtack's allotment, his young heart missed almost as often as his chugging engine. 3. Lillie Fineweather lived there. . . . 9. Lillie was okay. 10. One in a million. 11. But now he had to face old Mrs. Hardtack and her stuffy old man, and hurdle their objections. 12. Dakotah

and Crow had been enemies from away back. 13. When a Dakotah boy came courting a Crow girl, there was likely to be trouble. . . . 101. "Are you the kid I came all this way to marry?" . . . 139. "My grandson wants to marry your granddaughter." . . . 174. "She would not look at a Dakotah. 175. Your grandson must be crazy to follow her."

Problem of the Author   To indicate the conflicting emotions in the hero's mind, love for the heroine versus loyalty to his tribe.

Solution by the Author   References to these two emotions are placed early in the story and objectified throughout by the quarrel of the loving pair with each other and by their quarreling old folks.

Effect upon the Reader   The author intended sympathy for the lovers and amusement at the old folks fighting over again wars long since ended.

Student's Comment   In the early part of the story the quarrels of the other characters so obviously involve the hero, pulling him both ways, that little more need be said directly about his personal motives.

Heading · DEVICES OF THE BEGINNING · CONFLICT OF EMOTIONS

Clipping   From *Dakotah Courtship*—in Appendix

265. Joe groaned. 266. "Zowie! 267. Now Granddad is talking about the Custer Battle."

268. "The Custer Massacre," Lillie corrected him, sharply.

269. Joe bristled. 270. "Massacre nothing. 271. Them soldiers came looking for trouble, and found it. 272. They died fighting—with guns in their hands and cartridges in their belts. 273. That was a fair fight, and no massacre."

274. "That's what *you* think," Lillie snapped. 275. "I know. 276. Some of my relatives were there."

277. Joe swayed with restless irritation. 278. "They did not stay long," he countered. 279. Then, suddenly, he whirled on her. 280. "Hey, Lil. 281. Don't let it get you too. 282. We got to stand together. 283. I'm going to marry you."

284. "Maybe," she said, her eyes brimming with angry tears.

285. "Okay, Lillie, if that's the way you feel." 286. Joe turned his back on her.

287. "Oh, for the love of Mike, shut up," she scolded. 288. "The more we talk, the worse it is. 289. I can't help it, I tell you."

Problem of the Author To show the conflict of emotions in the minds of the hero and heroine and also between themselves as representing their respective tribes.

Solution by the Author The two are made to fight the tribal wars over again.

Effect upon the Reader Amusing, but not altogether happy, since by this time the reader is sympathetic with the young people.

Student's Comment This device also gives promise of trouble.

M. Promising Conflict

In addition to the conflict within his own mind, your hero usually has conflict with the outer world. In the course of the story he is commonly confronted with: (1) an obstacle to be overcome, (2) an opponent to be overcome, and (3) a disaster to be averted. Like everything else in the story, these conflicts must be pointed to, and it is most essential that quite early in the Beginning you somehow indicate these dangers. Without a Promise of Conflict your reader will hardly continue, however interesting your characters and setting may be.

Here follow devices of this sort:

Heading · DEVICES OF THE BEGINNING · PROMISE OF CONFLICT

Clipping From *Dakotah Courtship*—in Appendix
11. But now he had to face old Mrs. Hardtack and her stuffy old man, and hurdle their objections. 12. Dakotah and Crow had been enemies from away back. 13. When a Dakotah boy came courting a Crow girl, there was likely to be trouble.

Problem of the Author Quickly to make the reader aware of the hero's approaching conflict with his adversaries.

Solution by the Author A brief expository statement of the problem of the hero in general terms.

Effect upon the Reader The reader is now fully aware of what the conflict will be about.

70

Student's Comment Use of the phrases "stuffy old man," "from away back," and "courting" in this passage keeps the statement in the viewpoint of the hero, where it belongs.

These sentences also give Promise of Conflict: 18–31, 46, 47, 51, 52–55, 59–61, 70, 110, 116, 121–23, 140, 142–45, 151–52, 158–59, 171, 201, 205, 218–19, 230, 400–03.

N. Characterization

Having once introduced your characters, you must as promptly as possible characterize these more fully so that the reader becomes aware not only of their identity but also of their traits. A trait is a quality of mind or heart. Traits are:

1. human or natural; such as love of food, laziness, gusto, mother love, etc.
2. typical, representative of a group; such as fastidiousness in an aesthete, boldness in an explorer, daintiness in a lady, etc.
3. individual or peculiar to one character; such as zeal in a slave, honor in a thief, etc.
4. moral or social (selfish or unselfish); such as loyalty, courage, self-sacrifice, or spite, envy, cowardice.

Of all the elements of fiction, character is easily foremost as a source of interest. Human character is something we all naturally understand and so enjoy, since we are ourselves human. Moreover, broadly speaking, human character is the only thing we can fully understand; that is, grasp with our emotions as well as with our intelligence. In addition, character is so diverse that it offers us more variety than plot or setting ever can: there are only a few plots, only a few settings, but there are millions of people on this earth, no two exactly alike. Best of all, character, in fiction, can be made so vivid that the imaginary persons often seem more real to the reader than his own friends and neighbors.

With all these counts in its favor, it is hardly surprising that the reader loves good characterization. Thus, whether it is our desire to publish for a large, paying public, or to go down in history as great writers, immortals, the surest way to our goal is to create characters, for there is nothing the reader loves more.

There are several kinds of characterization and several methods

71

of creating character. These arise out of the nature of man and of his peculiar situation in the world.

When he is born, a man is a complete egotist, selfish, greedy, at the mercy of his emotions and his appetites. *A newborn baby has no more social feeling than a shark.* But society, in the person of the mother, the family, the neighbors, and the community, takes that baby in hand and, during its long infancy, instills into it more and more social feeling, until—if "well brought up"—that baby develops into an honest, hard-working, unselfish, public-spirited man, willing, if necessary, to sacrifice his own interests to those of others, and even to give his life for them. This amazing transformation is made possible by the fact that the baby cannot take care of himself for many years after he is born and so has to do as he is told and accept the standards of the group in which he finds himself. His naturally selfish egotism is overlaid by an unselfish, social loyalty to those who have made it possible for him to survive and grow to maturity.

This loyalty to the group may persist to the end if circumstances favor it. It may crack up under extremes of pain and suffering. But, in either case, the natural, original selfishness is there somewhere and craves expression—all the more because it has been controlled and suppressed. The natural man is still alive and kicking, and this vital principle is necessary if the man is to do a man's work in the world. Society attempts to turn it to the service of the group. *But the balance is always precarious.* And, not being allowed to indulge his natural egotism in group life, the poor wolf in sheep's clothing has to find release in his dreams—or in his fiction. He *has* to be *good*, but he *wants* to be *happy*.

This conflict of the desires of the natural, individual man and the demands of the social group is something man cannot escape from because of his long infancy and his gregarious habits, and so he turns to dreams and fiction for his release. You will find that every good story turns upon this point, that the conflict is inevitably between a man's natural, selfish interests and the artificial but none the less necessary interests of the group.

Human society is a necessary thing, something without which a man cannot survive, cannot even be normal. But, for all that, it is an artificial thing and often irksome to the natural man. In fiction the two things are reconciled: for in fiction, to be good is to be happy, or—sometimes—to be happy is to be good. In real life the thing is not so simple.

In real life, if a man kills his enemy, Nature says, "Attaboy! Let the best man survive." But Society says, "Hang him." In real life, if a man eats a bad oyster, Society says, "Poor fellow!" But Nature says, "Off with his head!" Man has to live under two codes that do not always coincide. It is only in fiction that the two can be made to coincide so that the man is entirely satisfied, both on his natural side and on the side of his social ideals.

Tags are marks by which a character may be identified. Tags are:

1. sensory (sometimes called the tag of appearance); such as how the character looks, sounds, smells, feels, or tastes. Thus the character may be blue-eyed, loud-mouthed, rank-smelling, hard as nails, or taste of lipstick.
2. of speech; such as the tone of voice, dialect, or a common expression used repeatedly: "Glory be!"
3. of gesture; such as a small characteristic mannerism: sniffing, or wagging a cigar.
4. habit of mind; such as stupid, quick-witted, etc.

The merely *human* trait wins our good will, makes us feel at one with the character. Thus, if he shows a natural weakness, a natural hunger or thirst, a natural laziness or selfishness (so long as it is not dangerous to society), we respond at once. When Abraham Lincoln wished to prevent the mob from lynching his client he made no attempt to appeal to the crowd's love of order and law; he appealed to them on the ground that he was a young lawyer, just getting started, and could not afford to have his first client lynched. That touch of human nature made them respond at once.

The *social* trait wins our respect. It is not easy to set aside our own good for the good of society, and we feel and have been taught to believe that unselfishness is the highest human virtue and selfishness the lowest vice. This conviction is almost universal. In short, we regard as a hero the man who puts our interests ahead of his own.

The *typical* trait wins our interest because it is something we recognize, something familiar and therefore delightfully easy to understand. Recognition is always a sure-fire device in fiction since it requires little or no effort on the part of the reader.

The *individual* trait wins our interest because it is, to some degree, novel. It adds *variety* to the merely human, merely typical, and merely social traits, all of which (by repetition) have become somewhat tiresome.

Therefore, to make your character appeal, you should give him a

73

warmly human weakness, such as a tendency to imbibe too much (as in *Rip Van Winkle, The Old Soak*), make him lazy (as in the old man in *You Can't Take It with You*), or just have him take off his shoes because his feet hurt! Any natural, normal, human feeling like that will win your reader's heart. It is all the better if this trait exhibits itself (though harmlessly) in violation of social custom.

The typical trait should follow quickly or be presented simultaneously, so that the merely human response will be connected with the easily recognizable type. The individual trait lends the interest of variety, and the social trait ties in with the story. The reaction of the reader should be more or less as follows: "He's natural, all right. Sure, I know that kind. But this one is different, a little. What will he do?"

So much for the traits of character. Now for the methods of characterization.

There are several, each appropriate to its own kind of fiction, its own purpose. There is, first of all, the method of creation suited to the "flat" character, usually found in short stories, for the simple reason that short stories do not afford room for the development of characters in "relief" or fully "round" characters.

By a *flat* character we mean one which exhibits a single social trait, one that is clear cut, distinct, and simple, a character that always behaves in the same way from the same motive, one that always displays the same mannerisms and the same appearance.

Such simplicity of characterization is, of course, extremely effective and vivid in short stories, where there is no room for too much tiresome repetition. Also, it is found in plays, in novels whose main resource is scene rather than plot, and in the works of such authors as John Bunyan and Charles Dickens. In fact, such authors often name their characters for the traits which they embody.

To create such a flat character it is necessary to decide definitely upon a trait for the character and to see to it that he always acts in accordance with his trait. In order to do this, you may, if you like, give your characters names suggesting the traits they embody—Mr. Busybody, Mr. Slow, Mr. Jealous, and so on. Later, for purposes of lifelikeness, you may change them to Mr. Smith, Mr. Brown, Mr. Jones. But while writing, it keeps you on the track to use the trait names for all characters.

The character in "relief" will have to have more than one trait, though these should be, as Aristotle remarked long ago, "consistent."

74

That is, the reader must be made to feel that the two traits belong together.

In the fully "round" character (generally found only in novels) you may have a number of traits, as you find them in real people, but you must take care to make these, however inconsistent they may appear, always appear "consistently inconsistent," to quote Aristotle once more.

The flat character is best adapted to short fiction, where it is extremely vivid, and to brief scenes, or for minor characters in a novel who do not hold the stage for long. Also in melodrama, or for bloodcurdling villains with whom the reader is not permitted to become acquainted. Such villains are created simply by denying them the *human* and the *social* traits, and emphasizing the *typical* and sometimes the *individual* traits, and of course by making their motives unsocial to an extreme.

The character in "relief" may be the principal character in a plot novel where real people rarely appear, or the major characters in a novel where the chief character is fully "rounded." There is seldom room for such a character in a short story.

The fully "round" character is useful for the long novel of character, for so-called "serious" fiction, where the reader demands characters approaching the complexity of real persons. In this you develop all traits, and sometimes several of each.

Thus, whether you use flat, relief, or round characters will depend upon (1) the length of the fiction you plan to write, (2) the amount of space you can devote to characterization, (3) the preference of your readers. It is all a matter of choice on your part and of ability to mix your traits judiciously.

But there is a second consideration to be studied: the *functions* of your characters. In a story or novel you must display character in action, you must have a plot, you must show conflict between the natural man and the social man. This means that at least some of your characters have a function to perform, something they must *do*, in your story. Hence they must have the ability to do it. Thus, if the hero is to shoot the bad man, he must be a marksman. If the girl is to win the millionaire, she must have the qualities and the technique to win him (preferably the quality, since women like to imagine that men fall at their feet, overwhelmed by charm, instead of being lured to love).

Naturally some characters will have no function to perform and remain merely passive—as in the case of suspects in a murder mystery, oftentimes. But the main characters, those who make things happen, must have a function and an ability to perform it. In short, they are actors hired to do a job, while the others are mere supers. Determine, therefore, what function each of your characters must perform, and provide each one with the necessary ability to do that, and that alone.

Naturally, if they have the ability to do something, they must be supplied with the tool or weapon with which to do it. Thus, your gunman must have a gun, your charmer must have beauty, your sleuth must have intelligence. To each his function, his ability, and his tool or weapon. Without these you have no story, only a lot of lay figures around.

Since the reader wishes to distinguish your characters, you must also provide each of them—at least each one of any importance—with labels or tags by which he may be recognized.

It is by means of tags that we remember people in real life as well as in fiction. For example, Theodore Roosevelt, the former President of the United States, had a tag of appearance: the teeth and the glasses; a tag of gesture or action: the strenuous movement of his head or arm; the tag of speech: "Bully!" and a decided habit of mind—at any rate, in the popular belief—determination.

Franklin D. Roosevelt also had a tag of appearance: the way he stood, his face; a tag of gesture: his grin; a tag of speech: "My friends"; and a cheerful habit of mind.

A little consideration will enable you to provide tags for General MacArthur, Joe Louis, Winston Churchill, Donald Duck, the Duke of Windsor—anybody, in fact, who is in the public eye. Once you have learned to recognize these, you will do well to make a habit of "tagging" everyone you meet, as a matter of habit. Practice at this until you form the habit of thinking in terms of tags about people, just as a doctor thinks automatically of people he meets in terms of symptoms.

These tags, you will find, are generally most interesting when they are connected in some way with the motives and purposes of the character. The tag should be in accord with the trait or appear to be in strong contrast to it. We can see tags, and traits we cannot see. Hence tags should help us see traits.

You may use this classification of traits, tags, abilities, and tools in imagining your characters beforehand. Or you may prefer to create your characters first and then check back to see if each one has all the necessary traits, tags, and that he has the tool or weapon, the ability, to perform his function in the story. Then if one character seems to be deficient in interest or truth to life, you may be able to discover what is lacking in him and make that deficiency good.

While you are learning to think in these terms it may be useful for you to read with these things in mind. Get a box of sixteen Crayola colored pencils. Then go through some magazine story you have recently read. Underscore the merely human traits (wherever indicated) in red; the social traits (selfish or unselfish) in green; the typical traits in blue; the individual traits in black. You may also use the same method for the tags which show the traits and identify the characters: tag of appearance, orange; tag of gesture, purple; tag of speech, yellow; tag of thought, pink. This simple exercise will teach you much about the methods and materials of character drawing.

A character may be presented in eight different ways. The author may characterize:

by *action* of the character: Pete slunk out of the battle.

by *speech* of the character: "Hiya, pardner!"

by *effect* of the character upon other characters: Her loveliness was breath-taking.

by the character's own reactions to persons, things, and surrounding circumstances: John adored her, especially in blue.

by reporting what other characters say about the character: Said Tom, "Of course Sam is a heel!"

by explaining the traits and motives of the character: He loved good food.

by describing the character (in terms of the five senses): He had blue eyes, spoke with a Southern accent, smelled of the smoke-house, and his muscles were hard as nails.

by analyzing the psychological processes of the character: He was unable to overcome his shyness, which was the result of his being the son of a famous and terribly egotistical father.

Sometimes, no doubt, you will use all eight methods of presenting your chief characters in the course of the story, and you may even use all of them quite early. Which you use first or how you combine them will depend upon your purpose.

Of course in exhibiting character in terms of action you must consider the reader you are attempting to please. In popular fiction,

77

where actions speak very loud and where conformity to social standards is identified with virtue, a character is commonly shown making the conventional choice in a great crisis. Thus, if compelled to choose between love and duty, he will be no hero if he puts love first. But in "serious" fiction (so-called) character is not shown in great crises but in little actions of which society takes little notice. Character there is shown in a series of "significant trivialities," because the readers of serious fiction know, or think they know, that in great crises people generally do what is expected of them, while in small matters they really do as they wish.

Here follow examples of devices for Characterization.

Heading · DEVICES OF THE BEGINNING · CHARACTERIZATION

Clipping From *The Cask of Amontillado,* by Edgar Allan Poe
1. You, who so well know the nature of my soul . . .

Problem of the Author To make the reader believe the story of the narrator hero of the yarn.

Solution by the Author A character witness is introduced to vouch for the truth of the hero's narration. The character witness is addressed as "you."

Effect upon the Reader Through this device the reader is identified with the character witness and therefore never doubts the truth of the narration.

Student's Comment This is a splended example of the use of a character witness, a very clever trick indeed—convincing, swift, and immediate. It is an axiom that the reader will not believe anything the author tells him, that he will believe only what the author shows him. This device is most convincing.

Heading · DEVICES OF THE BEGINNING · CHARACTERIZATION

Clipping From *Dakotah Courtship*—in Appendix
52. But when Joe laid eyes on the old woman, he held his breath. 53. Mrs. Hardtack was formidable. 54. She sat upright on the ground—one leg stretched straight out before her. 55. Her flat, uncompromising face was painted red. 56. She had a short hooked nose,

78

like the beak of an owl, and her dark gaze was so searching and hostile that Joe wondered what ailed him. 57. She wore an old-time calico dress with open flaps for sleeves. 58. A regular squaw—even if she was Lillie's grandma.

59. Nobody moved. 60. Nobody spoke. 61. Each party waited for the other to make the first move. 62. Chief Lone Bear would not enter until the Crow had made him welcome. 63. The Hardtacks were ready to sit still forever rather than welcome a Dakotah on such an errand. 64. In the silence, Joe heard the dog scratching himself.

65. Joe couldn't stand it. 66. He broke the ice. 67. *"How!"* he said.

68. At that word, old Mrs. Hardtack drew herself up triumphantly. 69. Her hard face set in lines of scorn. 70. "Dakotah!" she sneered.

Problem of the Author   To characterize an opponent of the hero (Mrs. Hardtack) from the hero's point of view.

Solution by the Author   Mrs. Hardtack is characterized as follows in this passage: by reaction of another character (sentences 52, 53, 56); by uncompromising action (54); by description (55–57); by gesture (56); by exposition (58–61, 63); by reaction of others (62, 65–67); by action or gesture (68, 69); by reaction to others, by speech (70).

Effect upon the Reader   The use of six of the eight possible methods of characterization in this passage (some of them repeated) can scarcely help being convincing.

Student's Comment   Six of the eight possible methods of characterization are used here. The more you use, the more vivid the characterization is likely to be.

Heading · DEVICES OF THE BEGINNING · CHARACTERIZATION BY REPORT OF OTHERS

Clipping   From *Dakotah Courtship*—in Appendix

118. Lillie raised her hand to stop him. 119. "Keep out, Joe. 120. If Grandma catches you alone with me, she'll sure raise hell. 121. She'll call the whole thing off. 122. She's terrible old-fashioned, like I told you. 123. She don't approve of necking."

Problem of the Author   To characterize one of the hero's opponents.

Solution by the Author   A creditable witness (the heroine) reports to the hero on his opponent.

Effect upon the Reader   The report of a character witness in quotation marks is generally regarded by the reader as reliable.

Student's Comment   Characterization by report usually seems valid.

Heading · DEVICES OF THE BEGINNING · CHARACTERIZATION BY REPORT OF OTHERS

Clipping   From *Dakotah Courtship*—in Appendix
172. Then Mrs. Hardtack charged. 173. "My granddaughter does not think of marriage. 174. She would not look at a Dakotah. 175. Your grandson must be crazy to follow her. 176. She is a wife for a chief. 177. She can cook and sew and wash and tan hides. 178. She makes fine beadwork. 179. She is beautiful and modest and strong as a horse. 180. On top of that she belongs to a family of warriors and feast-makers. 181. Her great grandfather was a famous horse-thief."

Problem of the Author   To characterize the heroine.

Solution by the Author   A second character passionately describes the heroine in highly laudatory terms.

Effect upon the Reader   The reader takes the laudatory description of the heroine with a grain of salt, yet accepts it on the whole. He is also amused by the vigor of the laudator and becomes more sympathetic both to her and to the heroine.

Student's Comment   An example of economy in writing. The characterization of the heroine achieves several things besides—directing the sympathies of the reader, characterizing the laudator (by speech), and providing a dash of color.

Heading · DEVICES OF THE BEGINNING · CHARACTERIZATION BY PSYCHOLOGICAL ANALYSIS

Clipping   From *The Cask of Amontillado*, by Edgar Allan Poe
1. The thousand injuries of Fortunato I had borne as I best could, but when he ventured upon insult I vowed revenge. 2. You, who so well know the nature of my soul, will not suppose, however, that I

gave utterance to a threat. 3. At length I would be avenged; this was a point definitely settled—but the very definitiveness with which it was resolved precluded the idea of risk. 4. I must not only punish but punish with impunity. 5. A wrong is unredressed when retribution overtakes its redresser. 6. It is equally unredressed when the avenger fails to make himself felt as such to him who has done the wrong.

7. It must be understood that neither by word nor deed had I given Fortunato cause to doubt my good will. 8. I continued, as was my wont, to smile in his face, and he did not perceive that my smile now was at the thought of his immolation.

Problem of the Author To make reader aware of the motives of the hero at once, so that the action of the story may begin.

Solution by the Author After a flashback, an introduction of the two antagonists, a statement of the hero's problem, and a promise of conflict (all in the first sentence), the author has his hero explain his own motives in the first person.

Effect upon the Reader Confession in the first person is convincing and has the advantage of being brief, thus projecting the reader into the action at once.

Student's Comment This is more effective than third-person narrative could be. It is also more natural, since the narrator was the only witness of the events of the story.

Conclusion

The devices given above were given separately so that you might see them clearly and realize how they are commonly handled. All these must be brought in somehow in the first two or three pages of your yarn, and the sooner the better—provided you can do it effectively.

In doing this you will often weave them together so that a single sentence may contain several devices and so serve several purposes.

It is not intended or supposed that you will be content with the examples given above but that you will in your own reading discover and collect many others, until you have a thick file of Devices of the Beginning. By studying these examples and looking for others in the stories you read you will soon become adept at recognizing them, and with a little practice of Finger Exercises you will be able to create combinations of your own for the particular story you have in hand. Thus, by study of the work of others, by *isolating, analyzing,* and *practicing* their devices, you may—sooner than you think— become familiar with and adept in the methods of the masters.

So much for the Devices of the Beginning.

WORK PROGRAM 8

1. In this story the hero, Joe Lone Bear, is characterized chiefly by action, speech, reaction of others, reaction to others, report of others, description, and exposition, in that order. He is characterized by action thirty times; by speech, twenty-nine times; by reaction of others, thirty times; by reaction to others, twenty-one times. Description and exposition are used only four times each. Can you find any example of characterization of Joe by psychological analysis?

    Scan the story *Dakotah Courtship* in the Appendix and locate every passage of characterization of Joe Lone Bear by sentence number, listing each under one of the methods given above.

2. Chief Lone Bear is characterized throughout the story as follows: by action in twelve passages; by speech, eight times; by report of others, five times; by reaction of others, sixteen times; by reaction to others, five times; by description, once; by exposition, none. Can you find any passage in which he is characterized by psychological analysis—that is, by an explanation of his motives?

    Scan the story *Dakotah Courtship* in the Appendix and locate every passage of characterization of Chief Lone Bear by sentence number, listing each under one of the methods given above.

3. How do you account for the fact that there is so little characterization by description and exposition here?

4. Now make up devices for yourself stating the Problem, Solution, etc., of each of the major passages in which Chief Lone Bear is characterized.

5. Mrs. Hardtack is characterized in a number of passages in this story. It is recommended that you search out the following passages, characterizing her as follows: she is characterized by

her actions nine times; by her speech in ten passages; by report of others in three passages; by the reaction of others to her in ten passages; by her reaction to others in ten passages; by description in two passages; by exposition in two passages. Can you find any passage where she is characterized by psychological analysis?

6. You will find Chief Hardtack characterized in the passages noted herewith. Check these in the story and prepare devices of your own, giving the Heading, Clipping, Problem, Solution, Effect upon Reader, and Student's Comment. Give examples of each of the methods used.

28–30, 48–51, 72, 81, 240–41, 251–55, 298, 306–17, 322–25, 326–64, 398–99, 412–15, 451–52, 455–59, 514.

7. In the story *Dakotah Courtship*, Lillie Fineweather is characterized in sentences as indicated below. Go through the story, checking the passages indicated. Then select for each method used in her characterization several of the passages here noted and use them as clippings. Prepare devices of your own according to the pattern.

5, 6, 7, 8, 9, 10, 13, 14–15, 44, 87, 91, 92–95, 96–99, 100–01, 104–06, 108–10, 118–23, 144–45, 159, 173–81, 183, 200, 201, 203, 224–25, 226–30, 235, 268, 274–76, 284, 287–90, 365–67, 372–74, 375–79, 382, 404–08, 416, 461, 462–67, 470–73, 475–77, 484–85, 497–500, 502–07, 509–19, 517–25, 529, 540, 554–56, 559, 566, 569–71, 572–79, 583, 592–96, 602, 612–14, 618–22.

8. In Chapter 8 you have been given examples of devices for most of the principal problems you will have to solve in writing the Beginnings of your own stories. In order to fix these in your mind it is advisable to study them and then write three Finger Exercises in imitation of at least one example of each device, always using different words and different subject matter but adhering to the pattern of the original. Do that.

9. Now study the Beginning of some other short story or a novelette or novel, looking for devices in the Beginning. Then make a list of the devices given in Chapter 8 and try to find passages which serve the same purpose in the other story, novelette, or novel. Make these up into devices for your file. Then practice each one in three Finger Exercises.

These exercises, if patiently worked out, will be rewarding; for they will not only teach you certain tricks, but, what is far more important, train you to recognize these in everything you read. Indeed, after serious study of this kind, you will find devices leaping at you from every page you read. When that happens, you are well on your way as a writer. All the secrets of the writers you admire will be plain as day to you, and your own technique will advance accordingly.

10. Turn to the Appendix, Section B, Notes on Chapter 8. Check your answers to questions 1 and 2 in Work Program 8 with what you find there.

11. Now record whatever you have learned about technique in general or in particular while doing the exercises suggested in this Work Program.

CHAPTER 9   FICTION • DEVICES OF THE MIDDLE

THE SHORT STORY

The Middle of a story, if you have a good plot, is comparatively simple and easy to write. It falls into two parts, each about as long or a little longer than the Beginning—three or four pages each.

In Part Two (the first half of the Middle) you develop your situation and problem by having your hero set about solving his problem as best he can. This brings about complications; things begin to look bad; he begins to sizzle in the frying pan.

In Part Three his jeopardy, his difficulty, his agony increase. Things become desperate. The hero is losing; the villain winning. The hero is brought to his black, agonizing moment where everything seems lost and he is out of the frying pan and into the fire. If your complication is well devised, the reader will not be able to see how the hero can solve it and escape. But you will have in mind a pat solution, at once surprising and plausible, to be used in Part Four.

But here we are concerned only with the Parts Two and Three—the Middle.

The Middle consists of a series of ups and downs in which the hero struggles to solve his problem. Each time he takes a step forward his opponents shove him back. Thus the Middle is a series of Hindrances and Futherances. Whenever the hero acts to carry out his purpose and solve his problem, or when he even plans to do so, though bound hand and foot, you have a Furtherance.

Whenever his opponents get the better of him or scheme to do him harm, you have a Hindrance. These alternate throughout the Middle, developing the problem to the complication and on to the verge of the decision.

The middle ends whenever the reader becomes aware how the story is coming out.

It follows that Continuity of interest and increasing Suspense are the important problems of the Middle. There must be an unbroken tie-up of cause and effect, with each part interlocking with what goes before and follows after, with gripping incident, powerful motives, and swift transitions. A spotlight of emotion must be focused on each important step as the plot unfolds, and each step should follow inevitably from what has gone before and lead relentlessly to what follows. And of course the whole must be made plausible.

Now for the devices commonly found in the Middle.

These are:

A. Furtherances
B. Hindrances
C. Complications
D. Scenes
E. Transitions
F. Devices for Continuity
G. Devices for Plausibility
H. Focus
I. Repetitions
J. Overlapping Paragraphs
K. The Gimmick
L. Dialogue at Cross-Purposes
M. Devices for Corroboration
N. Indication of the Speaker
O. Discovery and Reversal
P. Color
Q. Fact Feeling
R. Incident
S. Happening

A. The Furtherance

The Futherance has been explained as any action or thought or motive of the hero which furthers his purpose.

Here follow devices illustrating Futherance and

B. The Hindrance

This has been defined above. It embodies any action, thought, feeling, or motive of the hero's opponent in thwarting the hero's purpose.

In the short story *Dakotah Courtship*, Furtherances and Hindrances will be found in the sentences whose numbers are given below. They naturally, as a rule, occur in pairs and are so listed here for your convenience. Search out these examples of the device and make up a card, putting in the device used in the more interesting examples. See how many different methods you can find employed here.

FURTHERANCES	HINDRANCES	FURTHERANCES	HINDRANCES
1	2	210–13	214–19
4–10	11–15	221–23	224
16	17	225	229–30
18–22	23–37	231–38	241–50
38–43	44–64	251	252–55
65–67	68–70	256–64	265–66
71–75	76–84	267	268
85–90	91–98	268–73	274–78
99–101	102	280–83	284–86
106	108–10	287–90	291–97
117	118–24		298–325
125	128		326–64
133	137–41		365–67
	142–45	374–96	397–403
146–50	151–52	404–15	416
153–55	156–59	418–47	453
160–64	165	459	462–68
166–71	172–81	469	470
182	185–86	474	475
	182–97	481	484
198–99	200–01	486	487
202	203	491–96	497–500
204–07	208–09	501–04	505–12

FURTHERANCES	HINDRANCES	FURTHERANCES	HINDRANCES
513	514	560	561
521–22	523	562	562 (second part)
526	527–30		
531–32	533	563	564–65
535	537–40	566–68	
541–43	544	572–91	592
546	547–50	597	602
555	558	607–17	618–21

C. The Complication

The Complication (there may be several) has been described in Chapter 8 as the worst thing that could happen to the hero under the circumstances of his original problem. It was illustrated by the example of the man bound hand and foot in the lonely cabin. If there are several complications, each one must be worse than the one before, in order to maintain suspense.

We are all aware of the essential elements of a good plot: the setting, which includes a time and place and a social atmosphere; the state of affairs out of which the necessity for action arises, some problem or question pressing for an answer; a barrier or obstacle to be surmounted; an antagonist to be overcome; a threatening predicament or imminent disaster; contrasting characters torn by emotions pulling either way; a crescendo of emotion, with one or more complications to increase the tempo. Every writer grasps these essentials readily enough—that is, grasps the fact that they are essential. But sometimes the beginner and even writers experienced enough to understand fail entirely to comprehend the real nature of a complication.

Inasmuch as the Complication and its solution are the nub of the story, the high point of interest for the reader, and the chief difficulty of plotting, it seems important to understand it. Critics and agents and editors may be able to help on other parts of your work, but nobody can be expected to write the *story* for you, and creating complications is the principal task of the storyteller—*creating* complications and *solving* them. That is something you will have to do for yourself, and unless you can do it well and often you had better turn critic and leave the storytelling to someone with a more energetic and fertile intelligence.

Most of the failures in creating complications arise simply from the fact that the writer does not see clearly what a Complication amounts to. It is not easy to manufacture a thing when you do not know what it is.

The main Complication normally falls near the end of the story, where increased interest is desirable. Such a main Complication may be defined as a predicament or disaster so dangerous to the hero that it seems (to the reader) insoluble and *therefore* so dreadful that it contains its own solution. A Complication is, in fact, at once a disaster and its solution. One must involve the other, given the ability and weapon of our hero.

Finding or inventing complications is a principal part of the storyteller's art. It is for this that he gets paid. No matter how well you write, if you cannot create complications you are no storyteller.

Note that *a Complication is a disaster which contains its own solution,* but the reader must not be allowed to perceive this. Some writers fail simply because they do not understand the true nature of a Complication; for, oddly enough, the worse the disaster, the oftener one finds a solution for it.

Many beginners fail to grasp this and so "pull their punches," making it too easy for the hero, in order, as they imagine, to make it easy for themselves to provide a solution. This is fatal to interest. The reader goes to sleep, for he is paying the writer to make it hard for the hero, and the writer who fails in this respect will soon find himself without a public. Strangely enough, one way to find good solutions is to create the worst disaster possible. It is the halfway disaster that is difficult to solve. Really bad disasters almost always suggest a way out.

In fact, one may almost lay it down as a rule that, *the worse the disaster, the easier it is to find a solution.* Moreover, the more striking the disaster, the more striking the solution will be, particularly if the solution is a simple one. And the worse your disaster is, as a rule, the more *simply* it can be solved.[1]

Take for example the story of Snow White. You will remember how the villainous Queen determines to destroy Snow White. The Queen disguises herself as an old woman and gives Snow White a

[1] As Sherlock Holmes is made to say, "The very point which appears to complicate a case is, when duly considered and scientifically handled, the one which is most likely to elucidate it"—*The Hound of the Baskervilles,* by Sir Arthur Conan Doyle, Chapter XV. Bantam Books, N.Y., 1949.

poisoned apple to eat. Snow White takes one bite of the apple and falls dead. No disaster could be more complete than that.

But what would a green beginner have done? He would have made it appear only a little deadly in order (as he fondly imagines) to make it easy for the author to extricate Snow White from being poisoned. How foolish! But the writer who invented this disaster in the fairly tale had more sense than that. He made it *so* deadly that one bite of the poisonous apple would kill her. He made it as bad as he could. There seemed no way out. But actually it was the complete deadliness of the apple that saved Snow White in the end, for she died before she could swallow the bite of apple in her mouth. And so at last when it dropped from her mouth she immediately recovered. If some green beginner had written this story and made the apple only a little deadly, Snow White would have swallowed it, digested it, and so died beyond recovery. But in the fairy tale it was the utter poisonousness of the apple which saved Snow White's life. That example will show what we mean by a good Complication. It must be very bad; indeed, *so* bad that a simple solution naturally arises from it.

There is another advantage in making it hard for the hero. Great disasters lie outside the experience of most readers. Therefore, the farther your disaster gets from reality, the more willing the reader is to believe in it, since he can no longer check the author's imagination against his own experience. A really terrible disaster sets the author's imagination free, and this makes a solution much easier to find.

You see, then, that there is a good technical reason for treating your hero rough. It makes plotting far easier for you, believe it or not. Therefore, when you find you have your hero in a bad spot, so bad that you cannot get him out, the solution is not to "pull your punches" and let up on the hero, but to shove him into another even tighter corner, where the solution will more readily occur to you. Otherwise you have only two possible courses of action: you may "pull your punches" and lose the reader's interest, or you may destroy your hero absolutely and so confess failure. You may, of course, bring in Providence to save your hero, but this use of what the critics call "machinery" is not plotting. It is begging the question.

Here follow examples of devices for presenting a Complication:

Clipping From *Dakotah Courtship*—in Appendix
15. Lillie said Joe couldn't wrangle the old lady single-handed.
16. So Joe had brought along his own grandparents to make the match in the old-time way. 17. But now, as he rolled in through Hardtack's gate, Joe began to get cold feet about that.

18. Anxiously, he shouted to caution the aged warrior at his elbow.
19. Chief Lone Bear sat braced against the gale, clutching his splintered stiff straw hat with gnarled fingers, staring fiercely through the windshield. 20. "Grandfather," Joe yelled, "the wars are over.
21. We are friends with these people now. 22. Remember that!"

23. The old Dakotah shifted his moccasins to a firmer position upon the hot floorboards, turned red-rimmed eyes upon his grandson, and showed his yellow teeth in a grin of pleasurable anticipation. 24. "Make your heart strong, my grandson," he quavered. 25. "I know how to handle the Crows. 26. I have killed plenty of them in my day, and made them run like rabbits. 27. *He-han!* 28. Who is this Hardtack? 29. He has seen only seventy-six winters. 30. I have nothing to fear from that boy!"

31. The old man's words upset Joe. 32. Then and there he killed his engine. 33. The car jolted to a stop.

Problem of the Author To introduce a first complication.

Solution by the Author By having the persons whom the hero has brought to help him make peace begin a quarrel instead.

Effect upon the Reader In a story of this sort the effect upon the reader is amusing.

Student's Comment Up to this point in the story the characterization has been limited almost entirely to the hero and heroine. Now a disturbing factor in the person of the old chief is introduced. He is made as vivid as the author knew how to make him, thus enabling the promise of conflict.

Clipping From *Dakotah Courtship*—in Appendix
516. He was still trying to start it when Lillie Fineweather passed by on her way to the gate. 517. She sailed past in her new sneakers, blue dungarees, and a clean white shirt. 518. Her shining bob swung free.

519. Joe thought she looked swell. 520. She was headin' for town, sure. 521. Joe tried to catch her eye. 522. "Where you goin', Lillie?"

523. "Nowhere with you," she replied. 524. "And don't you follow me neither—if you ever do get that thing started. 525. You damn Dakotah, I'm through."

526. Joe stamped on the starter furiously, and held his foot down. 527. Lil went on, and he saw her halt at the gate. 528. A truck was rolling down the road in a cloud of dust. 529. Lillie raised her thumb and waggled it in the air above her head. 530. Joe saw the truck slow to pick her up.

Problem of the Author To present the worst complication of all (the disaster).

Solution by the Author The Wave Formula is used. The heroine is shown walking out on the hero. Here the motivation is implied, as the reader well knows what it is. She is shown in action, walking out on the hero, and caps her action with defiant dialogue and by thumbing the truck.

Effect upon the Reader Amusing, but more serious than anything felt so far.

Student's Comment This final complication forces the hero to his decision and sacrifice and to implementing these, thus pointing to a solution to his original problem.

D. The Scene

The Scene is a unit of dramatic action, like a round in a prize fight. It follows a definite formula as follows:

MEETING of the two forces (emotions and/or persons involved in the conflict).

PURPOSE of one or both.

ENCOUNTER, containing these possible elements: attempts—

to interrogate or seek information;

to inform or convey information;

to overcome by argument or logic, to convince;

to persuade;

to influence, impress;

to compel by use of physical force.

FINAL ACTION (win, lose, or quit).

SEQUEL state of affairs; state of mind.

The Scene is the dramatization of a conflict. Its use is to convince the reader of the state of affairs and state of mind in the Sequel. There is first a Meeting of the two parties to the conflict. One has a Purpose which the other resists. An Encounter results, with six possible steps, any of which may be omitted, or repeated as often as necessary. These steps may occur in any order you find convenient. As a result of the Encounter there is a Final Action in which the character with the Purpose either wins, loses, or quits trying. As a result of this final action there is a state of affairs and a state of mind in one or both of the contestants which constitute the Sequel.

The state of mind in the Sequel of one scene usually provides the Purpose which brings about the Encounter in a following scene. Thus scenes may be interlocked and tied together by a continuing motivation. Thus a plot consists of a *series of sequels,* each state of mind being established and made credible by the four preceding steps: Meeting, Purpose, Encounter, and Final Action in each case.

In short, you write a scene to make the reader believe in your character's motive (state of mind). You *show* the events which caused the state of mind instead of telling, and so your reader believes.[2]

Here follow examples of this useful device, the Scene:

Heading · DEVICES OF THE MIDDLE · THE SCENE

Clipping From *Dakotah Courtship*—in Appendix

16. So Joe had brought along his own grandparents to make the match in the old-time way. 17. But now, as he rolled in through Hardtack's gate, Joe began to get cold feet about that.

18. Anxiously, he shouted to caution the aged warrior at his elbow. 19. Chief Lone Bear sat braced against the gale, clutching his splintered stiff straw hat with gnarled fingers, staring fiercely through the windshield. 20. "Grandfather," Joe yelled, "the wars are over. 21. We are friends with these people now. 22. Remember that!"

23. The old Dakotah shifted his moccasins to a firmer position upon the hot floorboards, turned red-rimmed eyes upon his grandson, and showed his yellow teeth in a grin of pleasurable anticipation. 24. "Make your heart strong, my grandson," he quavered. 25. "I know how to handle the Crows. 26. I have killed plenty of them

[2]For a thorough discussion of the Scene, see *Writing Magazine Fiction*, by W. S. Campbell (Doubleday & Co., Inc., New York, 1940), Chapter III.

in my day, and made them run like rabbits. 27. *He-han!* 28. Who is this Hardtack? 29. He has seen only seventy-six winters. 30. I have nothing to fear from that boy!"

31. The old man's words upset Joe. 32. Then and there he killed his engine. 33. The car jolted to a stop.

34. It was a good long hundred yards across the blistering prairie to Hardtack's unpainted shack and the brush arbor alongside. 35. But Joe was too disheartened to try to start the car again.

Problem of the Author To show vividly the first complication—that our hero's allies (his grandparents) are eager to quarrel with the grandparents of his sweetheart.

Solution by the Author A dramatic scene with dialogue and action is used in sentences 18–35, as follows:

PURPOSE (of the hero): 16, 17
MEETING (of hero and the chief): 18
ENCOUNTER (between hero and chief): 18–35, including:
  Giving information: 20–21
  Persuasion: 22
  Impression: 23–24
  Giving information: 25–27
  Seeking Information: 28
  Argument: 29–30
FINAL ACTION: 32
SEQUEL:
  State of Affairs: 33–34
  State of Mind: 35

Effect upon the Reader Convincing and amusing; there is an obvious threat of conflict.

Student's Comment American readers have little awe of authors and do not choose to take much on their say-so. American readers like scenes which *show* what happens. This is one of the results of our national tradition of liberty and independence.

Heading · DEVICES OF THE MIDDLE · THE SCENE

Clipping From *Dakotah Courtship*—in Appendix
59. Nobody moved. 60. Nobody spoke. 61. Each party waited for the other to make the first move. 62. Chief Lone Bear would not

enter until the Crow had made him welcome. 63. The Hardtacks were ready to sit still forever rather than welcome a Dakotah on such an errand. 64. In the silence, Joe heard the dog scratching himself.

65. Joe couldn't stand it. 66. He broke the ice. 67. *"How!"* he said.

68. At that word, old Mrs. Hardtack drew herself up triumphantly. 69. Her hard face set in lines of scorn. 70. "Dakotah!" she sneered.

71. Hardtack now came suddenly to life. 72. *"Sho-da-gee!"* he cried, in hospitable greeting now that the others had begun the talk. 73. Chief Lone Bear stepped over the pots and firewood, grasped Hardtack's hand quickly, and seated himself on his host's left side— the side nearest his heart. 74. Mrs. Lone Bear, making a purring sound of pleasure, waddled in and found a place beside her hostess. 75. All four of them seemed to be in high good humor, eager to begin the business. 76. All four of them completely ignored Joe.

77. Joe felt like a rank outsider. 78. For a minute he stood still, not knowing what to do. 79. Then he turned hastily and retreated. 80. Nobody wanted him around.

Problem of the Author   To show the stubborn antagonism of the two parties and the anguished anxiety of the hero to have them be friends.

Solution by the Author   A dramatic scene with dialogue and action is used in sentences 59–80, as follows:

MEETING (of Sioux and Crow): 59–64
PURPOSE (of the hero): 65
ENCOUNTER (between hero and the Crows):
  Persuasion: 67
  Impression: 68–70
  Persuasion: 72
FINAL ACTION: 73–75
SEQUEL:
  State of Affairs: 76
  State of Mind: 77–80

Effect upon the Reader   Dramatic and amusing.

Student's Comment   Everything of which the reader must be convinced in order to believe in the story is usually best shown in a dramatic scene.

Clipping From *Dakotah Courtship*—in Appendix
87. Lillie Fineweather stood inside, looking anxiously out towards the arbor through the grimy windowpane. 88. Joe halted in his tracks. 89. "Hey, Lillie. 90. Is that you?"

91. She turned towards him, shamefaced. 92. "Believe it or not," she said defiantly. 93. "Go on and laugh. 94. I know I look awful. 95. Grandma made me do it."

96. She hardly looked the bobbed-haired beauty Joe had dated and dragged to the movies at school. 97. Her hair still had the lustre of a new gun-barrel, but it was parted down the middle now and plaited into two stubby braids made long with strands of colored yarn. 98. Instead of her usual shirt and dungarees, she had on a red calico dress with a yoke and frill—Crow Reservation, fashion 1890— and high button shoes too big for her. 99. Yet somehow, she was pretty in spite of it.

100. Joe could not help laughing. 101. "Are you the kid I come all this way to marry?"

102. "You don't have to," she countered. 103. Relenting, she added, "No kidding, Joe. 104. I thought you were never coming. 105. One more day in this lousy dump, and I'll be coocoo."

106. "Okay. 107. Let's skip," Joe prompted.

108. "Nothing doing, Big Boy. 109. Grandma's got me buffaloed. 110. I'm scared to marry without her okay—supposing you can get it."

111. Joe laughed. 112. "Me? 113. What I got to do with it? 114. I'm just a bystander." 115. He moved his pursed lips in the direction of the old folks. 116. "Well, I guess the war is on." 117. Joe started to enter.

Problem of the Author To show the affectionate relationship of the hero and the heroine at their first meeting in the story.

Solution by the Author An emotional scene is used not without some promise of conflict and further convincing information as to the hazards of the hero's enterprise, as follows:

MEETING (of hero and heroine): 87–89
PURPOSE: 88
ENCOUNTER:
  Seeking information: 88–90
  Giving information: 91–95

Heading · DEVICES OF THE MIDDLE · THE SCENE

Clipping From *Dakotah Courtship*—in Appendix
117. Joe started to enter.

118. Lillie raised her hand to stop him. 119. "Keep out, Joe. 120. If Grandma catches you alone with me, she'll sure raise hell. 121. She'll call the whole thing off. 122. She's terrible old-fashioned, like I told you. 123. She don't approve of necking."

124. Joe halted. 125. "Who said anything about necking?" he complained.

126. "Nobody. 127. But somebody might think of it. 128. Whyn't you set on the stoop outside? 129. It's shady there. 130. That way we can talk, and watch the old folks at the same time. 131. They can't understand each other's talk. 132. They'll have to use the sign language."

133. "Okay, sweetheart." 134. Joe sat on the stoop, and ran his fingers through his stiff black hair. 135. Looking sideways he could see every movement in the arbor—not a dozen yards away. 136. Lillie was watching through the window.

Problem of the Author To show emphatically the intimacy between hero and heroine and the danger which overhangs them in seeking to marry.

Solution by the Author A short dramatic scene is used with dialogue at cross-purposes, implications, and promise of conflict, as follows:

MEETING (of hero and heroine): 117
PURPOSE (of hero): 117

ENCOUNTER:
   Impression: 118–19
   Argument: 120–23
   Seeking information: 125
   Persuasion: 126–32
   Giving information: 133
FINAL ACTION: 134
SEQUEL:
   State of Affairs: 135
   State of Mind: 135–36

Effect upon the Reader   Humorous and convincing.

Student's Comment   The heroine's unprovoked protest is a clear indication of close personal relationship with the hero. Such methods of indicating relationship of characters save a great many words in explanatory flashbacks.

Prepare similar analyses of the scenes found in *Dakotah Courtship* in sentences 139–97, 198–203, 205–65, 266–90, 291–364, 365–73, 375–87, 388–96, 404–15, 446–59, 460–77, 478–95, 496–512, 519–29, 527–41, 543–52, 553–59, 560–64, 591–617.

E. Transitions

Transitions are passages in a story which transport the hero and the reader from place to place, from time to time, from emotion to emotion, from scene to scene. They usually are better if they are brief. Very often they are narrative, sometimes expository or descriptive. Not infrequently the sequel at the end of a scene serves the purpose of a transition, since it may provide the motive or the purpose of the scene which follows.

   Here follow examples of the device, the Transition:

Heading · DEVICES OF THE MIDDLE · TRANSITION—FROM TIME TO TIME

Clipping   From *Dakotah Courtship*—in Appendix
440. "But now she is dead, and these grandchildren of ours want to get married."

Problem of the Author To carry the reader from the past to the present.

Solution by the Author A speaker breaks off his flashback by a sentence in the present with the verbs in the present tense.

Effect upon the Reader This ends the flashback and brings him into the present.

Student's Comment A not unusual device.

Heading · DEVICES OF THE MIDDLE · TRANSITION—FROM TIME TO TIME

Clipping From *Dakotah Courtship*—in Appendix
237. For a while there was no sound in the arbor but that of resolute mastication. 238. Chewing, for the old folks, was a chore that demanded concentration.

Problem of the Author To indicate a lapse of time.

Solution by the Author A continuous sound is described as lasting "for a while."

Effect upon the Reader Relaxation and amusement.

Student's Comment The reader can imagine as long or short a period as he likes. Sentence 238 is perhaps unnecessary.

Heading · DEVICES OF THE MIDDLE · TRANSITION—FROM TIME TO TIME

Clipping From *Dakotah Courtship*—in Appendix
137. Already Mrs. Lone Bear had begun.

Problem of the Author To get the action in the new scene going immediately.

Solution by the Author He tells us that the action has already begun.

Effect upon the Reader Rapid.

Student's Comment This is a good device for continuity.

Clipping From *Dakotah Courtship*—in Appendix
239. The old men, having been served first, finished before the women. 240. Hardtack was host, and had to use both hands to fill and light his pipe. 241. Lone Bear had his chance at last.

Problem of the Author To indicate the lapse of time.

Solution by the Author Passage of time is indicated by gestures and manipulations following one another.

Effect upon the Reader Anticipation.

Student's Comment The motivation implied in this pantomime whets the reader's appetite for the dispute to follow.

Clipping From *Dakotah Courtship*—in Appendix
363. "I killed him. 364. I have heard that his name was Running Hawk."

Problem of the Author To bring the flashback (326–63) to a swift end.

Solution by the Author The narrator uses a perfect tense, "have heard," thus definitely putting the flashback into the past.

Effect upon the Reader This turns the reader's attention to the present time again.

Student's Comment Usually a flashback begins with a past perfect tense or some such form as "had been." Here, however, the flashback is in quotation marks and, being spoken, is in the past tense only. Hence the importance of using "have heard," a perfect tense, in the final sentence.

Clipping From *Dakotah Courtship*—in Appendix
417. But after a time, Lone Bear took the floor.

Problem of the Author To account for a lapse of time already suggested (410–15), but briefly, so that the story may proceed without delay.

Solution by the Author   Action is prefaced by a short phrase "But after a time."

Effect upon the Reader   Rapid and satisfactory.

Student's Comment   References to the passage of time are much more numerous in novels than short stories, as the development of character in a novel makes awareness of the passage of time on the part of the reader most essential.

Heading · DEVICES OF THE MIDDLE · TRANSITION—FROM PLACE TO PLACE

Clipping   From *Dakotah Courtship*—in Appendix
291. Joe said no more, and watched the old men.

Problem of the Author   To switch the reader's attention from the hero and heroine to their old folks.

Solution by the Author   The hero turns from the heroine and watches the other group in the other spot.

Effect upon the Reader   The hero, in whose viewpoint the story is being told, does not move from place to place. But his attention *does,* and this carries the reader from the shack to the arbor.

Student's Comment   This is an effective but not unusual device in fiction. It is not unusual *because* it is effective.

Heading · DEVICES OF THE MIDDLE · TRANSITION—FROM PLACE TO PLACE

Clipping   From *Dakotah Courtship*—in Appendix
515. Joe hitched up his jeans and stalked off to his car.

Problem of the Author   To get the hero away on his own with pleasure to the reader.

Solution by the Author   The character is pictured first as preparing to go, and then as going to a named destination.

Effect upon the Reader   The character's action, though briefly and factually stated, amuses the reader, who is already laughing at him
100

and wishes to enjoy his embarrassment, requires no elaborate device here to keep up his emotion. Therefore, the transition is given in plain narrative at a slow pace.

Student's Comment Plain narrative is all that is necessary if it makes a picture and the reader is already interested.

Heading · DEVICES OF THE MIDDLE · TRANSITION—FROM PLACE TO PLACE

Clipping From *Dakotah Courtship*—in Appendix

34. It was a good long hundred yards across the blistering prairie to Hardtack's unpainted shack and the brush arbor alongside. 35. But Joe was too disheartened to try to start the car again. 36. Chances were it wouldn't start, anyhow, and he did not want the visit to begin by Lillie's folks having the laugh on him. 37. It would be less humiliating to pretend that he had meant to stop right there, and walk the rest of the way.

38. Joe jumped out, landing on the heels of his tan Oxfords. 39. Chief Lone Bear stepped down, catlike, in the manner of a man who has worn moccasins all his life. 40. Old Mrs. Lone Bear, after a moment's silent dismay at the distance to be covered afoot, heaved her two hundred pounds up from the rumble-seat and slowly clambered to the ground.

41. The spry old man went first, bright-eyed, bow-legged, stooping over his polished cane. 42. Joe nervously hitched up his blue jeans and followed. 43. The old woman pulled her bright new blanket—the price of her participation—over her meaty shoulders, and plodded along behind.

Problem of the Author To get the hero and his companions from his car to the home of the Hardtacks.

Solution by the Author The distance to the goal is first stated, then the emotion and motivation of the hero, and finally the picture of action.

Effect upon the Reader The reader is led by the movement of the characters to a new place.

Student's Comment A standard device, often used.

101

Clipping   From *Dakotah Courtship*—in Appendix
16. So Joe had brought along his own grandparents to make the match in the old-time way. 17. But now, as he rolled in through Hardtack's gate, Joe began to get cold feet about that.

Problem of the Author   To transport the reader from one place to another (from the road to Hardtack's shack) without losing emotional continuity.

Solution by the Author   Passing from fact ("through Hardtack's gate") to feeling ("cold feet about that").

Effect upon the Reader   Combination of feeling with fact carries reader along.

Student's Comment   The "But now" helps propel the reader over mere *fact* to "cold feet."

Clipping   From *Dakotah Courtship*—in Appendix
502. Breathless, she stood poised, with open mouth, watching his face. 503. She whirled and ran. 504. The moment she moved, Joe was after her. 505. Two strides brought him close. 506. Lillie heard him coming, stepped to one side quickly, and stuck out her foot. 507. She tripped him. 508. Joe hit the grass on his face.

509. Lillie laughed at him. 510. "Don't you try to boss me, Big Boy. 511. You ain't big enough." 512. She ran into the shack and slammed the door.

Problem of the Author   To bring the hero and heroine from the dwelling into the open and separate them.

Solution by the Author   The characters are shown in pursuit of each other, one escaping.

Effect upon the Reader   Amusing.

Student's Comment   The highly emotionalized action—a chase—carries the reader along.

Clipping   From *Dakotah Courtship*—in Appendix

73. Chief Lone Bear stepped over the pots and firewood, grasped Hardtack's hand quickly, and seated himself on his host's left side— the side nearest his heart. 74. Mrs. Lone Bear, making a purring sound of pleasure, waddled in and found a place beside her hostess. 75. All four of them seemed to be in high good humor, eager to begin the business. 76. All four of them completely ignored Joe.

Problem of the Author   To bring the characters into position for the scenes to follow.

Solution by the Author   Action with motivation implied alternates in this transition.

Effect upon the Reader   Effect of rapidity and humorous anticipation with perhaps a little pleasure at the Indian color suggested here.

Student's Comment   This transition ends with a further complication for the hero (76).

Clipping   From *Dakotah Courtship*—in Appendix

77. Joe felt like a rank outsider. 78. For a minute he stood still, not knowing what to do. 79. Then he turned hastily and retreated. 80. Nobody wanted him around.

81. Chief Hardtack's allotment was a flat, uncompromising square of short Montana grass surrounded by a sagging fence of rusty barbed wire. 82. The sun beat down on it with all the steady purpose of an August afternoon. 83. Joe decided to wait in the car. 84. It would be hot—but what the hell!

85. To reach the car, Joe had to pass the shack.

Problem of the Author   To transport the hero from his companions to his sweetheart.

Solution by the Author   The motivation for action is first given, then the action, then the setting and the emotion it inspired, and then the progress of the action, in that order.

Effect upon the Reader   Sympathy for the hero and a better idea of the setting.

Student's Comment   The old people having been placed in position for a fight, it is necessary to transport the hero into the position for his fight and a post of observation where the reader may see both sides—a sort of two-ring circus.

Heading · DEVICES OF THE MIDDLE · TRANSITION—FROM PLACE TO PLACE

Clipping   From *Dakotah Courtship*—in Appendix
404. But Joe and Lillie were in the arbor, each talking as fast as possible—the one in Crow, the other in Dakotah, and both in the sign language.

Problem of the Author   To transport the hero and heroine at a dramatic moment from their former position into the midst of the other characters.

Solution by the Author   The hero and heroine are shown already arrived at their destination.

Effect upon the Reader   This device is about as swift as a transition can be, and the effect is one of release from the tediousness of a slow change of base.

Student's Comment   At such a dramatic moment a swift transition is essential.

Heading · DEVICES OF THE MIDDLE · TRANSITION—FROM MOOD TO MOOD

Clipping   From *Dakotah Courtship*—in Appendix
475. "I say it's a girl, Joe. 476. That's flat. 477. And you bet I won't have no girl named Sitting Bull!"
478. "Skip it, Lil. 479. Call her Prairie Flower, Milkweed, Sagebrush, Cactus, or Hollers All Night. 480. We got plenty of time to name the kid. 481. Let's get married. 482. Come on. 483. We can find the missionary in town in ten minutes."

Problem of the Author   To bring the reader into a new mood of livelier amusement.

Solution by the Author   One character placates the other with easy argument.

Effect upon the Reader   Amusement and sympathy.

Student's Comment   Making fun of Indian names is an old gag.

Heading · DEVICES OF THE MIDDLE · TRANSITION—FROM MOOD TO MOOD

Clipping   From *Dakotah Courtship*—in Appendix
446. "That boy must have a good name. 447. What shall we call him?"

Problem of the Author   To carry the reader from a quiet, colorful passage of peaceful feelings into bickering and dispute.

Solution by the Author   A question is proposed to which everyone is sure to disagree.

Effect upon the Reader   Curiosity and anticipation.

Student's Comment   Chief Lone Bear tosses down a golden apple of discord.

Heading · DEVICES OF THE MIDDLE · TRANSITION—FROM MOOD TO MOOD

Clipping   From *Dakotah Courtship*—in Appendix
96. She hardly looked the bobbed-haired beauty Joe had dated and dragged to the movies at school. 97. Her hair still had the lustre of a new gun-barrel, but it was parted down the middle now and plaited into two stubby braids made long with strands of colored yarn. 98. Instead of her usual shirt and dungarees, she had on a red calico dress with a yoke and frill—Crow Reservation, fashion 1890— and high button shoes too big for her. 99. Yet somehow, she was pretty in spite of it.

Problem of the Author   To bring the hero and the reader from a mood of amusement to one of sympathy.

Solution by the Author   The heroine is described in her ridiculous costume. The hero is shown amused and yet still admiring.

Effect upon the Reader   Amusement and sympathy.

Student's Comment   Here is a build-up with the twist at the end.

Heading · DEVICES OF THE MIDDLE · TRANSITION—FROM MOOD TO MOOD

Clipping   From *Dakotah Courtship*—in Appendix
371. "Running Hawk was a relative of mine," he said, sternly.
   372. "Joe! Is that true?" 373. Lillie turned to him, her face stricken. 374. "Oh, Big Boy, I'm so sorry."

Problem of the Author   To cause a reversal in emotion of the heroine toward the hero.

Solution by the Author   This is done by a discovery which makes personal what had formerly been a tribal attitude.

Effect upon the Reader   Deeper sympathy.

Student's Comment   The artificiality of the quarrel dissolves into strong, natural feeling.

Heading · DEVICES OF THE MIDDLE · TRANSITION—FROM MOOD TO MOOD

Clipping   From *Dakotah Courtship*—in Appendix
374. "Oh, Big Boy, I'm so sorry. 375. Look here, Joe." . . . 386. "They got together and insulted each other for all they were worth—to make sure the peace would stick!"

Problem of the Author   To switch the reader from the mood of sympathy to one of amusement.

Solution by the Author   A discovery and reversal is used.

Effect upon the Reader   The discovery of the young folks that they are being tested blows away the serious emotion and raises a practical problem. The tone is immediately lighter.

Student's Comment   Here (386) a historic fact is brought forward to convince the reader that the discovery and reversal is justified.

106

Clipping   From *Dakotah Courtship*—in Appendix
410. The old folks sat still, astonished at the outburst. 411. One by one they subsided. 412. They sat staring at the ground, with disappointed faces. 413. The women wiped their tears with the corners of their blankets. 414. The old men hung their heads. 415. The happy game of bluff and brag was over.

Problem of the Author   To set up a new situation and complication.

Solution by the Author   Done by putting the reaction of one close to the other in a passage with slow pace.

Effect upon the Reader   This sudden and prolonged quiet after the rapid-fire action and speech preceding induces a new and more thoughtful mood in the reader.

Student's Comment   Each sentence here is in the same mood, and the slow pace helps maintain it.

Clipping   From *Dakotah Courtship*—in Appendix
497. Stung by the shame of having him touch her in the presence of her relatives, Lillie struggled to wrench herself free. 498. "Let go of me," she raged.

Problem of the Author   To motivate a final quarrel between hero and heroine.

Solution by the Author   Done by reaction of the heroine to the hero's unconscious affront. The Wave Formula is used: first the motive, then the action, then speech.

Effect upon the Reader   Sympathy and amusement.

Student's Comment   It was necessary at this point to have something more violent than talk. The hero has adopted physical coercion, and the heroine's action is even more violent.

F. Devices for Continuity

Without Continuity of interest your reader will not continue to read. You must take pains with this problem. Continuity must not only be real—that is, a matter of ideas and actions—but apparent—a matter of words and phrases. The reader must not only feel Continuity, but should be able to *see* it.

Nearly all the devices found in the Middle of your story may be used for Continuity—which includes unity, coherence, and emphasis.

Of these the more common are:

1. Transitions
2. Repetitions
3. Overlapping Paragraphs
4. Furtherances
5. Hindrances
6. Sequels of Scenes
7. Pointers
8. Promise of Conflict

All these contribute to create suspense. With the exception of numbers 2 and 3, they have been explained already. These are illustrated later in this chapter.

G. Devices for Plausibility

Plausibility is absolutely essential to a good short story. The reader may accept the proposition (in the Beginning) of your story that there is an island of Lilliput where the men are only six inches tall, but he will never endure to have those men suddenly become six feet tall later on in the story. He expects you to play the game according to the rules laid down in the Beginning.

Of course you may say that in *Alice in Wonderland* Alice grows rapidly or shrinks to smaller size. But in that fantasy her change in stature is made plausible by having her swallow something guaranteed to produce that effect. Even in the most fantastic story the happenings must be made plausible, at least for the time being.

A good story is a tall tale made plausible. And a tall tale is made plausible by making each step as the story proceeds so reasonable that the imaginative reader can nowhere say, "This is incredible."

Of course there are readers who have no imagination, like the fellow who, having bought a copy of *Gulliver's Travels,* returned it to the bookseller and demanded his money back, saying, "This is incredible." Such fellows should not read fiction.

Most people know when they are reading fiction. They do not expect it to be true throughout, but they do expect it to be plausible enough to give them pleasure.

Yet Plausibility is not only a matter of externals, but also—principally—a matter of convincing motivation in the characters. Indeed, romance has been defined as "the adventures of an ordinary man in extraordinary circumstances." As everybody knows, the literature of English-speaking people has been for the most part romantic, and our readers are conditioned to expect the extraordinary circumstances and the ordinary motivation.

If the motivation is sound, the circumstances may be as fantastic as you like—provided these circumstances can be made plausible.

Here follow some devices for Plausibility:

Various devices may be used for Plausibility. The principal one is, of course, *motivation*, for if the reader can believe in the motives and passions of the characters, he will accept improbable incidents and fantastic settings. In the story *Dakotah Courtship* you will find motivation indicated in sentences 2, 5–10, 18, 23–31, 40, 59–63, 77, 89, 91, 122, 123, etc.

Plausibility through sensory impressions will be found in sentences 2, 19, 34, 39, 41, 43, 48–51, 52–58, 81–82, 86, 96–99, 255, 401, etc.

Plausibility through use of the familiar will be found in sentences 1, 11, 14, 42, 64, 67, 123, 254, etc.

Plausibility is not ordinarily enhanced by the use of the strange, for strangeness acts to produce surprise rather than Plausibility. However, in *Dakotah Courtship* strangeness is used for Plausibility in sentences 73–74, 76, 96–99, etc.

Plausibility is enhanced by calling in a witness or referring to historical fact, as in sentences 385, 386, 426, 435, etc.

See if you can find in the story other examples of these devices for Plausibility. Note the numbers of the sentences in which you find them and prepare cards showing each device.

H. Devices for Focus

Some parts of your story will be more plausible than others. Some may be more important than others. Each of these parts must have a focus of interest upon it—that is, it must be more brightly lighted, more exciting; you must turn a spotlight of emotion upon your main points, whether in fiction or non-fiction, so that the reader will be sure to see them clearly and so accept and follow the emotional path which you have laid out for him to follow.

This means that whenever an important point is to be made, such as the motive of a character, a crucial action, or an important piece of description necessary for Plausibility, you will take care to phrase that passage in such a way as to make the reader react emotionally. You will state the thing in such a way as to make him chortle, or catch his breath, or feel his throat constrict. You will make him fear and hope and laugh and blink back the tears. Only in this way can you be sure that he will give full value to your important Pointers and passages, for interest is *emotion*, and every important part of your story must be colored and warm with it. This is what we mean by Focus.

Devices for Focus will be found in *Dakotah Courtship* in the following sentences: 2, 6, 18–22, 23, 30, 41, 50, 52–58, 64, 81, 96–99, 123, 143, 152, 161, 179, 181, 237, 258, 292, 296, 386, 401–03, 422–30, 450, 499, 517, 611, 622.

Prepare cards showing the Problem and Solution of the author in each case with your comments.

I. Repetitions

Since, as Samuel Taylor Coleridge pointed out, a reader much prefers recognition to surprise, repetitions are a standard and frequently used device in all forms of literature. In poetry we have the refrain, the repeated stanza, the regular pentameter line, the clink of rhyme, the echoing vowels, alliteration, puns, and all those other verbal tricks which make it easy for the reader to follow.

Whenever you present a reader with a surprise, a puzzle, a question, something *new*, he has to attend closely to it and slow down in order to understand and feel it. But when you repeat something— whether a phrase or an idea, an action or a bit of dialogue—you make it easy for the reader because, having read the same thing earlier, he finds no difficulty in understanding and enjoying it again.

In literature as in music (both of which exist in time), repetition plays a most important part. The beating of time in music and the rhythm of good verse sweep you along. Of course, if we repeated the

110

same line over and over without change, the reader would soon become fatigued and find our verse boring. A refrain that never varies its meaning can become tiresome. It was for this reason that Poe in his *Raven* took care that "Nevermore," the word repeated by the bird, was the answer to a different question each time it was uttered and so had various meanings.

From this we can readily see that Repetition must not be mere repetition every time but should be varied in meaning, length, or sound. This variation often takes the form of adding something when the repetition is made, as in "That day, that day, that dreadful day"; or by subtracting something each time so that, on the third repetition, the shortened form implies the rest. Thus a character may first strike another down. A little later he may come in and merely raise his first; a third time he need only stick his head in the door. Everybody laughs to see his enemy wince.

This device is known as Incremental Repetition.

Too often beginners imagine that novelty is what delights the reader. Novelty may attract the reader, but it will never hold him. Recognition of the familiar is what he enjoys, and that is why Repetition, which gives him something to recognize, plays such an important part in good literature.

Here follow some devices of Repetition:

Heading · DEVICES OF THE MIDDLE · INCREMENTAL REPETITION

Clipping From *Dakotah Courtship*—in Appendix
34. It was a good long hundred yards across the blistering prairie to Hardtack's unpainted shack and the brush arbor alongside. . . . 82. The sun beat down on it with all the steady purpose of an August afternoon.

Problem of the Author To make the reader thoroughly aware of the season, time of day, and temperature of his setting.

Solution by the Author The reader is first given a sensation ("blistering") and then a picture of the "sun beating down" to reinforce the sensation.

Effect upon the Reader This double-barreled impression convinces the reader.

111

Repetition is a common and most useful device. Here follows a fist of some of the repetitions to be found in *Dakotah Courtship*. Some of these are plain repetitions, others incremental repetitions where something has been added to or subtracted from the first statement. There are a number of references to the starting of the car, beginning with sentence 35; to the hero looking in, 48, 52; to necking, 123, 124; to courting, 151, 165; to Sitting Bull, 204, 213, 220, 453; to running, 264, 294, 302, 303, 304, 314, 319, 359; to fighting, 299, 401; to trails, 422–30; to sex of the child, 468, 469, 472, 475, 477; to fun, 490, 491, 492; to shirt and dungarees, 98, 517; to tripping, 506, 555; to "Hop in," 539, 591, 610; to names and naming, 446, 448, 449, 450, 452, 609.

Prepare devices showing the Problem and Solution in each of these devices.

J. Device of Overlapping Paragraphs

In collecting devices you will sometimes find it necessary, remember, to include in your clipping more sentences than those which actually embody the device, simply because the device may not be clear without its context. In that case you may clip out a whole paragraph, only one sentence of which embodies a device. Then you should underscore the words which do embody the device so that they are clearly distinguished from the surrounding context when your eye falls upon them.

This technique is necessary in preparing the device of Overlapping Paragraphs.

The overlapping paragraph is a device for Continuity, is in fact a form of transition from paragraph to paragraph. It consists in using the same words or presenting the same idea at the end of one paragraph and at the beginning of the next.

This makes it easy for the reader to jump the gap between paragraphs, since he recognizes that the beginning of the paragraph ahead has the same words or the same idea which he has just read in the paragraph behind. You might think it would be simpler not to have paragraphs at all, but to print all the sentences one after another straight through the book as the ancients did. But I fear the modern reader would find this intolerably fatiguing, since he would have to find the breaks between the paragraphs for himself. Thus we have to write in paragraphs to keep our reader and therefore are confronted with the problem of tying these together.

Overlapping Paragraphs is one of the most effective means of doing this. The device may be supplemented by the use of connectives such as "Nevertheless," "And so," "But yet," "Accordingly," "Therefore," "It follows that"—and all the rest.

Here follow the examples of the device of Overlapping Paragraphs:

Heading · DEVICES OF THE MIDDLE · OVERLAPPING PARAGRAPHS

Clipping   From *Dakotah Courtship*—in Appendix
150. "He has many horses."
   151. "How many?"

Problem of the Author   Continuity.

Solution by the Author   The use of the same word in a question following a statement.

Effect upon the Reader   Amusement and curiosity.

Student's Comment   A standard device.

Heading · DEVICES OF THE MIDDLE · OVERLAPPING PARAGRAPHS

Clipping   From *Dakotah Courtship*—in Appendix
17. But now, as he rolled in through Hardtack's gate, Joe began to get cold feet about that.
   18. Anxiously, he shouted to caution the aged warrior at his elbow.

Problem of the Author   Continuity of emotion.

Solution by the Author   The same idea in different words is found in the last sentence of one paragraph and the first of that following.

Effect upon the Reader   There being no facts between feelings at this juncture, the reader sails right along from paragraph to paragraph.

113

Student's Comment   This tie is especially strong, as it is part of the problem of our hero.

Heading · DEVICES OF THE MIDDLE · OVERLAPPING PARAGRAPHS

Clipping   From *Dakotah Courtship*—in Appendix
196. "Always making trouble." 197. She beamed.
    198. "Hot dog! 199. What a naughty boy!" Joe jeered.

Problem of the Author   Continuity.

Solution by the Author   Satirical comment follows a serious boast. The same idea is expressed in both by different words.

Effect upon the Reader   Amusement.

Student's Comment   The childishness of the boast is mentioned by the juvenile phrasing of the satirical comment.

Heading · DEVICES OF THE MIDDLE · OVERLAPPING PARAGRAPHS

Clipping   From *Dakotah Courtship*—in Appendix
37. It would be less humiliating to pretend that he had meant to stop right there, and walk the rest of the way.
    38. Joe jumped out, landing on the heels of his tan Oxfords.

Problem of the Author   Continuity.

Solution by the Author   Similar steps of a continuous action are indicated in these paragraphs.

Effect upon the Reader   He is prompted to continue.

Student's Comment   Not too strong a tie.

Heading · DEVICES OF THE MIDDLE · OVERLAPPING PARAGRAPHS

Clipping   From *Dakotah Courtship*—in Appendix
234. "And put plenty of sugar in the coffee."
    235. Hastily, Lillie Fineweather caught up the kettle of stew and the pot of coffee . . .

114

Problem of the Author   Continuity.

Solution by the Author   Duplication of words and action following an imperative sentence.

Effect upon the Reader   Rapid.

Student's Comment   Action helps the duplication of ideas.

Heading · DEVICES OF THE MIDDLE · OVERLAPPING PARAGRAPHS

Clipping   From *Dakotah Courtship*—in Appendix
67. "How!" he said.
    68. At that word, old Mrs. Hardtack drew herself up triumphantly.

Problem of the Author   Continuity.

Solution by the Author   The new paragraph starts off with a phrase referring emphatically to the sentence preceding.

Effect upon the Reader   Anticipation keeps him going.

Student's Comment   A not unusual device.

Heading · DEVICES OF THE MIDDLE · OVERLAPPING PARAGRAPHS

Clipping   From *Dakotah Courtship*—in Appendix
76. All four of them completely ignored Joe.
    77. Joe felt like a rank outsider.

Problem of the Author   Continuity.

Solution by the Author   The same idea is presented and a double link is provided by a repetition of the name of the hero.

Effect upon the Reader   Focus upon the idea.

Student's Comment   A standard device.

Heading · DEVICES OF THE MIDDLE · OVERLAPPING PARAGRAPHS

Clipping   From *Dakotah Courtship*—in Appendix
141. We want a good wife for our grandson."
    142. Mrs. Hardtack smiled with marked condescension. 143. "Is that puny boy your grandson?

115

Problem of the Author   Continuity.

Solution by the Author   The same word is used but with contrasting emotions by two speakers.

Effect upon the Reader   Amusement.

Student's Comment   Dialogue at cross-purposes helps this device.

Heading · DEVICES OF THE MIDDLE · OVERLAPPING PARAGRAPHS

Clipping   From *Dakotah Courtship*—in Appendix
2. But as Joe gradually approached the gate of Chief Hardtack's allotment, his young heart missed almost as often as his chugging engine. 3. Lillie Fineweather lived there.

4. That motor trouble in Joe's fighting heart was not entirely due to Lillie's near presence, however.

Problem of the Author   Continuity.

Solution by the Author   A double overlapping of ideas and names is used.

Effect upon the Reader   The reader finds two paths over the bridge between paragraphs.

Student's Comment   So early in the story the author dared not rely on a single tie between paragraphs.

Heading · DEVICES OF THE MIDDLE · OVERLAPPING PARAGRAPHS

Clipping   From *Dakotah Courtship*—in Appendix
316. "A good warrior knows when to charge and when to retreat. 317. The Crows did both better than the white soldiers."

318. Lone Bear gave a hearty gesture of assent. 319. "The Crows ran well that day."

Problem of the Author   Continuity.

Solution by the Author   Repetition of idea from different points of view in the two paragraphs.

Effect upon the Reader   Amusement.

116

Student's Comment The mere word "ran" is here enhanced by its having been used a number of times earlier in this debate.

Heading · DEVICES OF THE MIDDLE · OVERLAPPING PARAGRAPHS

Clipping From *Dakotah Courtship*—in Appendix
399. "A Dakotah and a Crow will always be fighting," Hardtack declared, with satisfaction.
400. "True," Lone Bear assented, with gusto.

Problem of the Author Continuity.

Solution by the Author Two characters at odds agree to disagree.

Effect upon the Reader Amusement.

Student's Comment Even while agreeing the two men are trying to outdo each other in gusto over their alleged quarrelsomeness. This is sympathetic and amusing.

Heading · DEVICES OF THE MIDDLE · OVERLAPPING PARAGRAPHS

Clipping From *Dakotah Courtship*—in Appendix
429. "The old trail is lost. 430. The young men cannot find it.
431. "Yet it is good to remember the old ways. 432. Ours was a good trail."

Problem of the Author Continuity.

Solution by the Author The same word is used with emotion to refer to a way of life.

Effect upon the Reader Poetic passage, pathetic, or one of nostalgia.

Student's Comment Imagery may produce a poetic effect.

Heading · DEVICES OF THE MIDDLE · OVERLAPPING PARAGRAPHS

Clipping From *Dakotah Courtship*—in Appendix
123. "She don't approve of necking."
124. Joe halted. 125. "Who said anything about necking?" he complained.

117

Problem of the Author Continuity.

Solution by the Author The same idea is presented from the opposite points of view of two characters, and the same word is used in both paragraphs.

Effect upon the Reader The repetition of the word by the characters in this passage heightens the interest of the reader.

Student's Comment This is an example also of dialogue at cross-purposes.

Heading · DEVICES OF THE MIDDLE · OVERLAPPING PARAGRAPHS

Clipping From *Dakotah Courtship*—in Appendix
446. "That boy must have a good name. 447. What shall we call him?"
448. "Yes. 449. A good name," Mrs. Lone Bear assented.

Problem of the Author Continuity.

Solution by the Author The same word is used in both paragraphs, the characters assenting.

Effect upon the Reader Emphatic.

Student's Comment Nothing unusual here. This device is commonly used, as commonly effective.

Heading · DEVICES OF THE MIDDLE · OVERLAPPING PARAGRAPHS

Clipping From *Dakotah Courtship*—in Appendix
490. "I want some fun out of life."
491. "Fun!" Joe barked. 492. "They'll be plenty of fun, if you don't take care of my kid."

Problem of the Author Continuity.

Solution by the Author The same word is used three times in two sentences and with a good deal of emotion.

Effect upon the Reader Excitement as the quarrel mounts to its climax.

Student's Comment Dialogue at cross-purposes is always good.

118

Clipping   From *Dakotah Courtship*—in Appendix
614. "Big Boy," she whispered, "you're wonderful!"
    615. Joe Lone Bear made himself look even <u>bigger</u> than he was.

Problem of the Author   Continuity.

Solution by the Author   The same word is used in both sentences.

Effect upon the Reader   The reader is amused at the hero's accepting the tribute, as by this time the reader must expect the hero's pretensions to be punctured shortly.

Student's Comment   A good device.

Clipping   From *Dakotah Courtship*—in Appendix
155. "<u>Look</u>."
    156. Mrs. Hardtack laughed. 157. "I <u>see</u> it."

Problem of the Author   Continuity.

Solution by the Author   Similar idea in the first and last lines of the paragraphs.

Effect upon the Reader   The contrast in the mocking argument keeps up the reader's interest.

Student's Comment   In overlapping paragraphs the exact words need not be repeated if the idea is the same.

Clipping   From *Dakotah Courtship*—in Appendix
51. Hardtack was a <u>big</u>, vital man, and <u>tough</u> as a mule.
    52. But when Joe <u>laid eyes</u> on the <u>old woman</u>, he held his breath.
53. Mrs. Hardtack was <u>formidable</u>.

Problem of the Author   Continuity and increase of emotion.

Solution by the Author   Having presented an impressive character, the author immediately contrasts another even more formidable.

Effect upon the Reader   Suspense.

119

Student's Comment   Contrast where the characters are allied is a good device.

Heading · DEVICES OF THE MIDDLE · OVERLAPPING PARAGRAPHS

Clipping   From *Dakotah Courtship*—in Appendix
267. "Now Granddad is talking about the Custer Battle."
   268. "The Custer Massacre," Lillie corrected him, sharply.
   269. Joe bristled. 270. "Massacre nothing."

Problem of the Author   Continuity.

Solution by the Author   Repetition with variation (incremental repetition) is used. Middle paragraph ties in both to the one before and the one following.

Effect upon the Reader   Climactic.

Student's Comment   Incremental repetition gives an effect of easy progress.

Heading · DEVICES OF THE MIDDLE · OVERLAPPING PARAGRAPHS

Clipping   From *Dakotah Courtship*—in Appendix
522. "Where you goin', Lillie?"
   523. "Nowhere with you," she replied.

Problem of the Author   Continuity.

Solution by the Author   The same idea, "going," is used in both sentences—stated in one, implied in the other.

Effect upon the Reader   No break is felt here.

Student's Comment   Question and answer also help to tie the two paragraphs together.

K. The Gimmick

A gimmick is a device for objectifying the pivot on which a plot turns, the decision which the hero makes at the crisis. It consists in an objectification or personification of that pivot or point on which the story turns. It makes the decision seem more real. Usually it is some small physical object—for example, a wedding ring.

120

Suppose a woman has a quarrel with her husband and prepares to leave him. While packing she has time to think things over, yet persists in her purpose. But on leaving the house her wedding ring catches on the key in the door and she is reminded by this physical thing of her deepest motive, which is love for her husband. By the time she frees herself, her deeper motive prevails over her temporary one and she turns back into the house. The wedding ring in itself is there only so that the reader may see, as it were, the motive in objective form. A gimmick might be a familiar scent, a gesture that recalls a dear one, an old medal that arouses a veteran to remember the courage of his war days and so to face his peacetime troubles more bravely. Obviously the gimmick should not be a huge thing, but something small. Desdemona's handkerchief is a classic example of the gimmick.

Here follow examples of the device called the Gimmick:

Heading · DEVICES OF THE MIDDLE · THE GIMMICK

Clipping From *Dakotah Courtship*—in Appendix

526. Joe stamped on the starter furiously, and held his foot down. . . .

531. "No you don't," Joe muttered, and jumped from his seat.

Problem of the Author To objectify the hero's decision and sacrifice at the crisis.

Solution by the Author He makes the hero abandon his most precious possession (his car) to prevent disaster (the loss of his sweetheart).

Effect upon the Reader Convincing.

Student's Comment A gimmick is usually a smaller object than a car. If the heroine were the viewpoint character, her change of costume, indicating her change of purpose (517, 518), or the name Mickie Mouse (611), on which she bases her decision to go and marry Joe, might serve as gimmicks.

L. Dialogue at Cross-Purposes

In most stories a certain amount of dialogue is necessary. Usually there is too much of it, and nowadays there is a tendency among

121

some writers to use altogether more than their story demands. The effect in such cases is like that one gets in a picture theater when the lights go off and the screen is dark, while the sound track plays on: we hear voices but cannot tell who is speaking because we never see them.

Writers would be wiser to plan their stories as though the characters were all deaf-mutes, showing the action and the motivation and using only as much dialogue as is absolutely necessary. As Edith Wharton in discussing the Wave Formula declares, dialogue should ordinarily occur only at the crest of the action.

But even with scanty dialogue you will write dully and lose your reader unless you try wherever possible to make it dialogue at cross-purposes. By this term is not meant that the characters are in conflict, though of course they should be that ordinarily. By dialogue at cross-purposes we mean that *the characters do not understand each other*—that each attaches a different meaning to what is said. Then you have a real misunderstanding and a conflict that may be continued indefinitely, for neither character is right or wrong. They are simply at odds. I think you will find that wherever dialogue is really good and thoroughly enjoyable it is of this sort.

Thus a child may say something innocently which rocks adults with laughter, because for them it has another meaning. That is an example of dialogue at cross-purposes. Another would be where two characters meet, each imagining that the other is someone else. An old man and a young man, for instance, meet at a club. The young man thinks the old man is his prospective father-in-law. The old man takes the young man for a traveling salesman. The resulting dialogue could be very funny. Whereas, if the two men understand each other, nothing worth listening to would be said.

Again when characters are very close together and have been intimate in some way as friends, enemies, or lovers in the past, it is easy to introduce dialogue at cross-purposes, since people who have been intimate with each other in work or war or love understand each other's thoughts and so can leap over or omit logical steps in their conversation. They can come in at a tangent or far ahead of the argument. This makes for much livelier and entertaining dialogue, partly because it carries such a load of implication. And implication is one of the greatest delights a reader may enjoy. The rate of pay an author receives in sophisticated markets is in direct ratio to the amount of implication he offers.

Now for some examples of the device of Dialogue at Cross-Purposes:

Heading · DEVICES OF THE MIDDLE · DIALOGUE AT CROSS-PURPOSES

Clipping From *Dakotah Courtship*—in Appendix
20. "Grandfather," Joe yelled, "the wars are over. 21. We are friends with these people now. 22. Remember that!"

23. The old Dakotah shifted his moccasins to a firmer position upon the hot floorboards, turned red-rimmed eyes upon his grandson, and showed his yellow teeth in a grin of pleasurable anticipation. 24. "Make your heart strong, my grandson," he quavered. 25. "I know how to handle the Crows. 26. I have killed plenty of them in my day, and made them run like rabbits. 27. *He-han!* 28. Who is this Hardtack? 29. He has seen only seventy-six winters. 30. I have nothing to fear from that boy!"

Problem of the Author To present friendly characterization in unconscious antagonism.

Solution by the Author Dialogue at cross-purposes is used. Our hero sees the expedition as an effort to make friends. His grandfather sees it as an opportunity for conquest. Neither understands the other completely.

Effect upon the Reader The effect is amusing and dramatic by contrast. It also characterizes swiftly and points up the problem of the hero in the conflict to come.

Student's Comment Nearly all good dialogue is at cross-purposes. Nothing is so dull as dialogue between persons who have nothing but a conversational relationship.

Heading · DEVICES OF THE MIDDLE · DIALOGUE AT CROSS-PURPOSES

Clipping From *Dakotah Courtship*—in Appendix
65. Joe couldn't stand it. 66. He broke the ice. 67. *"How!"* he said.
68. At that word, old Mrs. Hardtack drew herself up triumphantly. 69. Her hard face set in lines of scorn. 70. "Dakotah!" she sneered.

Problem of the Author To show the hero's opponent as warlike and quick to take advantage.

Solution by the Author The author uses dialogue at cross-purposes by having the hero's opponent, Mrs. Hardtack, reply to his well-meant words of greeting with a sneer.

Effect upon the Reader Suspense at this promise of conflict.

Student's Comment The swift stepping up of the encounter advances the story.

Heading · DEVICES OF THE MIDDLE · DIALOGUE AT CROSS-PURPOSES

Clipping From *Dakotah Courtship*—in Appendix
100. Joe could not help laughing. 101. "Are you the kid I come all this way to marry?"
102. "You don't have to," she countered.

Problem of the Author To show the intimate relationship of the hero and heroine.

Solution by the Author Dialogue at cross-purposes is used.

Effect upon the Reader The reader is convinced that the characters are sufficiently intimate to kid each other about personal matters.

Student's Comment This is a rather mild example of this device but better than straight logical dialogue. The function of the device is to come in at a tangent or leap over logical steps.

Heading · DEVICES OF THE MIDDLE · DIALOGUE AT CROSS-PURPOSES

Clipping From *Dakotah Courtship*—in Appendix
118. Lillie raised her hand to stop him. 119. "Keep out, Joe. 120. If Grandma catches you alone with me, she'll sure raise hell. 121. She'll call the whole thing off. 122. She's terrible old-fashioned, like I told you. 123. She don't approve of necking."
124. Joe halted. 125. "Who said anything about necking?" he complained.
126. "Nobody. 127. But somebody might think of it."

Problem of the Author To make his dialogue vividly interesting.

124

Solution by the Author By having one speaker impute a familiar thought to another not then actually entertained, thus producing dialogue at cross-purposes.

Effect upon the Reader The effect is amusing, as indicating convincingly a previous intimacy. The reader feels that he is on the inside and in the know. There is nothing a reader likes better.

Student's Comment Dialogue at cross-purposes may be used between characters who are very close and take so much for granted that they can skip intermediate steps and carry the story forward much faster. Dialogue at cross-purposes is an excellent device to prevent dullness and a plodding plot.

Heading · DEVICES OF THE MIDDLE · DIALOGUE AT CROSS-PURPOSES

Clipping From *Dakotah Courtship*—in Appendix
181. "Her great grandfather was a famous horsethief."
    182. Joe looked over his shoulder. 183. "Attagirl, Lillie. 184. Grandma and me think you're tops."

Problem of the Author To contrast the standards of the older Indians with those of the young people.

Solution by the Author Dialogue at cross-purposes is used.

Effect upon the Reader The old Indian's phrasing (181) and the American slang (183, 184) help to point up the contrast.

Student's Comment The author was enabled to interest the reader in the old-time Indians by using the younger ones as a sort of chorus to interpret by contrast.

Heading · DEVICES OF THE MIDDLE · DIALOGUE AT CROSS-PURPOSES

Clipping From *Dakotah Courtship*—in Appendix
192. "When he was little he used to steal his mother's butcher knife and slash holes in the tent. 193. She could not stop him. 194. He was bad. 195. Heap bad. 196. Always making trouble." 197. She beamed.
    198. "Hot dog! 199. What a naughty boy!" Joe jeered.

125

200. Lillie stiffened. 201. "Lay off my folks," she cautioned.

202. "How about mine?" Joe demanded.

203. "They ain't so hot, I guess," she answered, and kept her face to the window.

Problem of the Author To point up the contrast between the old Indian and modern standards and at the same time indicate that the young folks have not entirely abandoned old-time attitudes.

Solution by the Author This is done by double-barreled dialogue at cross-purposes. The old Indian view is stated (192–97); modern (198, 199). Then by swift reversal the young folks join the quarrel (200–03).

Effect upon the Reader This double-barreled reverse-action dialogue advances the plot rapidly at this point.

Student's Comment The contrast of old-time Indian speech with modern slang helps the device here.

Heading · DEVICES OF THE MIDDLE · DIALOGUE AT CROSS-PURPOSES

Clipping From *Dakotah Courtship*—in Appendix

314. "When they saw that the soldiers could not win, they ran away. 315. If the soldiers had been smart, they would have run away too. 316. A good warrior knows when to charge and when to retreat. 317. The Crows did both better than the white soldiers."

318. Lone Bear gave a hearty gesture of assent. 319. "The Crows ran well that day." 320. He laughed. 321. "I chased them."

Problem of the Author To keep up the quarrel between two characters who should be friendly.

Solution by the Author One character who might be expected to object apparently agrees with the other, only to cap his agreement with a nasty remark (321).

Effect upon the Reader The effect intended was one of amusement and surprise.

Student's Comment Dialogue at cross-purposes can be used for almost every purpose in plotting, characterizing, or building good scenes.

Clipping From *Dakotah Courtship*—in Appendix
398. The old men beamed at each other. 399. "A Dakotah and a Crow will always be fighting," Hardtack declared, with satisfaction.

400. "True," Lone Bear assented, with gusto. 401. "They are like two mean dogs. 402. If they fight, you can pull them apart. 403. But if you turn them loose, they will go right back to fighting again."

Problem of the Author To prepare for a reversal in the next paragraph, when the hero and heroine put an end to the quarreling of the other characters.

Solution by the Author Dialogue at cross-purposes is used. The quarrelers enjoy the fight so much that they become positively friendly.

Effect upon the Reader The turning from personalities to generalities here and the genuine emotion emerging prepare the reader for the paragraph to follow.

Student's Comment The essential point here is the contrast between the bitter argument and the actual friendliness of the characters engaged in it. Some such contrast is essential for this device.

Clipping From *Dakotah Courtship*—in Appendix
460. "My woman goes with me," Joe gestured, positively. 461. "She does not like it here."

462. Lillie turned on him. 463. "Oh, yeah? 464. That's what *you* think. 465. What's the matter with Crow country, I'd like to know?"

466. "Why, Lil, you told me yourself——"

467. "You're crazy."

Problem of the Author To get the young people in a quarrel now that the old people have made peace, and so keep the plot moving.

Solution by the Author Dialogue at cross-purposes is used, contrasting what the characters really think with their pretensions before their relatives.

Effect upon the Reader It is amusing to see the old quarrel revived after it has apparently been laid to rest.

Student's Comment   One way of producing good dialogue at cross-purposes is that used here: to have one character assuming a new point of view while the other continues in the old one.

Heading · DEVICES OF THE MIDDLE · DIALOGUE AT CROSS-PURPOSES

Clipping   From *Dakotah Courtship*—in Appendix
468. "Anyhow, if we did marry and have a kid, like as not it would be a girl."
   469. "My kid a girl?" he protested, grappling with the new idea.
   470. "Sure. 471. Why not? 472. What's wrong with a girl? 473. I thought you was modern."
   474. "But Lillie——"
   475. "I say it's a girl, Joe."

Problem of the Author   To make the quarrel between the lovers seem ridiculous.

Solution by the Author   Dialogue at cross-purposes is used for a dispute about something which may never come to pass and over which the two parties have in any case no control.

Effect upon the Reader   Effect here is amusing but sympathetic. The reader perceives that if they can find nothing better to quarrel about they will soon make peace.

Student's Comment   This dialogue at cross-purposes also serves as a pointer to the twist at the end of the story (621, 622).

Heading · DEVICES OF THE MIDDLE · DIALOGUE AT CROSS-PURPOSES

Clipping   From *Dakotah Courtship*—in Appendix
   484. "Don't get tough, Big Boy. 485. We got to make the old folks like it, or the kid won't have no grandparents to look after it."
   486. "Lucky kid," Joe groaned.
   487. Lillie's eyes blazed. 488. "You think I'm going to stay home all day with that baby? 489. I ain't no squaw. 490. I want some fun out of life."
   491. "Fun!" Joe barked. 492. "They'll be plenty of fun, if you don't take care of my kid. 493. Let's get going. 494. All this fuss makes me sick. 495. Come on."

Problem of the Author To revive the reader's interest after the letdown of the preceding paragraphs.

Solution by the Author After letting the reader see the hero and heroine quarrel about nothing in the preceding passage, the author's problem here is to give them something more definite to fight about lest the reader lose interest. He accomplishes this by dialogue at cross-purposes.

Effect upon the Reader Amusing and enlivening.

Student's Comment One trick here is often found in dialogue at cross-purposes, the using of a word ("fun") in two senses.

Heading · DEVICES OF THE MIDDLE · DIALOGUE AT CROSS-PURPOSES

Clipping From *Dakotah Courtship*—in Appendix
496. Joe took her by the arm.
    497. Stung by the shame of having him touch her in the presence of her relatives, Lillie struggled to wrench herself free. 498. "Let go of me," she raged. 499. "Where do you think you are anyhow?" 500. She slapped him hard across the cheek. 501. Joe let go.

Problem of the Author To motivate the disaster on the final complication of the story, the heroine's leaving the hero.

Solution by the Author Dialogue at cross-purposes is used along with action.

Effect upon the Reader Dramatic. The plot thickens.

Student's Comment Here the contrast is that of feminine and masculine viewpoints admirably suited to display through dialogue at cross-purposes.

Heading · DEVICES OF THE MIDDLE · DIALOGUE AT CROSS-PURPOSES

Clipping From *Dakotah Courtship*—in Appendix
522. "Where you goin', Lillie?"
    523. "Nowhere with you," she replied. 524. "And don't you follow me neither—if you ever do get that thing started."

Problem of the Author To indicate that the separation of the lovers is not to be final.

129

Solution by the Author   Dialogue at cross-purposes (524) is used. The heroine in one sentence forbids her lover to follow her and then suggests that he might get the car started.

Effect upon the Reader   Amusement and satisfaction.

Student's Comment   Here we see that dialogue at cross-purposes can be indicated in a single speech by one character.

In dealing with the Middle, then, you have to consider primarily your fictional style.

The goal of the fiction writer is continuity of emotion, continuity of interest. Fiction is subjective writing. Words, grammar, and formal style being essentially objective, true fictional style is at first rather baffling to the writer trained to write objectively—he cannot see the forest for the trees. He is trained to amass facts and deal with parts rather than to fuse the whole array into a flowing stream of emotion. But the guiding principle of the fiction writer is the text: "The letter killeth, but the spirit giveth life." Therefore, the fiction writer tries to use as few words as possible to convey or create his effect—whereas the objective writer uses as many as possible.

All fiction is in the actual First Person, whether it is written in formal First Person or not. Formally it may be—and in fact usually is—in the Third Person. No matter. Correctly written, the viewpoint character is thought of as "ME" even though the author writes "HE" or "SHE" on the page. The objective word does not matter.

The majority of the sentences in objective writing begin with the fact. In fiction, on the contrary, most sentences begin with the feeling, thus determining the direction of attack. Of a dozen sentences on the ordinary page, about seven will begin thus: "Horrified, he turned," or "The horror of it striking him, he flinched," or some such arrangement, putting the emotion out in front at the start of the sentence. In fiction almost every sentence contains *both* a fact and a feeling. (See my *Writing Magazine Fiction*, pp. 125, 285. Also my *Professional Writing*, p. 60.)

Ordinarily you have a rhythmic succession of *feeling fact, feeling fact* (or *emotion motion, emotion motion*) for your pattern; or, less often, in reverse order—*fact feeling, fact feeling* (*motion emotion, motion emotion*). Sometimes it is possible to imply the feeling or emotion, or—rarely—to imply the motion or fact. You will have to

130

decide—if necessary, by trial—which order suits your material best. But you must NOT string together a series of facts without interlaced emotions; you must NOT lump emotional items together without interspaced facts.

In choosing words to carry emotion, remember that in English the oldest, commonest words serve best—and these are nearly always short words—what we call Plain English. When a man is serene he will use long-handled words of foreign derivation; but get him angry and see how quickly he drops into Plain English—short words that carry emotion! If you wish to write good fiction, go and do likewise.

In the sentence take care—as a rule—that verbs and subjects are not separated. Do not write, "He bitterly regretted." Make it, "He regretted bitterly," or "Bitterly he regretted."

In the paragraph you must forget what you were taught when learning to write exposition. Make formal but not actual breaks between paragraphs—that is, use just the reverse of the objective method of paragraphing. What would be—in objective writing—the *first* sentence of the next paragraph is—in fiction—used as the *last* sentence of the present paragraph. Or a question may end the paragraph, to be followed in the next paragraph by the expected answer. Note that in fictional style the paragraph does NOT indicate a subtopic neatly divided from the remaining material. Usually, though by no means always, a fictional paragraph ends on the *motion*, or *fact*-beat, leaving the *feeling*, the *emotional note*, for the start of the next paragraph. In fiction nothing is chopped off and finished; everything carries through; everything is "continued in our next." Fiction is a non-stop flight.

Transitions, difficult for the beginner, are handled much like paragraphs; that is, the writer bears down heavily on a sustained emotional note, adds the necessary fact or motion, makes the transition, and begins anew on the other side with the very same emotional note. For example: "Bitterness in his heart, he turned away" (the last sentence before a transition, both in space and time). Now leave your three-line gap on the typed page to indicate that a transition is taking place. Then add as your first sentence after the transition: "And somehow, curiously, he was still bitter even five years later when he met her again." The transition must be a bridge of emotion. And the sustained and unchanged emotional note makes the reader feel that the story has continued and that nothing of importance has happened in the dropped space and time. All that is worth remembering in life is the poetry of it—the emotion. So in fiction.

Remember, *popular fiction is NOT intended to make the reader think.* Reading fiction is an act of faith.

This brings us to the final, basic law of writing.

This natural law or basic principle is so important that in my classes in Professional Writing at the University of Oklahoma we make a ritual of it; every few days the whole class stands and repeats in concert: *"The reader will not believe, because he cannot imagine, what I tell him; he will only believe, because he can only imagine, what I show him."*

By *telling*, of course, we mean referring to a thing by its name—as "a rattlesnake." By *showing*, we mean presenting the thing through its qualities, sensory (as "lithe, squirming, venomous") or emotional ("that hellish beast"). Omit, or at any rate withhold, the name, offer only the sensations and emotions—and you make your reader *experience* the reptile.

Avoid, when you can, using articles, copulative verbs, verbs like "seems," "appears," "becomes," which *do* nothing and *show* nothing; also past perfects, subjunctives, and passives. Almost NEVER describe your viewpoint character passively: do not say "became angry," but say, "Rage swept him," or "Suddenly furious, he struck." Use simple words, simple sentences, as a rule, and unmistakable constructions. KEEP 'EM READING!

THE SHORT STORY · DEVICES USEFUL THROUGHOUT

In addition to devices particularly adapted to the Beginning, the Middle, and the End, there are many which may be used to advantage in any part of your story.

Among these are devices for Plausibility, Continuity, the Wave Formula, Transitions, Repetitions, Focus, and Scene. All these have been discussed already in this book.

Here follow a few others which you should master:

M. Device for Corroboration · The Character Witness

It is a curious fact that the reader will not believe anything the author tells him. That is because he cannot imagine it. He can only imagine what the author shows him—that is, makes him realize by calling attention to its qualities, or, in other words, by making it an experience instead of a mere statement. You cannot afford merely to tell the reader. You must show him.

Thus the reader will not believe you if you declare that your hero was a brave man. But if you bring in a character (whom you yourself, of course, have invented) in whom the reader feels he should have confidence, and then let this new character bear witness to the courage of the hero, the reader will believe that he is brave. Whenever, therefore, you think it doubtful that the reader will take your word about one of your characters, you must invent a Character Witness to testify to what you wish the reader to believe.

Heading · DEVICES USEFUL THROUGHOUT · CHARACTER WITNESS

Clipping From *Dakotah Courtship*—in Appendix

14. Lillie had warned Joe that her grandma was terrible old-fashioned. 15. Lillie said Joe couldn't wrangle the old lady single-handed. 16. So Joe had brought along his own grandparents to make the match in the old-time way. 17. But now, as he rolled in through Hardtack's gate, Joe began to get cold feet about that.

Problem of the Author To make sure that the reader believes in the danger in which our hero stands.

Solution by the Author A character witness (the heroine) is brought in to declare the character of one of the hero's adversaries.

Effect upon the Reader When the author's statement of one character's opinion might be doubted by the reader, his doubt is removed by bringing in another character to bear witness to the facts.

Student's Comment This is all the more convincing because the phrases "terrible old-fashioned" and "wrangle the old lady" keep the testimony in character.

Heading · DEVICE FOR CORROBORATION · CONJURING WITH GREAT NAMES

This device is used whenever you feel that the reader will not believe you about some incident in the story. Then you mention the name of some important person whose quoted words or whose

133

example may persuade the reader that your incident or your idea (of which he was so doubtful) is, after all, plausible.

This device, of course, makes the reader feel that the author is modest because he calls in as witness more famous and important people to testify in his behalf.

Other examples of the device of using a Witness for Corroboration may be found in *Dakotah Courtship*. Among them, the following: 23–30, 108–10, 123, 160, 163, 172, 188, 244, 259, 294, 326, 385.

Examples of conjuring with great names may be found in *Dakotah Courtship* in sentences 204, 213, 220.

Here follows one device taken from the story:

Heading · DEVICES USEFUL THROUGHOUT · CONJURING WITH GREAT NAMES

Clipping From *Dakotah Courtship*—in Appendix
217. "That is the way when Dakotah and Crow marry. 218. They are never happy."

219. Mrs. Lone Bear could not resist that opening. 220. With gusto she signaled, "That was what Sitting Bull said."

Problem of the Author To convince the reader of the truth of an idea. In this case a hindrance to the hero (that when Dakotah and Crow marry they are never happy).

Solution by the Author The idea is first stated as agreed upon by the parties conferring, one of whom corroborates it by quoting a famous man, as in agreement.

Effect upon the Reader To emphasize the danger to our hero and the possibility of peacemaking to spoil his hopes.

Student's Comment This is a device constantly used both in fiction and non-fiction.

N. Devices for Indicating the Speaker

One of the problems of the author who writes stories containing much dialogue is that he must continually tell us who is speaking as the talk goes on.

There are, of course, scores of words in the English language which indicate that someone is speaking: "he said," "he lied," "he squawked," "he whispered," "he grumbled," etc. The gender of pronouns will often tell the reader which character is speaking, as, for example, "he laughed" or "she chirped."

Again, dialect may be used where one speaker speaks in dialect and the others in formal English, or where each of the speakers has a different dialect or vocabulary. In some instances the tone of voice may indicate the speaker, or his characteristic expletives. Sometimes the pantomime or gestures which accompany the speech identifies the speaker. There are dozens of ways in which the speaker may be indicated.

These will be better if they characterize, and the best of all methods of indicating the speakers is to have your characters so individualized that no one is ever in doubt as to the identity of the person speaking. Some authors prefer merely to say "he said," "she said," and let it go at that. Others believe that this fails miserably to present a picture and that such bare dialogue is apt to be a bore.

Some methods of indicating the speaker may be listed herewith. Proper names may be used in addressing the other character in a dialogue. Personal pronouns may be used, or some reference to the sex, age, appearance, occupation, dress, habits, or character of the person addressed which will tag the speaker.

Sometimes a mere alternation of passages in quotation marks will keep the reader clear as to who is speaking.

Again one party may ask a question and the other answer it.

The speaker may also be indicated sufficiently by words indicating that a speech is forthcoming, a warning given of a reply to a speech. Such a reply may include the circumstances of the former speech, a brief summary of what was in an argument. The speaker may be indicated by a surprised exclamation at a remark made previously, by objecting or taking exception to what has just been said, by the implied need for a reply, by the statements made by another, by a few words of indicated emotion such as, "He shook his head," or "She seemed reconciled." Or it may be indicated by the reaction to a previous speech, or again by indicating a felt need for a remark such as, "He knew he had to interrupt her without delay."

Success comes from having your characters speak naturally and convincingly and then setting their remarks in such phraseology as will make sure that the reader knows to what speaker every speech belongs.

Examples in *Dakotah Courtship* of the Indication of the Speaker will be found in the following sentences:

The simple use of a personal pronoun with the word "she" is found in sentence 67.

Use of the proper name indicating the speaker is found in many passages, such as 153–54, 188, 189, 400.

Where two people are speaking and one uses the name of the other in addressing him; this device may be found in 119, 466, 570, 591, 602, and elsewhere.

A gesture indicating the speaker, followed by dialogue, will be found in 88–89, 100–01, 111–12, 388–89.

Manner of speech with the name classification, or personal pronoun may be found in 20, 23, 24, 70, 92, 125.

No indication of the speaker is necessary when what is said is obviously the reply to a question proposed by the other character in a dialogue. See sentence 421.

A question with the name of the party addressed, followed by an answer, may indicate the speaker of the answer in a dialogue: 125–26, 223–24, 153, 366, etc.

A name indicating sex of the person addressed may serve, as in 539, 552.

Sometimes several of these devices are combined, as in 251–52, where the proper name of the speaker is given along with his characteristic gesture and the words he uttered.

O. Device of Discovery and Reversal

Life consists of stimuli and reactions. We discover something and then think or feel something as a result of it. This goes on continually so long as we are alive and conscious, since life consists of such discoveries and reactions.

And since life is more dramatic when the discovery is followed by a change or reversal of the original attitude, it is obvious that literature must use this discovery and reversal as the basic pattern if it is to give the reader anything like the experience of real life.

Aristotle, first to point out the usefulness of Discovery and Reversal in plotting, in his *Poetics* explains this device. He defines Discovery or Recognition as a change from ignorance to knowledge, producing love or hate between the persons destined by the poet for

136

good or bad fortune. The Reversal is the effect of his change from ignorance to knowledge—the love or hate created thereby.

Such a Recognition and Reversal will produce either pity or fear.

Aristotle says further that when a man kills his enemy, it is only what the reader expects; when a man kills a stranger, that is merely a pitiful incident; but when a man kills or wishes to kill his friend, you have a tragic story.

The basic principle here is that all strife in a story must be between persons who are naturally and properly "near and dear" to each other.

Thus, if the families of Romeo and Juliet had not been at war, there would have been no story—only a happy meeting between two lovers. And since the natural habitat of man is trouble, the reader could take no interest. A happy love is of interest only to the happy lovers, whereas their tragedy is known to the wide world.

The course of fictional love never did run smooth!

Man can only act or not act, knowingly or unknowingly. This fact provides us with four patterns of Discovery and Reversal.

Thus a man may kill his brother, knowing that he is his brother.

Again the killing may be done in ignorance and only discovered afterward.

A third method: A man may be about to do such an irreparable deed and then—just in time—discover that the victim is a dear one, and refrain.

Finally, a killer may be about to kill his brother, knowing that he is his brother, yet fail to act. This, of course, is such a feeble device that it is seldom used. It is shocking without being dramatic.

Whenever, therefore, you have one character find out something which causes a change in his attitude toward another—as when Hamlet discovered that the King had murdered his father—you have the makings of a story. Moreover, at any stage in your story a Discovery and Reversal provides you with new interest, new drama, new plot—even though the "change" or Reversal is merely an intensification of the original motive of the character.

Thus a man undergoing torture, rather than reveal a secret which will make his sweetheart unhappy, may be ready to talk, when in she comes, because she loves him, to beg him to confess.

The discovery of her presence will then steel his heart to endure the more and he refuses to tell. Such a scene will have the added appeal of dialogue at cross-purposes.

137

A thorough study of Recognition and Reversal, or Discovery and Reversal, as it is sometimes called, is of the utmost value to anyone who wishes to make story plots.

In *Dakotah Courtship,* Discovery and Reversal is found in these passages: 32–37, 53–67, 371–74, 377–93, 405–21, 496–501, 506, 530–32, 551–56, 561–64, 602–14.

Heading · DEVICES USEFUL THROUGHOUT · DISCOVERY AND REVERSAL

Clipping From *Dakotah Courtship*—in Appendix
371. "Running Hawk was a relative of mine," he said, sternly.

372. "Joe! Is that true?" 373. Lillie turned to him, her face stricken. 374. "Oh, Big Boy, I'm so sorry.

Problem of the Author To bring about a change in the attitude of one character toward another.

Solution by the Author The hero gives information (the discovery) in 371 which brings about a change which causes the heroine to turn from hate to sympathy (reversal, 374).

Effect upon the Reader Sympathetic and convincing.

Student's Comment Whoever hopes to write fiction should understand and use discovery and reversal.

Heading · DEVICES USEFUL THROUGHOUT · DISCOVERY AND REVERSAL

Clipping From *Dakotah Courtship*—in Appendix
375. "Look here, Joe. 376. The old folks know we are watching them. 377. I bet they are trying us out. 378. That's what! 379. If we can't take it, they don't want us to marry."

380. Joe stared at her. 381. He looked quickly at the group in the arbor. 382. "Kid, you're smart. 383. You've said a mouthful. 384. That's it, all right. 385. It's just like them old-time peace treaties Granddad tells about. 386. They got together and insulted each other for all they were worth—to make sure the peace would stick!"

387. Lillie nodded.

388. Joe got up. 389. "Look here, Lil. 390. This has gone far enough. 391. If they keep on, they'll make saps of us. 392. We got to stop it. 393. Come on."

138

Problem of the Author   To motivate an about-face of two characters.

Solution by the Author   In sentence 377 the characters make a discovery leading to a change of heart or new purpose (the reversal) in sentence 392.

Effect upon the Reader   Convincing and suspenseful.

Student's Comment   You can do anything with discovery and reversal in a story, and you can do nothing without it.

P. Devices for Interest · Color

Not every story requires color, or, at any rate, not much of it, but it is a useful thing both in arousing emotion and for Plausibility.

By color we mean whatever convinces us of the locality, the time and place and kind of life—not merely setting, but typical incidents which make us feel that the story is real and vivid.

Some authors make much of color and go to a great deal of trouble to find and use it, not only in a regional or travel tale, or in stories of foreign lands, or settings unfamiliar to most readers; for there may be color in any story, no matter what the background.

In fact, a reader is apt to judge a story's authenticity by its color. He expects a certain type of people, certain kinds of incidents, certain settings. He will not expect luxurious and voluptuous romance in a covered-wagon train. It is conceivable—indeed, it is true—that some of the people who crossed the Plains in early days traveled in luxury, with tents and servants, silver and china, expensive foods and champagne, and everything handsome about them. It is true that on military marches from one post to another the troops carried sectional dancing floors along so that the officers and their ladies could dance every evening while the regimental band played. But this sort of thing, though true, will not appeal to readers who like to think of the Old West as a rough frontier life. And so color plays quite a part in fiction.

In *Dakotah Courtship* we have the color of old-time Indian life and customs contrasted with the color of young Indians trying to live a modern life. Examples may be found in every paragraph. Consider the following sentences as examples: 1, 3, 6–8, 15, 23–30, 34, 36, 38–39, 41–42, 48–50, 55–58, 67–70, etc. Record as many other examples as you can find in this story.

139

Clipping   From *Dakotah Courtship*—in Appendix 181. "Her great grandfather was a famous horsethief."

Problem of the Author   To contrast old Indian standards with the new.

Solution by the Author   He brings in a striking bit of color.

Effect upon the Reader   Amusement.

Student's Comment   Having the old woman boast of what would now be criminal points up the contrast.

Q. Devices for Continuity · Fact Feeling

Since your readers have both minds and hearts, since words have both denotation and connotation, it follows that the writer inevitably deals in part with ideas and facts and in part with emotions or feelings. The reader likes to have these well mixed up and to experience them alternately. A passage which consists entirely of facts and ideas without any emotional appeal repels him; he calls it "dry as dust." On the other hand, when someone writes pure gush, eliminating all the facts and ideas and presenting only colorful, meaningless words and emotions, the reader is likely to gag. He says such writing "does not make sense." Your reader does not wish to be drowned in emotion nor to thirst among the facts.

He likes his facts and feelings dished up alternately at short intervals.

That is to say, he wants a fact and a feeling, an idea and an excitement, a motion and an emotion in every sentence and clause and the writer who wishes to hold his reader and keep him reading will have to accept that natural law and act accordingly.

If we could put both the fact and the feeling in one word, as in the word "ouch"—which has the meaning "I am hurt" and also the feeling "I don't like it"—we could all be poets all the time. But since there are very few words like "ouch" in the language, we have to speak in sentences. And in a sentence, the fact and feeling get separated, so that one precedes the other.

Thus we are continually faced with the problem of whether to put the fact first and the feeling second, or the feeling first and the fact second. Fortunately we can readily solve that problem by writing our sentence both ways and judging which form will serve us better.

As a rule sentences in a given sequence or paragraph are similar. Thus if the paragraph starts off *fact feeling, fact feeling,* the following sentences will duplicate the pattern clear to the end of the paragraph or sequence. If it starts off *feeling fact, feeling fact,* or *emotion motion, emotion motion,* then the following sentences will continue in that pattern to the end of the paragraph or sequence as a rule.

Sometimes, of course, for purposes of jolting the reader and making him realize a conflict in the hero's mind, you may set up your paragraph *fact feeling, feeling fact, fact feeling, feeling fact.* But this problem of the sequence of fact and feeling, of emotion and motion, of idea and excitement, of stimulus and reaction, is the basic problem of style. Solve that and you can hardly lose your reader.[3]

You will be wise to go through first *Dakotah Courtship* and later stories by your favorite authors, underscoring in each clause or sentence the facts, ideas, or motions once and the feelings and emotions twice. This you will find most instructive and helpful. Note how often in the same sequence the sentences are all of the same type Note how the mood changes with a change in the order of fact and feeling in the sentences.

In *Dakotah Courtship* you may profitably study the passage 487–90. Here follows one device as an illustration:

Heading · DEVICES USEFUL THROUGHOUT · CONTINUITY · FACT FEELING

Clipping From *Dakotah Courtship*—in Appendix

421. "My grandson is right. 422. The trail behind is lost. 423. The rains and snows of many winters have filled it with mud. 424. It is covered with grass. 425. Here and there it has been plowed under. 426. When I was young, I used to come upon the bones of a man lying on the prairie. 427. Sometimes they were the bones of a Crow, sometimes of a Dakotah. 428. But now I never find bones lying on

---

[3]This problem has been already discussed in *Writing Magazine Fiction,* by W. S. Campbell, Doubleday & Co., Inc., 1941.

the prairie. 429. The old trail is lost. 430. The young men cannot find it."

Problem of the Author   To introduce a new and quieter mood into the story as a transition to another lively conflict yet to come.

Solution by the Author   A character delivers a monologue in which all the sentences are arranged in the order of *fact feeling*.

Effect upon the Reader   Since the fact is not seen through the feeling, but stated before the feeling is indicated, the effect here is much less violent, more calm.

Student's Comment   Very often in fiction the feeling comes first and the fact afterward, so that the reader, seeing the fact through the feeling, gets a double shot of emotion.

To indicate agitation in a character's mind it is possible to express his thoughts in sentences alternating *fact feeling, feeling fact, fact feeling, feeling fact*. An example of this in *Dakotah Courtship* is found in the passage 31–37.

R. Device for Meeting and Purpose without Conflict · The Incident

In addition to the Scene there is what is commonly known as the *incident* or *episode*, in which there is a meeting and purpose but no conflict. This, however, may be very useful to an author at any stage of his story.

Here follow devices presenting Incidents:

Heading · DEVICES USEFUL THROUGHOUT · INCIDENT

Clipping   From *Dakotah Courtship*—in Appendix
388. Joe got up. 389. "Look here, Lil. 390. This has gone far enough. 391. If they keep on, they'll make saps of us. 392. We got to stop it. 393. Come on." . . . 404. But Joe and Lillie were in the arbor, each talking as fast as possible—the one in Crow, the other in Dakotah, and both in the sign language.

Problem of the Author   To bring about united action of hero and heroine and so end conflict of their opponents.

142

Solution by the Author   One character makes a proposal that they both act in a certain manner. There is no conflict. The second character agrees to act with the first, and so they do act.

Effect upon the Reader   Dramatic, and promising further conflict by a union of forces.

Student's Comment   A promise of conflict with the old folks makes the agreement between hero and heroine dramatic.

Further examples of Incident in *Dakotah Courtship* will be found in the following passages: 409–11, 446–52, 578–81, 610–14. Look for similar passages in other stories and make up devices from them, showing their purpose and function in the tale.

S. Device for Meeting without Purpose · The Happening

In addition to Scene and Incident (or episode) there is what is called a *happening*. Here there is a meeting but no purpose, no encounter, no final action. Thus the wind slams a door and you jump. There was a meeting of forces there but no purpose.

Here follow devices for presenting a Happening:

Heading · DEVICES USEFUL THROUGHOUT · MEETING WITHOUT CONFLICT · THE HAPPENING

Clipping   From *Dakotah Courtship*—in Appendix
32. Then and there he killed his engine. 33. The car jolted to a stop.

Problem of the Author   A hindrance to the hero.

Solution by the Author   The hero, without purpose, causes his car to stall. Here hero and car meet, but without purpose on the part of either.

Effect upon the Reader   Amusing.

Student's Comment   This device enables an author to use the forces of nature and accidents to carry the story forward from one conflict to another.

143

WORK PROGRAM 9

In Chapter 9 you have been given certain standard devices useful in the Middle of your story. You will do well to master these as you did in the previous chapter and to collect similar ones from your own reading for your notebook of technical devices.

1. (a) List the Devices of the Middle given in Chapter 9. (b) Write three Finger Exercises, using different words and subject matter of your own in each case.
2. Now read the Pieces for Analysis in the Appendix (other than *Dakotah Courtship*) and discover what Devices of the Beginning and what Devices of the Middle are used therein. Prepare cards for these and imitate each one, as time permits, in three Finger Exercises.
3. As opportunity permits, collect similar devices from your own reading and put them in your notebook in the proper form with the Heading, Clipping, Problem, Solution, Effect, and Comment, in each case.
4. Record here what you have discovered about technique in general and in particular by doing the exercises in this Work Program.

CHAPTER 10   FICTION • DEVICES OF THE END

THE SHORT STORY

In the Fourth Part of the short story your hero, having already attempted to solve his Problem (getting out of the frying pan) and so leaped into the fire (the Complication), arrives at the Crisis. At the crisis in his Black Moment he is forced to a Decision between what he wishes to do and what he ought to do, between the two conflicting emotions in his mind and heart, between the self and the not-self.

In a well-plotted story it must seem to your hero in this crisis that —whatever he may do—he will surely regret it.

Yet the right decision, the unselfish decision, should also seem to be that for which he must sacrifice the most; he must feel that his decision to turn to the right is dangerous to him and to what he holds dear.

But if he is a hero—one who prefers the good of others to his own selfish desires—he will decide to make the Sacrifice. And because of this he will receive his Reward—though not until he has himself fought or found his way out of his difficulties by some heroic feat or exhibition of courage, or by some ingenious scheme which he himself conceives and executes. That is, he must not be rewarded merely for making the right decision. He must also work it out or fight it out, earn and so make it effective.

In other words, you must not use "machinery" to save your hero. By Machinery we mean the intervention of supernatural beings, of Providence, Fate, or Luck. The name comes from a machine used by the ancient Greeks in their theaters, a kind of derrick or crane with a rope and a basket depending from it by means of which actors impersonating supernatural beings could be lowered down upon the stage, there to solve a hopeless situation for the hero and so bring the story to an acceptable end. This intervention of supermen and deities, of Coincidence and Providence, should play no part in the solution of the hero's problem in a short story. You must not save him by "machinery." He must solve his problem with his own brawn and brain. Otherwise your reader will never be satisfied.

For example, in a triangle plot, it will not do to eliminate the odd man by a convenient motor accident.

However, should your principal character or chief sufferer (whom for convenience we call your "hero") not make the right decision or be unwilling to make the sacrifice required of him at the Crisis of the story; should he take the wrong turn and choose to follow his selfish desires instead of his duty, preferring wrong to right, selfishness to unselfishness, he must then be made to recognize his mistake and accept and suffer his punishment, fully realizing that he has lost out and made a bad bargain.

For a well-plotted short story is an artificial thing not found in real life. As Dr. Samuel Johnson sagely wrote, "Seldom is any splendid story wholly true."

A short story has more pattern, more coherence, more unity—which all arise from its consistency in sticking to the statement and solution of *one* problem until it obtains the correct answer.

Suspense in a story arises from the balanced struggle between the two emotions in the hero's mind and the reader's uncertainty whether the hero will turn to the right or the left in the Crisis. Suspense is not a mere curiosity as to what will happen next.

It is this conflict of emotions in the hero's heart that keeps him and the reader sticking to the problem and fighting it out to the end. It is this concentration on that *problem between the self and the not-self* which makes for unity, coherence, and emphasis, which brings character to life and makes action significant. It gives a story a Beginning, a Middle, and an End, a Problem, Complication, Crisis, Decision, Sacrifice, Final Conflict, Solution, and Reward. In short, it makes the short story a definite art form.

English-speaking people are men of action, living for the most part in the world of affairs, where a man must continually answer the question for himself, "What shall I do?"

Whoever acts must first have a motive, and that motive usually involves some moral principle—at least where other persons are concerned.

Therefore, every well-plotted story turns upon the pivot of a moral choice, and without a moral choice there can be no story form. Without a moral choice you have only a character sketch, a setting, an incident, or the illustration of a theme; you cannot have what is called a short story.

The problem of the story writer, then, is to combine the free will of his character with the predestination of the plot. This can be done only by grace of imagination, and this grace of imagination is found only where the author is so familiar with and so interested in his materials, his subject matter, that every fact he recalls about it suggests a dozen facets—a dozen possible points of departure—a dozen angles—so that he is never at a loss for natural motives, natural characters, natural incidents and scenes from which to build a convincing plot. That is why an ignorant writer who writes without enthusiasm writes so badly. He sees only one facet to his one fact— and that one facet rarely serves his need.

A *successful piece of writing is simply the correct answer to a technical problem.* And unless you are aware of many devices that might be used, how can you choose the best and so solve your technical problem correctly?

You need not fear the loss of your originality. You are an individual, and your temperament and talent are of necessity individual too. You can no more get rid of your originality than you can change the color of your eyes. It is always with you and part of you. Thus, to use the popular phrase, you are forever "stuck with" your particular kind of talent and type of originality. But you are *not* "stuck with" your amateurish technique. You can improve your technique and make it professional *if* you will only take the trouble.

Remember that a short story is a definite pattern requiring its own tools and techniques, just as an etching requires different tools and techniques from those used in producing a water color.

One thing you can do toward your success in publishing is to study the magazine in which you would like to have your stories appear. Read the short fiction pieces in that magazine, and when you encounter a love scene or a fight scene, circle it with your pencil. Afterward study all these love scenes and fight scenes to discover what happens in them—and in what order. For readers of a given magazine come to expect certain kinds of love scenes and fight scenes, and it is well for you to know what is typical of them in the magazine you wish to write for.

Thus in a love scene: are the sensations of the kiss described or are they merely implied? Does the lover begin by praising or admiring his sweetheart's hair, or is he first attracted by her sportsmanship and high ideals? Discover, in short, what happens and in what order in your love scenes.

Likewise in a fight scene. Does the hero defend himself with his fists, or with a gun, or in some other manner? Do the contestants wrestle, or shoot, or knife each other? Does the fight begin in talk and end in violence, or the reverse? Just what goes on in the typical fight scene in that magazine?

Such inquiries will help you in your efforts to write your own stories. You will be wise to collect a scrapbook full of love scenes and fight scenes, making an analysis of each alongside your clipping, and finally concluding the book with a digest of what you have discovered. You may not wish to follow these patterns in your own work; you may wish to vary from them. But unless you know what they are, you can do neither.

When writing the End of a story you should consider that it must plausibly follow the Beginning and the Middle and must seem inevitable. Thus it is bad art and cheap craftsmanship to take such a tragic story as *Hamlet* and give it a happy ending, with a sane Ophelia wading out of the brook and Hamlet on the throne, for the whole story before the last act points irresistibly to tragedy. Such a story must have a tragic end.

147

On the other hand, you need never avoid a happy ending, provided your story justifies it and leads up to it. The real point about the happy ending is that it must be a *happy one for your reader*. What happens to the hero, good or bad, is irrelevant; but what the reader expects is final. You must satisfy your reader—or you will lose him.

We have already discovered that the desirable qualities of the Ending of a Short Story are that it be (1) brief and (2) satisfying.

You must always remember, in writing the End of a story and contriving devices to carry it, that the End of any short piece must give satisfaction to the reader and that it must be brief.

It must be brief because the reader, seeing how the story is turning out, will not tolerate a long-winded finish. The End must be satisfying to the reader because otherwise the reader feels cheated and the author has failed.

Of course many of the devices used in the Middle of the story and in the Beginning can be useful in the End. You may use Characterization, a new Setting, a Complication, a different Emotional Tone, a Flashback, a new Conflict in the hero's mind, a Promise of Further Conflict.

You may use Hindrances and Furtherances, Scenes, Transitions, devices for Continuity, Plausibility, and Focus, Repetitions, Overlapping Paragraphs, and Dialogue at Cross-Purposes.

In short, nearly all the devices used in other parts of the story may serve you here. Therefore, it is unnecessary to give examples of all of these things set up as devices, since you are already familiar with them.

However, one may call attention to passages in the End of *Dakotah Courtship* in which such devices appear, and at the end of this chapter you will find references to these.

We have said that the End must be brief. How is that to be achieved?

Brevity is largely a matter of style, the selection and arrangement of words.

There are certain practices—or, rather, principles—of style, which are generally observed by the better writers, whether of fiction or non-fiction. It is helpful to consider these and occasionally to check one's own work by these, line by line and word by word, to see how one is handling the language.[1]

[1] Some of these principles have been set forth in a pamphlet, costing only five cents, which may be obtained from the Superintendent of Documents, Govern-

For clarity, the writer of English should generally prefer:

1. The familiar word to the unfamiliar word, as: "redden" to "incarnadine."
2. The concrete word to the abstract word, as: "hammer" to "implement."
3. The single word to the phrase, as: "He *splashed* through the ford" to "He *waded noisily* through the ford."
4. The short word to the long word, as: "home" to "domicile."
5. The Saxon or Old English word to the word derived from a foreign language, as: "drunk" to "intoxicated."

Of course it is not always possible to follow these principles[2] as rigid rules, since a great many things have been invented and a great many words have come into our language since the Norman Conquest for which no Saxon words exist.

Your principal concern in the End of your story must be to achieve Brevity without squeezing the emotion out; for a story is not fact but feeling, not motion but emotion. And if you save only the facts when you compress the Ending, you will find that you have squeezed all the blood out of it and instead of a story have a mere account.

Therefore, the best means of abbreviating the end of your story is through the use of implications, by choosing such phrases and words as will suggest far more than they explain. This is a most important matter, and you must give it serious consideration. Study the Ends of good models and make note of apt implications wherever you find them in your reading, with a view to imitation.

As a rule in beginners' work, the Beginning and End of his story are overweight and overladen with fact—wordy, diffuse, not fully imagined, not succinctly phrased. You must therefore learn to cut.

How true the adage is: *"There is nothing sacred about mistakes."* The fact that you wrote something does not make it a masterpiece, and you must learn to be relentless in pruning away everything which does not make your story as good as it can be. A story is like a stream—a continuous emotional movement—a steady and unceasing journey from the opening problem to the final answer.

Therefore, cut relentlessly all parts where your characters merely

---

ment Printing Office, Washington, D.C., entitled *To Government Writers: How Does Your Writing Read?* This pamphlet contains some interesting information and a test by which you may determine with fair accuracy what public is most likely to understand your style and what markets you may hope to reach with it.

[2]These principles are derived from those given in *The King's English* by H. W. Fowler and F. G. Fowler (Oxford. 1906). Chapter I.

149

jump up and down in the same place or—worse yet—merely stand still. Beware of chunks of facts like boulders in a stream blocking the flow of emotion. Keep your story moving, flowing, emotional. Cut away the physical movement, not the emotional movement. Whatever you eliminate, do *not* eliminate emotion.

Setting and scenery, long-winded physical descriptions of characters, most psychological analysis, places, and props can generally be cut to the bone. Do not use "he said" or "she replied." Instead, offer the reader the stage business—" 'Indeed!' He whirled angrily around. 'Then why are you here?'" Dialogue should be in broken phrases—not long grammatical sentences—as all good dialogue at cross-purposes will be. Strike out many adjectives and more adverbs, but remember that adverbs and particularly verbs, because they suggest movement, are the life of your story.

Often enough you can reduce the number of characters by letting one person perform several functions in the story.

Cutting a story is a fine art and one requiring much practice and thought. But primarily you either *cut to space* or *cut to speed up story movement*.

Since literature exists in time, since words and phrases flow into the reader's mind one after the other in time, movement is the basic and essential principle of the art. And since the reader will not continue to read unless his emotions are excited, this movement in fiction must be emotional.

Here are listed passages in the story *Dakotah Courtship* which illustrate devices found in the End.

Characterization: 516–22

Setting: 528

Complications: 516, 530, 533–37, 538–40, 548, 550

New Emotional Tone: 569

Flashback: 579, 585

Hindrances: 508, 509–12, 514, 516, 520, 523, 524, 527, etc.

Furtherances: 513, 515, 519, 521–22, 526, etc.

Scenes: 519–29

Transitions: 532, 564, 588, 616

Dialogue at Cross-Purposes: 597–611

Repetitions: 539, 558, 560, 591

Consider which devices are found in these passages:

Crisis: 508–17

Black Moment: 529

Decision: 531
Sacrifice: 543
Final Conflict: 560
Solution: 611
Reward: 612
Twist: 622

The secret of writing good Ends for your stories is not to use devices different from those used elsewhere in the story, but to use them differently. By that I mean use them to serve the purpose of making the End *brief*—and also *satisfying* to the reader.

Anything that makes for compression helps here. Those devices that enable you to state something in a few words are good; those that enable you to suggest something (and it may be something that would require a whole page, if stated) are better. And of these methods of suggesting matters not stated, and so saving words, Implication is the handiest and best.

Here follow a few devices of Implication.

DEVICES OF THE END · IMPLICATION

The dictionary defines the word "imply" as "to involve in substance or essence, or by fair inference, when not expressly stated in words or by signs; to contain by implication; as, war implies fighting; to express indirectly; to suggest; to hint or hint at."

In literature, implications are delightful to the reader and very useful to the author.

They are delightful to the reader because he gets two meanings for the price of one—that is, two meanings for the same effort he would normally make for one. And of course there may be multiple implications which multiply his pleasure.

Implications are useful to the writer not merely because the reader delights in them, but because by delivering a different meaning in a few syllables he is enabled to abbreviate his endings and cut the number of words in his story. Since the conveyance of ideas and emotions is the writer's aim and job, any device which simplifies the process is useful.

It follows that implications are golden, and the subtlety and cleverness which produces them—though perhaps overrated—nevertheless are rewarded by the editor and the public.

Here follow some examples of Implication. You will, of course, collect many more in your notebook from your favorite authors. Study them and create others of your own.

Heading · DEVICES OF THE END · IMPLICATION

Clipping From *Dakotah Courtship*—in Appendix
123. "She don't approve of necking."

Problem of the Author To indicate the relationship of two characters swiftly.

Solution by the Author A single word is used to suggest an idea more usually proposed by the other party to the conversation.

Effect upon the Reader Amusing and convincing.

Student's Comment All the world loves a lover, but it is tedious to watch them perform. Implication is quicker and leaves the imagination of the reader free.

Heading · DEVICES OF THE END · IMPLICATION

Clipping From *Dakotah Courtship*—in Appendix
499. "Where do you think you are anyhow?"

Problem of the Author To emphasize the intimate relationship of two characters who, though quarreling, are to be reconciled, and to do it in a few words.

Solution by the Author The first word of the sentence implies an intimacy between hero and heroine which both parties take for granted.

Effect upon the Reader Amusing and reassuring.

Student's Comment Though the characters are raging at each other, the implication tips the reader off that they are really friends.

Heading · DEVICES OF THE END · IMPLICATION

Clipping From *Dakotah Courtship*—in Appendix
537. The big roughneck looked Lillie up and down. 538. "Goin' to town? 539. Hop in, Sister."

Problem of the Author   At the end of a story to indicate clearly the motives of a newly introduced character without slowing down action.

Solution by the Author   The motive is implied by a gesture and a word.

Effect upon the Reader   Convincing.

Student's Comment   This device of impiication enables the author to let the reader in on thoughts and motives which could be offensive to some readers if explained at length.

THE SHORT STORY · CONCLUSION

In the preceding chapters you have been given examples of standard devices used in short stories, each of which may be used for solving some technical problem. Of course the subject matter and vocabulary, the pace and sentence structure used in each of these devices may be varied almost infinitely. But the pattern is established and effective for its purpose. If you will faithfully study the patterns and devices already given and imitate each one three times or more, using your own subject matter and vocabulary, yet sticking to the pattern, you can master these devices and will know how to use them whenever you find it helpful.

When you have mastered those devices given here and learned how to use them, you will soon find yourself scanning everything you read, looking for new tricks and new devices which you can add to your arsenal. Finally, having become master of many devices old and new, you will be prepared to handle any subject matter for any reader. Then you will be truly a professional writer.

Sound technique means doing the right thing in the right way at the right time.

Choose subject matter which appeals to you strongly, then choose a style and technique which will carry that subject matter appealingly to your public.

Remember that everything which has once appealed to the public will appeal again if properly rewritten to their taste. There is no form of literature so completely outdated that it has no chance of a comeback. Everything that has been done belongs to any writer who can do it better.

1. What are the necessary parts of the End of a story?
2. Indicate by number the sentences in *Dakotah Courtship* in which the essential parts of the End are found.
3. Go through a page of *Dakotah Courtship*, marking in each clause and sentence the phrases expressing facts and feelings or motions and emotions in each case. Underscore facts once, feelings twice.
4. (a) What is the basic law of writing given in this chapter? (b) Explain its application to writing.
5. (a) If you had to cut 100 words out of *Dakotah Courtship*, what words, what passages would you cut? (b) Explain why you made the cut in each case.
6. (a) Scan the stories in a current magazine and underscore the implications you find. (b) Make up devices for your notebook using each of these passages as the Clipping.

CHAPTER 11   FICTION • ANALYSIS

You have now had some opportunity to study a number of the standard devices commonly found in fiction of all kinds, whether short stories, short short stories, novelettes, or novels. We have gathered these devices from a single story, as this method has proven most fruitful in training writers.

It is now time for you to analyze other pieces of fiction and to study the devices found in them.

For this purpose a short story, a novelette, and a short short story have been included in the Appendix of this book. We shall now turn our attention to each of these in turn, beginning with the story by Miss Naomi John White entitled *A Very Valuable Quality* found in the Appendix, Section A-2.

When you have read the introduction to that story and the story itself, turn back to Work Program 9 and write out the answers to the questions found therein.

Answers to some of these questions will be found at the end of the book in the Notes for Chapter 9, Section A-2. Do *not* consult these notes until you have written out your own answers to the questions. Then compare your answers to those given in the Notes. In like manner we shall then study the novelette *Eva? Caroline?* by Allan Ellston, and after that *Bargain Hunters* by W. L. Heath, a short short story.

If you will faithfully work out your own answers to the questions in the Work Program to follow, before you compare them with those offered in the Notes, and then follow this experience with practice in writing Finger Exercises in imitation of those devices you think good, you will be ready to analyze other stories which you find in magazines in the same manner. Thus you will become fully aware of what is happening to a reader and how an author makes it happen. In short, you will become aware of many devices, many niceties of technique.

And that is what every writer *must* do if he is to have any solid success.

WORK PROGRAM 11

Section A-1

No further study of *Dakotah Courtship* is required here. Proceed to Section A-2 of this Work Program, which follows immediately.

Section A-2

After reading the story *A Very Valuable Quality* in the Appendix, Section A-2, you should first analyze it by asking yourself these questions.
1. How long is this story—that is, how many words does it contain?
2. What type of story is this (action, atmosphere, idea, or character)?
3. Every story is somebody's story. Whose story is this? That is, who is the chief sufferer (the hero or heroine)?
4. What is the chief sufferer's problem?
5. What is the main complication? What other complications do you find?

6. What emotions clash in the mind of the chief sufferer?
7. What obstacle has the chief sufferer to surmount?
8. What opponent has the chief sufferer to overcome?
9. What disaster has the chief sufferer to avert?
10. What decision does the chief sufferer make and what sacrifice for the chief sufferer is involved in that decision?
11. What is the solution of the chief sufferer's problem?
12. How is this managed?
13. What, if any, is the chief sufferer's reward?
14. What are each character's identifying tags, traits, function, and weapon in the story?
15. What is the setting (time, place, and social atmosphere) of this story?
16. How many scenes does this story contain? How many incidents? How many happenings?
17. What transitions can you find (a) from place to place, (b) from time to time, (c) from mood to mood?
18. What types of discourse (exposition, description, narrative, dialogue, dramatic action, etc.) are used, and in what proportion?
19. What do you think of the title of the story?
20. What reader is this story aimed at?
21. Why did the editor buy this story?

Write out your answers to the questions above.

Consider now the devices used in the story *A Very Valuable Quality.*

DEVICES OF THE BEGINNING

22. Indicate by number the sentences comprising Bait.
23. There are nine characters in this story, not counting "our cat Violet." Give the numbers of the sentences in which each of the following characters is first introduced and identified as heroine, opponent, etc.:

a. Suzie
b. Henry
c. Elsie
d. Bessie
e. Walters
f. Tomlison
g. Burke
h. Janet
i. Laurie

156

24. The main problem of the heroine is to hold her man. Indicate by number the sentences in which this main problem is (a) first introduced and (b) made entirely clear to the reader. When the reader reaches the point where he fully understands the problem facing the chief sufferer in a story, he has reached the end of the Beginning.

25. Indicate by number the sentences in which the solution of the heroine's problem is hinted at.

26. List by number the sentences in which the light emotional tone of the story is indicated.

27. Most stories fit into one of four types (action, atmosphere, character, or idea). How would you classify this story?

28. A Plant indicates that some fact, condition, person, or thing exists. A Pointer indicates that a certain event or kind of event may, can, or will happen later on in the story. The following numbered sentences contain either a Plant or a Pointer, or both. Please indicate which contain Plants and which Pointers, or both.

1, 2, 3, 4, 5, 6, 7, 8, 9, 10, 11, 12, 15, 18, 19, 20, 26–28, 31, 34, 40, 41, 43, 46, 48, 57, 58, 59, 61–62, 63, 75, 76, 82, 89, 92, 94, 98, 103, 112, 117, 119, 120, 122, 128, 129, 133, 137, 141, 144, 148, 154, 155, 157, 158, 160, 163, 165, 166, 170–72, 183, 184, 186, 189, 194, 198, 201, 202, 207, 210, 214, 216, 219, 221, 228, 230, 235, 241, 248, 252, 255, 259, 267, 272, 274, 275, 280, 283, 291, 296, 297, 305, 317–19, 326, 337, 340, 345, 351, 358, 361, 362, 367, 370–72, 375, 376, 378.

29. What flashbacks are found in this piece of fiction? Indicate by number the sentences which embody flashbacks here. What type of flashback is used in each case? (See earlier discussion of flashbacks in this book.)

30. What two emotions are in conflict in the mind of the chief sufferer's opponent (Henry) here?

31. Indicate by number the sentences in which a promise of conflict occurs.

32. Characters in the story *A Very Valuable Quality* are characterized as indicated below in each case. Try to find the sentences in which each of these characterizations occurs and indicate them by numbers under the appropriate heading.

Suzie is characterized by her action 28 times, by her speech 34 times, by her reaction to others 9 times, by others' reaction to her 76 times, by the report of others 13 times, by description 7 times, by exposition 5 times, by psychological analysis not at all.

Henry is characterized by action 29 times, by speech 29 times, by reaction to others 22 times, by reaction of others 35 times, by report of others 17 times, by description 4 times, by exposition twice, by psychological analysis not at all.

Elsie is characterized by action 5 times, speech 3 times, reaction to others once, by reaction of others to her 8 times, by report of others 17 times, by description twice, by exposition twice, and by psychological analysis never.

Bessie is characterized by action 17 times, by speech 20 times, by reaction to others 11 times, by reaction of others to her 19 times, by report of others 10 times, by description 3 times, by exposition 3 times, by psychological analysis twice.

Walters is characterized by action 4 times, speech 5, reaction to others 12, reaction of others to him 10, report of others 9, description 1, exposition 1, psychological analysis none.

Tomlison is characterized by action 6 times, speech 5 times, by reaction to others 10 times, by the reaction of others to him 12 times, by the report of others 3 times, by description twice, by exposition twice, by psychological analysis never.

Burke is characterized by action 4 times, by speech 4 times, by reaction to others 7 times, by reaction of others to him 4 times, by report of others 5 times, by description once, by exposition twice, by psychological analysis not at all.

Janet is characterized by action 9 times, by speech 8 times, by reaction to others 3 times, by the reaction of others to her 12 times, by the report of others 5 times, by description 4 times, by exposition once, by psychological analysis never.

Laurie, the narrator, is characterized by action 14 times; by speech all the way through, but particularly in 7 passages; by reaction to others 16 times; by the reaction of others to her 3 times; by the report of others never; by description never; by exposition twice, by psychological analysis not at all.

DEVICES OF THE MIDDLE

33. What main Hindrances and Furtherances do you find here? Indicate by numbers the sentences in which these appear.

34. There are a number of repetitions here. Indicate by sentence number where these occur.

35. Indicate by sentence number the last line of one paragraph and the first line of the paragraph following where Overlapping Paragraphs occur.

36. What is the Gimmick used in this story? Indicate by number the sentences in which it is mentioned.

37. Indicate by sentence numbers passages in which dialogue at cross-purposes occurs.

38. Do you find any device for corroboration in this story? If so, indicate by number the sentences in which such a device occurs.

39. How many different devices for indicating the speaker do you find in this story? How many instances of each device?

40. The device of Discovery and Reversal occurs several times in this story. Indicate by number the sentences where you find it.

41. What "color" do you find in this story and in what sentences does it occur?

42. Take your pencil and underscore in each sentence or clause (or at least one page of the story) the fact and the feeling, the motion and emotion. Underscore the fact or motion once, the feeling or emotion twice. Which precedes the other as a rule?

DEVICES OF THE END

43. What implications do you find in this story? Indicate by number the sentences in which these implications are found.

44. You have now discovered the principal examples of standard devices in this story. But you will doubtless also have found some devices not included here. In order to fix these in your mind you should now write them up in the proper form with Heading, Clipping, Problem, Solution, Effect, and Student's Comment. Afterward write three Finger Exercises in imitation of each, following the same pattern but using fresh subject matter of your own. The same method is recommended for every device which you feel good enough to use in your own work.

Having written out your answers to the questions given above, you may now turn to the Notes for Chapter 11 in the Appendix and check your answers against those in Section A-2.

In the Appendix of this book, Section A-3, you will find a novelette by Allan Vaughan Elston entitled *Eva? Caroline?* reprinted here from the *Woman's Home Companion* for April 1949, by permission of the author. Turn now to the Appendix, Section A-3, read the remarks preceding the novelette proper, then read the novelette. Afterward turn to the beginning of Work Program 11, Section A-2, containing the questions which you answered in studying the short story *A Very Valuable Quality*. Write out your answers (as they apply to the novelette *Eva? Caroline?*) to questions 1 to 21 inclusive down to the heading, DEVICES OF THE BEGINNING.

Under DEVICES OF THE BEGINNING in the questions in Work Program 11 answer question 22.

Then answer question 23 given just below. As is natural in a novelette (longer than a short story), there are fourteen characters here besides the "supers," such as the counsel for the defense, witnesses in court—grocery boy, hotel clerk, and former maid—stewardess on plane, florist, Ruth Paxton, Jake Blythe, Mrs. Blythe, the wife of Colonel Cox, Dr. Joyce, and the three gangsters. The main characters are as follows:

a. Roger Marsh	h. Duke Smedley
b. Inspector Whipple	i. Lucile Dutton
c. Caroline	j. Police matron
d. Dr. Cawfield	k. Uncle Carey
e. Effie Foster	l. Leslie Paxton
f. Aunt Harriet	m. Colonel Cox
g. Evelyn (Eva Lang)	

Give the numbers of the sentences in which each of the fourteen characters is first introduced and identified.

24. What is the main problem of the hero, Roger? Indicate by number the sentences in which his main problem is (a) first introduced, and (b) made entirely clear to the reader.

Now answer questions 25 and 26 as given earlier in Work Program 11.

Omit 27.

28. You should by this time be able to discover without mistake the Plants and Pointers in a story. Indicate in what sentences Plants occur and in what sentences you find Pointers.

Answer questions 29 and 31 as given previously. Omit question 30.

32. Now indicate by number the sentences in which the characters in the novelette are characterized, placing the number in each case under whichever of the eight methods of characterization it uses.

DEVICES OF THE MIDDLE

Answer questions 33 to 43 inclusive as given in Work Program 11.

44. You have now discovered the principal examples of standard devices in this novelette. But you will doubtless also have found some devices not included here. In order to fix these in your mind you should now write them up in the proper form with Heading, Clipping, Problem, Solution, Effect, and Student's Comment. Afterward write three Finger Exercises in imitation of each, following the same pattern but using fresh subject matter of your own. The same method is recommended for *every* device which you feel is good enough to use in your own work.

Having written out your answers to the questions given above, you may now turn to the Notes for Chapter 11 in the Appendix and check your answers against the answers and suggestions in Section A-3.

45. Now set up, as formal devices complete with Heading, Clipping, Problem, Solution, Effect, and Student's Comment, whatever devices you find particularly effective in the novelette you have been studying.

46. Finally write three Finger Exercises (using different words and subject matter in each) on the pattern of the devices you have set up in answering question 45 above.

Section A-4

1. You have read *Bargain Hunters.* Now analyze this story by writing your answers to the first twenty-one questions given in Work Program 11, Section A-2.
2. (a) What is the Twist in this story? (b) the Back-twist? Indicate by sentence numbers.
3. Set up as many of the devices we have studied as you find in *Bargain Hunters,* using the correct form (Heading, Clipping, Problem of the Author, Solution, Effect, and Student's Comment).

4. Now write three Finger Exercises for each of the devices you have found and set up, following the same pattern but using different subject matter in each of the three exercises.

This should be the beginning of a collection of devices of your own. These you will collect from the work of other writers, and so learn to follow right methods. Once you have found and familiarized yourself with a dozen good patterns of every kind of device, you will have less difficulty in finding a solution to your own technical problems.

5. Now consult the Notes for Chapter 11 in Appendix, Section A-4.

CHAPTER 12   NON-FICTION • DEVICES

Most of the reading matter in English is non-fiction. Publishers draw most of their income from books of non-fiction—history, biography, books of science, books on the arts, and on every phase of living. For of these they can predict with a fair degree of certainty how many copies they may hope to sell. Thus a cookbook or a book on gardening, popular science, or current history can be counted upon to sell and go on selling to those interested in the subject. Whereas a novel may find no buyers whatever, though, on the other hand, it may be a best seller. In short, from a publisher's point of view a book of fiction is a speculation, whereas books of non-fiction are simply good business. In like manner most popular magazines publish two or three times as many articles as stories. In short, everybody reads non-fiction throughout life, whereas only a few limit themselves to fiction or read any great quantity of it.

It follows that the author who is skilled in this field has a big market before him.

He also has a far wider range of subject matter. Fiction is limited to human relationships, but non-fiction may be written about anything known to man in the whole universe. It is this vast range of subjects which makes it necessary for the writer of an article to sound out the editor before he offers the script; for unless the editor believes that the subject will please his readers, there is no use writ-

162

ing it. Thus it has been said that the only valid distinction between fiction and non-fiction lies in the fact that fiction is first written and then offered for sale, whereas non-fiction is first offered for sale and then written.

The popularity of non-fiction has been greatly increased within the last few years. For editors, following the lead of the *Reader's Digest*, which sells more copies than any publication known to history, have discovered that readers like human company and that the introduction of people into an article, book, or essay may make it as readable as fiction. In other words, the introduction of fictional techniques into non-fiction has put the article into first place.

"The magazine article has come of age, technically and stylistically. Non-fiction writers have outstripped the field in the race for the coveted, limited space available in periodicals. . . . While somnolent or absent, they [the short-story writers] have allowed article writers to steal many of the stylistic qualities and techniques which they themselves have developed and perfected. The best magazine articles today are more meaty than short stories and just as entertaining. . . .

"More and more editors and authors are learning that truth is not only stranger than fiction but that it can be made more entertaining. Thirty or twenty or even ten years ago, much periodical non-fiction was ponderous; think-pieces and philosophical essays appeared in polysyllabic and involved dullness. Quality magazines carried them because of their importance and to add 'tone,' but they relied upon short stories to furnish entertainment and sell copies. Not so today. . . . The article writer is in the saddle."[1]

The non-fiction writer then must not only know his subject, but may use quite as much imagination and emotion as any novelist.

In an earlier chapter of this book[2] it was pointed out that every fact has many facets and that every subject may be seen from many angles.

It follows that he who wishes to become a writer of articles should first of all be something of an expert on some subject or some field of knowledge and that he have a sufficient number of other interests to provide him with a variety of positions from which to view his main subject. For of course each point of view provides a new angle

[1]Harry Shaw, "Some Clinical Notes," in the *Saturday Review of Literature*, Vol. XXIV, No. 31, Nov. 22, 1941, p. 24.

[2]Chapter 2.

on that main subject, and each angle or approach may become a separate article. Thus a man who has some expert knowledge of meteorology and has also been a flyer, a farmer, and a sportsman has at least three points of view from which to write of the weather:

a. that of the farmer on the land trying to make a crop;
b. that of a flyer fighting storms; and
c. that of a golfer who has to contend with rain and wind on the links.

And so with every subject which an author knows: the more varied his interests, the more points of view he will have from which to view his main subject and the more articles he can write about it.

As Dr. Samuel Johnson remarks, "Knowledge of the subject is to the poet what durable materials are to the architect."

The writer of non-fiction then should make it a point to inform himself about those fields of knowledge which particularly interest him so that he can in time be rated an expert. For when an editor wants an article about a subject on which you are known to be an expert, you are likely to get the assignment.

Thus, if you know and write a good deal about dogs, or fishing, or college life, or sports, your expertness will in time be recognized and you will be asked to submit scripts.

Of course there are a certain number of celebrities whose famous names assure them of publication. But the vast majority of articles published are written by authors who have only their knowledge and their skill to offer.

The knowledge you must acquire for yourself. Systematic reading, supplemented by firsthand experience, will enable you within a few months' time to know more than most people know about almost any subject within your comprehension.

Acquiring the skill to present your knowledge effectively to readers may take a little longer.[3]

And now let us consider the patterns and techniques of the non-fiction article.

An article, like a short story, must have:

a Beginning that is clear and arouses curiosity;
a Middle that is coherent and arouses increasing interest or suspense;
an End which is brief and satisfying.

[3]For advice on reading and research, see *Writing Non-Fiction,* by Walter S. Campbell (The Writer, Inc., Boston, 1944), Chapter III.

But the pattern of an article differs somewhat from that of a short story, even though every fictional device found in the short story may be employed in an article.

This is because the article has no plot and may, indeed, make no mention of people whatever.

THE OVER-ALL PATTERN

In an earlier chapter we discussed the basic over-all pattern for every type of literary composition. Here it has a particular application.

This pattern, you will remember, has four parts:

1. getting the attention of the reader
2. assuring the reader that what you have to say concerns him
3. telling, or rather showing, the reader the points which you have to make
4. leaving him with something—an idea, a program, an attitude—which will satisfy him that he has not wasted his time in reading your piece.

For example, a salesman might first say, "My product is the best on the market." Then he might add, "You deserve the best." Then he will say, "My product costs less, wears longer, looks better than any other." Finally he will suggest, "Buy my product!"

One of my students in Professional Writing at the University of Oklahoma suggested that this formula may be more conveniently expressed in the four words which follow:

(1) HEY! (2) YOU! (3) SEE? (4) SO!

If you will *memorize* this formula, you will always have in mind the pattern on which you must create your article, story, or sonnet. Everything which people read must conform to this pattern, since it represents the actual process or behavior pattern of the human mind, beginning with attention, proceeding to concentration, and arriving at a conclusion.

In analysis of articles you must school yourself to look for and mark in the margin of the magazine the exact sentence where each of these four steps begins, and also the other sentences throughout the piece in which any one of them reappears.

And in writing an article you will do well first to block out your material according to this pattern. Afterward, when you have completed your first draft, you will check it over to make sure that each of the four steps given above is effectively stated.

The type of article you write will determine the emphasis you place upon each of these steps. Thus, if you were writing a "How-to-do-it" or Practical Article, informing the reader how he may solve some problem or accomplish some feat, like making a garden or flying a plane or caring for a child, it is obvious that the steps most important are the second, YOU, and the fourth, SO, since the theme is "Do it this way."

Again if you are writing a Formal Essay about public affairs, on which the reader can have no great influence but about which he is eager to make up his mind, the important steps are the third, SEE, and the fourth, SO, for you are showing him how he must think, presenting the facts and arguments in the SEE and suggesting the stand he must take in the SO.

Again in writing an Informative Article (such as one finds in an encyclopedia), which makes no strong appeal for reader interest but concentrates upon the facts, it is obvious that here the emphasis falls chiefly on the third step, SEE. The HEY and the YOU may be taken more or less for granted, though the SO is slightly more important.

Or, if you are attempting an Informal Essay, in which you share an experience with the reader or remind him of one which both of you have had, you would normally emphasize steps three, SEE, and four, SO. However, the Informal Essay, which may be whimsical or humorous, allows you greater freedom in choosing those parts of the formula to be stressed.

Of course almost any subject can be written up in any one of these four major types.

You might, for example, if writing about cats, first do an Informative Article, telling all that is known and agreed upon concerning the cat as a species, with its physical peculiarities, its history, origin, diffusion, etc. Then you might write a Practical Article on the care and feeding of cats, telling how to take care of them, feed them, and raise them. After that you might conceivably write a Formal Essay in which you weigh the advantages and disadvantages of having a pet cat and so arrive at some conclusion as to whether or not the reader should keep a cat. Finally, you might write an Informal Essay describing in a humorous, reminiscent, or whimsical manner your experiences with a given cat, which would remind

166

the reader of his own experiences, thus sharing an amusing experience with him.

You might conceivably write a personality article about a certain famous cat, showing how he became successful in catching mice and made himself necessary to someone who did not like cats. Such a personality article could be made into an Informative Article with fictional devices, a Practical Article suggesting how the reader might make better use of his mouser, or a Formal Essay contrasting or comparing the methods of mousing and showing how this cat excelled others, or—last of all—an Informal Essay relating the amusing idiosyncrasies of this particular cat.

So much for the over-all pattern.

But an article, like a story, has four parts with a slightly different emphasis. First, the Beginning which includes the HEY and the YOU; second, the Middle which embodies the SEE.

This Middle commonly has two sections: (a) that in which you state the problem and build suspense and interest. This section is likely to be more amusing and lighter in tone than the second part of the Middle (b), in which you solve the problem, answer the questions, and get down to serious cases. This second part of the Middle as a rule is more serious and informative, more solid and factual than the first part of the Middle.

The SEE, the Middle, as you will readily understand, gets down to cases in an interesting and logical manner. In fact, any article of any length will have a number of such cases arranged in such a manner as to build up the interest and lead the reader on.

Finally you come to the fourth part or End which embodies the SO.

THE OUTLINE

In preparing an article the first thing to do is to gather your material and prepare an outline. To do this you take a blank sheet of paper and jot down everything you can think of on your subject just as it comes to mind until you can think of nothing more. These jottings will be a list of words, or phrases, or sentences. It is only intended to remind you of all the items and points you have thought of.

When you have thus jotted down all you find both from firsthand knowledge and reading, you are ready to make your outline. To begin with, you first read over your jottings, underscoring those important enough to serve as main divisions or cases in your Middle or SEE. These main divisions will probably not appear on your sheet of jottings in the order in which you will wish to place them in your article, so the first thing you have to do is to decide what the order will be and so number the underscored items with Roman numerals (I, II, III, etc.). This gives you the skeleton of your cases, your main points in the SEE or Middle of your outline.

But you have left many jottings besides, and these also must be classified to fall under the main heads you have already underscored. You therefore go down the page and number each jotting or item with an Arabic numeral (1, 2, 3, etc.) according to which one of the main heads (I, II, III, etc.) each item belongs under.

If any items seem not to belong under *any* of your main heads or cases, it must be either because such items do not belong in your article and should be struck out or because these items ought to be main heads. If so, you will underscore these, too, and then renumber your main heads.

At this point a further step is necessary: to indicate by the use of letters (a, b, c, etc.) in what order under each main head those items which fall under that head are to appear. When this is done, you have all the material classified with indications as to just where it will fall in the completed outline.

You then proceed to make the outline for the SEE or Middle from these items, writing a topic sentence for each of the main heads or cases, listing under the main head in the correct order each of the items you have already tagged with 1a, 1b, or 2b, 2c, etc.

Thus you complete your outline for the Middle or SEE of your article. This is by far the easiest and simplest way to make an outline.

THE WORK SHEET

With the outline of the SEE or the Middle before you, you can then consider what the other three parts of the over-all pattern are to be. What kind of HEY can you write to catch the attention of your reader? Again, what kind of YOU will be sure to hold his interest? And finally, what is the SO to be at the End of the piece?

This done, you are ready to begin writing your article.

It is often helpful (since articles are usually written in a predetermined number of words—that is, "written to space"—according to the requirements of your editor) to prepare a work sheet in advance, indicating the approximate number of words you think necessary for each step in the over-all pattern, in this manner:

HEY	25 words	
YOU	50 words	
SEE	First Case:	100 words
	Second Case:	200 words
	Third Case:	300 words
	Fourth Case:	60 words
SO	90 words	

Such a Work Sheet enables you to construct your article on sound principles, emphasizing what requires emphasis and slighting what does not.

In this way you allot beforehand approximately the number of words which will be required to present effectively each item—head and subhead—in your article.

If you will take the trouble to find out how many words you average to the page when typing double-space on your machine, you will readily be able to determine at any time just how much you have written and how much you have yet to do. In this way you will learn to write to space—that is, to plan beforehand the number of words to be used on any project. A non-fiction writer must learn to say his say in the number of words allowed by his editor, otherwise he will have to do a great deal of rewriting. You will then have to consider what your transitions must be from case to case and how you will tie the whole thing together.

WRITING THE ARTICLE

Having planned the pattern of your piece, study your work sheet and your outline until you have it all firmly in mind. Then, next day, sit down and write your piece with only the work sheet to go by. Do not consult your notes or outline. Then you will write freshly in your own words. Never write from notes.

If your article is to introduce people or characters or have to deal with personal relationships, or even with only one person, you may —if you desire—use any or every device employed in writing fiction. If you have studied the devices offered in this book and fulfilled the requirements of the Work Programs up to this point, you are thoroughly familiar with these devices and will know how to use them.

If, on the other hand, your article brings in no characters whatever and has nothing to do with human relationships but is confined to facts or ideas about cosmic rays or ocean deeps or the like, you will have little need for fictional devices as such. In that case—though you cannot take your reader into the mind of a character—you may still keep him in human company by taking him into the mind of the author—yourself—treating your subject in a personal or autobiographical manner.

UNITY

However, this will not relieve you from the necessity of holding the reader's interest and tying everything together so that the continuity will carry him through from start to finish.

These devices are first of all devices for unity, and unity is achieved by choosing one subject and sticking to it, avoiding digressions and irrelevancies, however attractive. You may achieve unity by confining yourself to a series of related events, or to one kind of life, or to related facts, or to a progress through space or through time, or to a comparison of theories or ideas relating to the same facts, by sticking to a limited field of knowledge, or by expressing your own personal views, by logical progression, by uniform style, or by repetition of pattern in the different cases.

Having made sure of unity by excluding everything which is not pertinent to your subject and purpose, you have then to consider a second problem of maintaining reader interest through Continuity or Coherence.

COHERENCE

The devices for Continuity consist of transitions, plausibility, repetitions, overlapping paragraphs, corroboration (by citing witnesses and conjuring with great names); of color, incidents, happenings; of discovery and reversal, plants, pointers (to ideas or facts coming up later); of flashbacks giving the facts behind your article; of promise of conflict (which may take the form of contrasting ideas); of bait, setting the emotional tone, and indicating the type of article (Informative, Practical, Formal Essay, Informal Essay), as the case may be.

You are already familiar with all these devices from your study of *Dakotah Courtship*.

But in an article in which no people appear you are still not freed from the necessity of the device of *fact feeling*. In truth this must be a main reliance in keeping the reader reading.

In addition you must strive for *intellectual* suspense, never answering one question or solving one problem until you have raised an even more interesting question or problem to follow. The threads of interest in an article, like the threads of interest in a story, are never broken but continue throughout. So you must beware of chopping your piece up into independent paragraphs, each of which can stand alone. Every paragraph must tie up with the one which follows.

This means that you must take care to make your transitions effective and use overlapping paragraphs wherever necessary.

Of course if you have a definite reader in mind, a kind of person for whom you are writing, your problem will be much simpler.

Finally, you must consider devices for emphasis—or, as you may prefer to call it, devices for Focus. Descriptions of standard devices for Focus follow here.

Dialogue is one of the best for this purpose. Indeed, any words set off within quotation marks are likely to revive a reader's failing interest. For even though no characters appear in your article, some authority may be quoted.

EMPHASIS

Focus is a form of emphasis and therefore includes many of the tricks of emphasis.

To emphasize a passage, to focus a spotlight of emotion upon it, the following devices are useful:

1. Devices for Focus · Space

To emphasize an idea or a fact, you may give it more Space than you give to other matters. This makes it loom larger in the reader's mind.

2. Devices for Focus · Isolated Statement

Again you may emphasize an idea by giving it in very few words indeed, thus setting it apart as an Isolated Statement, a paragraph of one sentence only—or even just a phrase. This focuses attention upon it effectively.

171

3. Devices for Focus · Position

Another method of attaining Focus is by Position. The most emphatic position for any idea is at the end of the sentence, the end of the paragraph, the end of the piece, because whatever is at the end lingers in the mind of the reader for a time.

Next to the end position, the beginning of a sentence, of a paragraph, of a sequence, of the whole story is most emphatic. For the reader at the beginning is alert, and first impressions are strong.

4. Devices for Focus · Inversion

Another method for obtaining Focus is the emphasis of Inversion—done by turning a phrase over or setting the words in an unusual order which arrests the reader's eye and mind. Thus one may say, "She was exceedingly beautiful," without exciting the reader's attention. But if one says, "She was beautiful exceedingly," the inversion makes the reader attend more closely and satisfies him that the lady referred to must have been unusually lovely.

5. Devices for Focus · Choice of Words

Another device for Focus is the careful choice of words. All unusual words are generally apt or in some way striking, in sound, in denotation, in connotation, or unexpectedness. And here a world of rhetorical devices springs to mind. Of all devices for Focus, the choice of words is most constantly used.

6. Devices for Focus · Contrast

Contrast, whether of subject matter or form, is always effective in catching attention, for it is a kind of conflict—even though only a verbal conflict—and conflict is always arresting. White always seems whiter placed next to black.

7. Devices for Focus · Repetition

Repetition, one of the devices of Continuity described above, is also most effective for Focus. For an idea or phrase that is repeated tends to multiply itself in the reader's mind.

8. Devices for Focus · Rhythm

Cadence or rhythm can be a most effective device for fixing attention or making the reader feel the importance of what is said, as in much great poetry. Pace, Timing are essential to all good writing.

You will be wise, too, if you take care to make your sentences, your words, and your paragraphs no longer on the average than

172

those commonly found in articles in the magazine for which you wish to write.

Finally, there is a device for heading off the reader who may be tempted to jump to conclusions when a familiar idea is raised. This device we may call Road Block.

Non-Fiction Devices · Road Block

It sometimes happens that the reader, owing to some prejudice or fixed idea or emotional attitude already established in his mind, will automatically run down a bypath instead of following the trail laid out for him by the author of the article. Thus, for example, in an article about housing in which the writer wishes to call attention to a new development of better housing, he might well begin with a description of the discomforts most people suffer in old-fashioned apartments. This would contrast nicely with what follows.

But in such a case the instinct of the reader would be immediately to blame the builder for his sufferings, whereas the writer intends that the reader shall forget the past and turn his attention to the new development. Accordingly the author throws up a *road block*— that is, a paragraph urging the reader not to blame the builder and pointing out that the builder is himself a creature of circumstances. In this way the reader is prevented from following his first impulse and is instead led down the path laid out for him by the writer of the article. . . .

I hope I have made it clear how to construct and write an article. But you must not stop here or rely merely upon the methods and devices already explained in this book. By this time you should have become so aware of the devices that are used in what you read that a study of good models of the kind you wish to write will provide you with many new ones. In fact, if you are wise, you will go on collecting these throughout life, practicing and perfecting what you find until your handling of devices of every sort will become habitual.

Among these devices you might do well to consider the rhetorical figures of speech which you were taught in school.

If your knowledge of these has grown rusty, you may readily refresh your memory by taking up *A Dictionary of English Usage*, by H. W. Fowler, published by the Oxford University Press: they are listed there under the general heading "Technical Terms."

Never forget that a mastery of devices and of rhetorical figures of speech will make you master of your pen, so that you can push it instead of following it.

It was thus that Shakespeare and other great masters of writing learned their art and craft.[4]

Your knowledge of these devices and rhetorical figures will in time come to be second nature, so that you will know almost automatically which one will best serve your purpose in any given passage.

You need not rely upon inspiration to help you handle them. You can always try several devices for the same purpose, writing them all out—and then choosing *that one* which serves your purpose best.

This practice, this experience, will give you confidence, the sure knowledge that you know what you are doing. And if at times you find you cannot put your hand upon a device or rhetorical figure which serves your immediate purpose, you can always read good models and so pick up new tricks which have been tested and found useful by more experienced writers.

When you find a good device, take time to practice it in three Finger Exercises, and so fix it forever in your memory. There is no destiny for the lazy.

It is this experience in details which makes the successful writer. For every writer, whether he takes a writing course or blindly blunders along on his own, must have certain experiences before he knows what he is about.

With such understanding born of sufficient experience, you may confidently attempt any form of writing which appeals to you.

WORK PROGRAM 12

1. Select an article from the *Reader's Digest* or any good magazine, read it, and try to answer the questions given below.
2. Queries to be used in analysis of a magazine article:
   a. What is the subject?
   b. What is the author's angle?

[4]Christopher Beeston was one of the actors in Shakespeare's company. His son, William Beeston, reported to Aubrey that Shakespeare was a country schoolmaster before he went to London. If so, Shakespeare not only studied, but taught, rhetoric. Certainly he never ceased to delight in it. See *Shakespeare's Use of the Arts of Language*, by Sister Miriam Joseph, C.S.C. (Columbia University Press, New York, 1947), Chapter II *et passim*.

c. What is the Hey?
d. What is the You?
e. What is the See?
f. How many cases in the See?
g. What are these cases?
h. What is the So?
i. How long is the article?
j. How long are each of its parts, including the cases?
k. Make a work sheet of the article.
l. Is there dialogue? How much?
m. Is there exposition? How much?
n. Is there description? How much?
o. Is there narrative? How much?
p. Style: What is the average length of words, sentences, paragraphs? How many references to persons?
q. How many scenes, if any?
r. How many characters, if any?
s. What is the emotional tone?
t. Is the Beginning clear, and does it arouse curiosity?
u. Is the Middle coherent and interesting?
v. Is the End brief and satisfying?
w. Why did the editor buy this article?
x. What kind of article is this?
y. Classify this article, if possible, as Informative, or Practical, or Formal Essay, or Informal Essay.

CHAPTER 13 NON-FICTION ANALYSIS

Inasmuch as most non-fiction—both books and shorter pieces—may use the same devices found in fiction, there is no need to discuss the use of fictional devices in non-fiction here. You are familiar with these devices already.

But there are some devices more necessary or more frequently used by the writers of non-fiction. To these we must now give some consideration.

175

Non-fiction is intended primarily to instruct, though it should also entertain the reader. Instruction implies understanding.

Of course there are writers who deliberately obscure their meaning—if any—in the hope of seeming mysterious and therefore profound. Such writers, writing for themselves, are—to paraphrase Samuel Butler—as silly as people who talk to themselves. But such writers are seldom writers of non-fiction, the object of which is communication and the virtues of which are clarity, logic, coherence, and euphony.

There are, then, two kinds of non-fiction writing: (a) that which, like fiction, deals with human relationships, people, and therefore requires fictional devices; and (b) that in which persons are rarely mentioned and where the subject matter is abstract or factual; here fictional devices will not serve. But most articles nowadays, except scientific or scholarly papers,[1] manage to bring in people and so use fictional techniques.

In the Appendix you will find pieces for analysis.

The first is a practical article entitled "A Formula for Presence of Mind," by Fulton Oursler, reprinted here by permission of the *Reader's Digest*, in which it appeared, January 1949.

The devices used in non-fiction of every type are the same. By this time your understanding of devices should make it easy for you to discover or recognize devices of every kind.

Of course you should not rest content with the examples found in this textbook; you should study current magazines, new books, and classic masterpieces of non-fiction writing. Thus you will enrich your knowledge and learn the methods of the masters firsthand.

This book only attempts to make you fully aware of certain standard devices. Experience in the courses in Professional Writing offered by the University of Oklahoma both on the campus and by correspondence demonstrates the wisdom of this method. I would not presume to dictate what devices any other writer should use. Having learned to recognize and understand devices, it will be your privilege and pleasure to search out and perfect the best of these wherever you find them.

Turn now to the Appendix, Section A-5; read the first item there, "A Formula for Presence of Mind." Then turn to Work Program 13.

[1] I have already treated the writing of such papers in my book *Writing Non-Fiction*.

WORK PROGRAM 13

1. Having read the article "A Formula for Presence of Mind" in the Appendix, Section A-5, write out your answers to the questions on it, which are to be found in Work Program 12.
2. a. What device is seen in sentences 10, 11, 34, 39, 47, 65?
   b. What sentences constitute the Bait?
   c. What devices for Focus do you find here?
   d. What fictional devices do you find here?
3. Having read the article "Why Medicine Is Not a Science" in the Appendix, Section A-6, write out your answers to the questions on it, which you will find in Work Program 12.
4. a. What device is found in sentences 12, 13, 14, 31, 40, 45-47, 85, 100?
   b. What devices for Focus do you find here?
   c. What overlapping paragraphs do you find here?
   d. What devices for Continuity are used here?
   e. What fictional devices do you find here?
5. Now set about making a grand collection of hundreds of devices from your own reading.

PART 4 THE WORKSHOP

CHAPTER 14 TYPES

Literature began a great while ago, and a multitude of experiments in fiction and non-fiction were performed long before men had learned to write and so record what they had to say. Out of these manifold experiments certain types of literature were developed, each best adapted to a certain purpose. And so it comes about that most authors work in the light of that experience, casting their ideas and emotions, their subject matter and interpretations into those types of literature, those forms long since established as best suited to achieve their aims.

It is obvious that one cannot put the subject matter, much less the sweep and power of epic, into epigram. It is equally manifest that the tight pattern of the short story is not adapted to displaying the slow development of character and situation for which the novel serves.

In choosing a type of literature in which to cast your words you should consider: (a) the nature of your chosen subject matter, (b) what particular gifts you have, (c) what kind of writing seems most worth while to you.

Thus you might wish to write a novel because you are chiefly interested in people, their motives and behavior, and character; again you might prefer the short story, feeling that your gifts are those of a precise and careful artist, delighting in a neat pattern, with a distaste for long and sprawling narratives. Or verse may be your passion, so that prose seems lackluster and uninviting to you.

There are, however, other considerations which may enter into your calculations in choosing a type of literature to practice. Assuming that you wish not merely to write something but to become a skillful writer, you might choose a type which (d) will provide the best training and so lead you to your distant goal.

Thus, if you wish to become a novelist, you may consider the fact that most first novels are badly written, and so prefer to perfect your technique by writing the more technically exacting short story, rather than produce a half-baked novel and so waste the subject matter which you have in mind. For a book publisher who buys a first novel (and options on the next two) from a beginner is not so much buying a book as, he hopes, adding a writer to his "stable." The publisher may know that your first novel will make no success either in sale or critical acclaim. He may take you on because he wants a new novelist and hopes that your third book will reimburse him for his losses on the first two. He regards a book of fiction as a speculation.

On the other hand, the editor of a magazine cannot afford to publish stories which fall below a high technical standard. When he does so, his readers are annoyed, the circulation of the magazine falls off, and the business manager begins to look for a new editor. It is for this reason that you might decide, even though you feel that you have a novelist's talents—a love of people, a comprehension of human character, and a tendency to overwrite (that is, make things longer than you intended)—to begin your career by mastering the short story and so sharpening up your technique, learning to compress, to be adroit, to place your shots with care, to perfect a pattern, and to handle with skill and ease all the devices useful to a writer of fiction.

With that training behind you, your talents will stand a far better chance of creating a novel that is fine and lasting.

And then, of course, another factor may enter into your calculations as a writer—namely (e) the demands of the public, the competition which you have to face.

As everyone knows, Sir Walter Scott, after perfecting his skill in narrative verse by a study and revision of border ballads, made his first success with lays, long narratives in verse. But when Lord Byron sprang to fame, Sir Walter realized that he was being outdone and outmoded in verse, and promptly turned to writing the Waverley novels, thus making his own a field into which Lord Byron never ventured.

Not all writers write with the aim of making money. Yet it is a curious fact that, in every period of literature, you find the great writers working where the harvest is richest, writing the kind of thing—novel, satire, or play—which is most profitable and most in demand. Had Dickens lived in Shakespeare's time his theatricality and mastery of scenes would surely have led him to write for the stage. In like manner it is highly improbable that, had Shakespeare been a Victorian, he would have written tragedies in blank verse; the novel would have offered him a much more fruitful field.

The fact that in any given age most great writers are found writing the thing that pays the best does not indicate that great writers are more mercenary than minor poets; it simply points to the fact that men do their best work when they are most appreciated. You will recall the lines from Robert Browning's *Andrea del Sarto* in which that gifted painter, who had thrown away his chances, declares enviously that it is no wonder his rivals paint so well, with admiring kings and great men at their elbows.

The fact is that when a would-be writer scorns the great public and writes only for a clique, it is generally because he despairs of saying what he has to say in such terms as most men can understand and appreciate. For nothing was ever so well written that nobody could appreciate it. The greatest books are those most widely read.

After all, what you are offering to the reader is *skill*, not subject matter. Ninety-nine times out of a hundred the subject matter is nothing new.

You may conceivably say something new about cosmic rays or atomic power if you alone have discovered it. But people have been living together for a long, long time, and if you write of human nature the chances are astronomical against your having observed anything no other person ever thought or said about that subject. Modern psychologists can think up new terminology, but the facts they describe are as old as the hills and are to be found more plainly stated in the Bible and other ancient books. For what do all the findings of the psychologist amount to more than the old text: "Hope deferred maketh the heart sick"?

You may imagine that you have discovered something brand new about *homo sapiens*, but those who know the history of literature can point out a dozen authors who have published the same discoveries long ago. The same thing may be said of the technical tricks of writing. They were all familiar to men before printing or even writing had been invented.

But this is what gives writing so much dignity—that good work is in the great tradition of mankind. That good work is good not only because it conveys great and lasting truths, but because it employs a craftsmanship perfected by multitudes of artists down the centuries.

And now to consider briefly some of the types you may choose from for your own early work.

Autobiography

Christopher Morley has wittily remarked:

> This is all we ever say,
> *Ego, mei, mihi, me*.[1]

And I suppose everything one writes is to some extent autobiographical. Beginning writers particularly are likely to go in heavily for autobiography in their first work.

It is reasonable to suppose that one should live a lifetime before writing one's autobiography, but few young writers consider that. Yet autobiography is in itself perhaps the most difficult of all forms of non-fiction if, indeed, autobiography be not a form of fiction! It is difficult enough to write objectively of other things and people, but to write so of oneself is well-nigh impossible to anyone with a shred of imagination. And of course an autobiography written by an unimaginative person can only be a memoir. If, then, you have an autobiography in you, you may as well write it and get it out of your system, so that you can turn to what will probably be projects more within your powers and more worth while.

Biography

Biography also requires a wide knowledge of life if you are to imagine truly the motives of other men, particularly men older than yourself. Thus we find Carl Sandburg declaring that he was glad he wrote *The War Years* of his series on Abraham Lincoln in his fifties and early sixties, when his judgment of men was better. He says

[1] Quoted, or misquoted (from memory—since neither the author nor I can recall just where, in his many works, this appeared), by permission. W.S.C.

181

that he had to rewrite the notes he had set down on certain members of Lincoln's Cabinet because he understood them so much better at that age than he could when he was a younger man.[2]

Biography, however, is a rewarding task for the very reason that it compels the author to get outside himself and try to understand men with different backgrounds and different experiences. A biographer thus adds many rooms to his house of life and finds himself bigger and wiser than he was.

The Novel

A good novelist also has to make this effort but can avoid it in some measure by sticking to characters more like himself and neglecting the contradictions which to him are incomprehensible. He should not yield to this temptation but all too often does, because he has no stubborn facts which force themselves upon him and must be considered and included whether he understands them or not.

The novel is long because space is required in which to present character developing. In a short piece any change in character must be presented as a sudden conversion, which cannot be made convincing and so rings false. In a novel, on the other hand, character may be displayed in all its slow progress and change, with every pressure and motivation slowly developed and accounted for, and this long process makes the story seem real. For Nature does nothing by jumps but always through slow developments. Even a sudden revolution in our affairs has its roots and causes far back—so far back in history and culture that you and I cannot possibly account in full for our own motives and behavior. All these grow out of centuries of slow change among our ancestors and the influences which bore upon them.

It is obvious that since a novel is long and normally deals with slow development of character over a considerable period of time— sometimes years and even generations—the reader must be kept aware of the passage of time. Someone has remarked, "There is always a clock in a good novel."

And the reader must be made continually to hear that clock *ticking*. The reader must *always* be kept aware of the passage of time.

Thus it is easy enough, when you look at a short story in a maga-

[2]Robert van Gelder, *Writers and Writing* (Charles Scribner's Sons, New York, 1946), p. 286.

zine by an unknown author, to tell at once whether that author has spent his life writing short stories or whether he is a novelist who has turned to short fiction. For the short story writer is under no such continual necessity of keeping the reader aware of the passing of time as is the novelist. And by counting the references to the passing of time on the page one can readily discover what the author's training has been. For even in a short story a novelist will use far more references to passage of time than a short story writer. That is of necessity a novelist's habit, and when he writes a short story he goes right on doing it.

These are the two problems that must be met by every successful novelist: (a) he must show character and situation gradually developing; and (b) he must keep the reader aware of the passage of time.

Of course there are long narratives *called* novels, such as detective stories and tales of adventure, whose action takes place within twenty-four hours or less and whose characters remain essentially unchanged. These narratives are perfectly legitimate and often popular, but they can be called novels only by courtesy, since they ignore the two main problems of the novelist.

Romance

There are, of course, romances in which plausibility and true character development are sacrificed to adventure, sentiment, and the appeal of the strange. Romance has been aptly defined as the adventures of an ordinary man in extraordinary circumstances. Therefore, romance makes a strong appeal, for the reader readily understands the ordinary character and also delights in extraordinary circumstances, whether these circumstances be the adventures of mythical knights or the strange emotions of falling in love.

Drama

Some forms of literature, like farce and melodrama, amuse the reader through situation, through incident. In these what happens to the character is not caused by any peculiarity of the character but by external circumstances, as in romance the character is subordinate to the action. And since most readers sooner or later realize that character is destiny, these forms of literature are sometimes regarded as inferior and classified as mere entertainment.

183

In tragedy and high comedy, on the contrary, we have character dominant and fighting either Fate, as in the ancient Greek tragedies, or men, as in the Elizabethan plays, or environment, as in so many modern dramas. Not every age can produce good tragedy, and high comedy is even rarer. It is found only, if we may believe George Meredith,[3] where women are free or dominant. For high comedy shows mankind as *absurd*.

The perception that man is absurd and the acceptance of that fact are generally found only in sophisticated and cultivated societies. One may quote the French proverb here—that the degree to which a man is civilized may be estimated by the degree to which he can endure hypocrisy.

For to a civilized man it is obvious that there is a good deal of pretense about social life, that nobody dares present himself absolutely in his true colors, that even the best of men are by custom pretending and acting part of the time, while even the worst of men are not as tough and ornery as they let on to be. This discovery that man, with all his evil and selfish impulses, must live with others and so assume a virtue if he has it not is the first thing that must be understood if civilization is to be appreciated. For civilization is the result of men assuming virtues and then struggling to live up to them.

This struggle is imposed upon us in our infancy and youth, when we are unable to take care of ourselves. We have to learn what is expected of us and act accordingly. And if we are intelligent, however much we may be aware of the absurdity of these pretenses, we also see clearly that, without such pretending, community life would be impossible. And so high comedy deals with the foibles and follies of mankind, with the contrast between what men really are and what they pretend to be or try to become. But because the authors are civilized enough to realize that *all* men are to some degree absurd, they are not bitter or indignant about it, only delighted and amused. Of course this approach is not limited to stage plays. High comedy may be found in almost every form of fiction.

The Magazine Serial

Long ago editors discovered that by running a serial in several installments they could maintain a reader's interest over a number

[3] See his *Essay on Comedy*.

of issues. Since then the serial has been an established form of popular fiction. It may be as long as a magazine novel, but a good serial has special qualities that a good novel often lacks. In short, an inferior novel may sometimes make a good serial; yet a good serial is not necessarily an inferior form of fiction.

Among the special qualities a serial requires is that it have a number of places where it may be divided so that each sequence or installment may appear separately. Since it is to be published in a magazine, it must not deal too crudely with the facts of life or offend good taste or present things considered by the unsophisticated magazine reader as disagreeable. Of course, too, it must not be too long, though editors are very free in cutting serials to suit their requirements, and sometimes ask the author to make his serial much longer than it would be in a magazine. They do this because they feel that by cutting it they can heighten the interest.

The main requirement of the serial, however, is an engrossing story which will maintain continuous interest from one installment to another.

Some excellent writers have presented their work serially, as Charles Dickens did. Though of course most magazine serials cannot rate with *The Pickwick Papers*, there is no point in turning up one's nose at them. Nothing is more absurd than to dislike something because it is not something else. Each type of writing has its own peculiar merits, its own appeal. For my part, though I must, by temperament, prefer some types to others, it seems a pity to neglect any form of excellence.

The Novelette

And now we may consider shorter forms. After the novel we have the novelette. Here character plays a larger part than in the short story. The length permits that. But for the most part the novelette pays more attention to the situation. It differs in that respect from the novel. In its more sophisticated form the novelette often shows character in a single situation, reversing itself as the story goes on. Then it is made up of a series of discoveries and reversals. In the more popular form of the novelette the emphasis is more on action, on what happens, and the process is not so much a change of character in a given situation as a series of complications—more complications than are possible in a short story. The novelette maintains its popularity because it does in comparatively small compass something neither the short story nor the novel can do so gracefully. It has stricter form than the novel and more character development than the short story.[4]

The Short Story

The short story is a pattern, an artistic whole, something to be appreciated at one sitting. It divides its interests among character, situation, setting, and theme. It is a tight design and requires of its author deftness, a sure hand, and a clear head. Well written, the short story can produce a vivid effect, and its popularity—particularly in the United States—bears witness to the American love of efficiency, mechanics, dexterity, something shiny and foolproof. For the beginner in fiction, few forms offer so ready a market and such excellent technical training.

The Short Short Story

The short short story is a form little written by old hands and more often attempted by beginners. Beginners are attracted to it because of its brevity, its snap, its surprise ending. Too often they imagine that because it is brief it will be easy to write.

But a little experience soon convinces the beginner of his error. For the short short story, though popular, is by no means easy. It requires—in addition to all the merits of a short story—a compression and point which few beginners have the skill to create. But if one has an idea suited to this form, trying to write it is a valuable exercise. And though the check for a short short is never so great as that of a short story in the same market, the writer with the gift for such things can do very well with them.

The Article

The short article is another very popular form which we have discussed already.[5]

[4]For a more extended treatment of the serial, novel, novelette, story, and short short story, see *Writing Magazine Fiction*, by W. S. Campbell, Doubleday and Co., Inc., New York.

[5]For a complete discussion of non-fiction types, see *Writing Non-Fiction*, by Walter S. Campbell, The Writer, Inc., Boston, 1944.

The Epigram

The shortest of all literary forms in English is the epigram—a brief, pithy, usually witty saying—"what oft was thought but ne'er so well expressed"—usually cast in a single line or couplet. The soul—or rather body—of wit is brevity, so here compression and a piercing insight into some phase of life are the requirements. For wit, being truth well expressed, is far more lasting than humor, which is timely and therefore perishable. When Oscar Wilde wrote, "A cynic is a man who knows the price of everything and the value of nothing," he cast an ancient truth into a few vivid words; they will be quoted, one may suppose, as long as English is read. One way to create epigrams is to take old proverbs, saws, and platitudes and rephrase them briefly and effectively.

We have glanced here at some types of writing which you may wish to attempt. There are others, of course. Each type serves a certain purpose. The wise author chooses the right type for his purpose.

WORK PROGRAM 14

1. (a) Which of the types mentioned in this chapter do you feel you would like to master? (b) Why?
2. Which type do you wish to attempt first—or most—of all?
3. And now for some practical hints in the chapter which follows on the mechanics of getting into print. Turn the page.

CHAPTER 15   WHEN YOU PUBLISH

Literature, like music, exists in time, not in space. Musical notes written or printed on paper are not music. For music is what happens to a listener when the notes are played.

In like manner a page covered with printed words merely occupies space until it is read and appreciated in time. Only then can it truly be said to exist. For a story or article does not consist of words written on paper. A story or article is what happens to a person while he reads it—a series of effects produced upon the reader.

Therefore, to be a writer at all you must have a reader, you must publish.

Preparing your Manuscript

Your first necessity is a legible manuscript. Editors and publishers do a great deal of reading, and they expect your manuscript to be letter-perfect, clearly typed double-spaced on white bond paper 8½×11 inches, and to have an inch-wide margin all around the page.

On page one, in the upper left-hand corner, the name and address of the author should appear; in the right-hand corner the approximate number of words in the piece, in round numbers. Number other pages consecutively in the upper right-hand corner.

The first paragraph should begin about one third of the way down the page, and above this you should type the title in capital letters with the author's name below. For example:

Stanley Vestal   4,000 Words
University of Oklahoma
Norman, Oklahoma

DAKOTAH COURTSHIP

by

Stanley Vestal

(Begin your first paragraph here.)

You should make a carbon copy of your story and also of any letters you send out with regard to it. The carbon copy is your protection against loss in the mails. It is very difficult to hold editors and publishers legally responsible for unsolicited manuscripts. Like other people, they are not infallible and sometimes lose or missend scripts. But in such a case, if you have retained a carbon copy, you lose only the cost of having a new copy made.

In offering your piece for publication, clip the sheets together with a paper clip, lay them flat in a stout manila envelope slightly larger than the sheets on which the story is typed. Enclose postage for return, seal the envelope, and send it by first-class mail to the editor or publisher of your choice.

Heavy book manuscripts may be sent by express prepaid with a covering letter requesting the publisher to return the script—if he rejects it—by express collect.

Writers of fiction may be content with ordinary postage, but writers of non-fiction, whose work is sometimes perishable, will prefer air mail. It is necessary to get a perishable article to the editor quickly before it loses its value or before he grows "cold" to the idea.

Marketing

It is possible to offer your play or movie script to several producers at one time. But manuscripts offered to book publishers or magazine editors cannot be so put up at auction but must be—as it were—peddled from door to door; that is, offered to one editor or one publisher at a time.

It is usual to query the non-fiction editor before you write your article—that is, to write him a letter inquiring whether or not he would be interested in a piece on the subject you have in mind, suggesting also the angle from which you would like to treat it, and asking him, if he is interested, how long a piece he would consider.

Sometimes a brief synopsis of the article is sent with the query; in that case the synopsis should be written in the same style as the finished article so that the editor can get the "feel" of the finished piece of work.

Editors, however, are busy men who have to spare their eyes and so do not relish long autobiographical letters. What you write to them should be short, courteous, and to the point, having to do only with your story and its selling points.

If the editor approves your idea, you should then write it at once and send it in.

In offering fiction, no covering letter is necessary if the author's name is known.

But a beginner may find it an advantage to send a covering letter to the editor with his story, saying that he has published before or, if he has published in that magazine before, casually reminding the editor of it.

This insures the manuscript's being sent directly to the editor's desk and not stacked with the other unsolicited scripts to wait its turn. Editors receive a great many manuscripts and naturally favor those by authors who have published before.

Of course no editor can maintain the circulation of his magazine or the income of his publishing house by depending altogether on well-known authors. He has to have new blood for that and is therefore eager to discover good work by newcomers. Moreover, the beginner has yet another advantage over the "big name" author—namely, that the editor can buy his work for less. Do not imagine that editors and publishers are in a conspiracy against beginners. That is mere superstition. Most editors and their readers read everything that comes to them, if it is at all the kind of thing they use.

It is impossible to copyright a short story, article, or poem before sending it to a magazine. The editor will copyright the entire issue of the magazine in which it appears. In like manner, reputable publishers will copyright your book for you either in your name or their own.

For all that, every author should familiarize himself with the law of copyright. Books covering this topic will be found listed in the Bibliography of this book. But authors are commonly most in need of information as to what constitutes infringement of copyright, for infringement of copyright is a crime which sometimes brings severe penalties upon those guilty of it.

In general, make it a rule always to ask permission to use any passage—however brief—from another man's book or story. As a rule, there will be no charge for a short piece of 100 words or less of prose, or in most cases only a nominal fee.

In this book you will find samples of footnotes acknowledging permission to use certain passages which may serve as examples.

There are six big markets for literary wares in this country. These are: book publishers, smooth-paper magazines or "slicks," the pulp-paper magazines, Hollywood, radio, Broadway.

In selling plays, radio scripts, or movie scripts you will require a literary agent to act for you unless you are personally known to the producers; even then an agent can be of great service in negotiating the contracts.[1]

Books and magazine stories may also be handled by agents, but many writers prefer to peddle their wares for themselves. Certainly beginners will be wise to do so, as in this way they learn about markets firsthand. Once they begin to publish consistently, good agents will contact them and offer their services. It will then be time enough to use an agent for such literary properties.

A good survey on the six big markets is *The Writing Trade*, by Paul R. Reynolds, one of the foremost New York literary agents, which you will find listed in the Bibliography.

Another market is now developing, television. To sell to this, too, in all probability an agent will be necessary.

Addresses of those who buy manuscripts may be found in market lists published by the writers' magazines or in the annual *Writer's Market*, prepared by Aron M. Mathieu and Ruth A. Jones, Writer's Digest, Inc., 12 East 22nd Street, Cincinnati 10, Ohio.

Editors vary in the speed with which they report on manuscripts. Weekly magazines of large circulation such as the *Saturday Evening Post* or *Collier's* usually report within a week or ten days, large monthly magazines within thirty days. Book publishers, if interested, may take more time. In general, when times are good, editors report more quickly than at other times.

History of Your Manuscript

Some record should be kept of what you send out and when you send it. If you will put the carbon copy in an envelope like that in which you sent off the original, along with your notes for the piece and carbon copies of any letters concerning the script, you may scribble the record on the outside of this envelope and so have it and everything pertaining to it in one place.

The beginning writer often feels frustrated when his script comes

[1] I have discussed working with literary agents in my book *Writing Magazine Fiction*, pp. 189–95. Copyright will also be found treated in that book, pp. 195–98.

back with a printed rejection slip. Even a letter from the editor seldom fully explains why the story was not purchased. Writers cannot know all that goes on in editorial offices.

Yet this frustration is largely due to inexperience, ignorance of how to sell and how to write, and ignorance can be overcome.

Just because an editor rejects your story you must not hastily conclude that your story is unreadable. Many good manuscripts have gone the rounds and been rejected by nearly every editor and publisher in the business before they found a home. Editors do not have unlimited budgets; they cannot buy every good thing that comes their way: they can use only so many love stories, articles, or poems in one issue.

Perhaps the editor had just bought an article on the subject of your article. What of that? There are other markets. Never say die!

Of course if your script requires revision or can be improved, you should attend to that before you mail it out again. But if it is as good as you can make it, you should never allow it to remain overnight on your desk, but keep it in the mails until someone makes you an offer.

The better firms pay "on acceptance." This does not mean that you will receive a check, as a rule, in the same envelope with the acceptance, for the editor who makes you the offer is not the business manager who draws your check. It takes several days and sometimes several weeks for the check to come through after the story has been accepted.

There are publications which pay only on publication. Most writers feel that this arrangement is quite unfair and prefer markets which pay on acceptance.

It is a curious fact that a story or article looks quite different in print from what it did when typed. Just what this difference is, is difficult—if not impossible—to explain, and for that reason alone you should wish to have your work printed until you become aware of this difference and can allow for it in your written work.

While you are learning your craft and until you begin to publish with regularity, you should have some other means than writing for subsistence. For, of course, though you have nominated yourself a writer, whether or not you become one rests with the suffrage of your readers. Choose your reader and your market wisely and go ahead courageously; and rest assured that, if the public approves your work, the editors will be happy to print it.

But your greatest satisfaction will come from the actual practice of your craft—getting things down as they ought to be, saying what you mean, sharing your thoughts and feelings with the readers who enjoy your work—and the glorious, though often agonizing, privilege of practicing the greatest art in the world.

PART 5 APPENDIX

A. PIECES FOR ANALYSIS

SECTION A-1

In this Appendix you will find several pieces of fiction and non-
fiction.

A short story is first offered for analysis. More than ten years'
experience in teaching my courses in Professional Writing at the
University of Oklahoma has convinced me that, when striving for an
understanding of technique, a student learns more—and learns more
rapidly—if he at first confines himself to the close study of a single
example.

This study will call attention to many of the standard technical
devices in use. But it is not intended to display them all. That would
be as tedious as it is unnecessary. And it would only deprive you of
the fun and benefit of making your own discoveries.

Such intense study of a single story should soon develop in you a
keen eye for technical devices and the effects produced by them on
readers. You will then wish to test your powers by analyzing the
other examples offered here, in order to increase your skill. And of
course once you have acquired an alert awareness of devices of
many kinds, you will wish to study other examples chosen by yourself.

194

These may be of various types, because you must stock your arsenal of devices with the best you can find in the works of many writers. For, once you have learned to recognize devices and understand their use, you will be able to analyze any piece of writing, take it all to pieces, and discover how it works.

Finally, when you have practiced and made your own all the good devices you have discovered, you will doubtless create others of your own, polishing and perfecting them until you acquire a style of your own—effective, flexible, apt for whatever purpose you may have.

But to begin with, you must study *one* example.

Therefore, I have chosen a short story for your first analysis: (a) because most beginning writers wish to attempt the short story; (b) because a short story has a definite pattern, definite requirements, and so is packed with technical devices; (c) because a short story is a type of manageable length; (d) because the fictional devices found in a short story are the same in the main as those found in a novel, biography, or long narrative poem; (e) because the devices used in fiction are now commonly used in non-fiction; nine in ten of the non-fiction books and articles published today employ fictional techniques—dialogue, scenes, characterization, and all the rest— sometimes even plot. Without some mastery of these it is almost impossible to sell or publish a non-fiction book or article in the United States.

I have chosen this particular story, *Dakotah Courtship:* (1) because this story—though having a regular plot and all the usual parts —was styled for and published in a quality magazine or literary quarterly, *The Southwest Review;*[1] (2) because this story exhibits many of the standard devices usually employed, both in fiction and non-fiction; (3) because I wrote it and therefore know why every device employed was introduced; (4) because this particular story has been repeatedly tested in my classes for its effects upon readers, and these have been rather definitely determined.

Whether you enjoy or admire this story—or *any* story—which you are analyzing is entirely beside the point. The best works of the greatest writers all have their flaws and imperfections, and the most horrible examples by inept writers offer some devices and effects worth noting. Even the most commonplace author will be good at some things.

We must therefore study work of all kinds and learn from every-

[1]Reprinted by permission.

thing we read. Most successful writers are omnivorous readers, for before they can be successful they must have discovered that they can learn from *all*.

Therefore, I warn you not to assume that the story *Dakotah Courtship* is offered here as in any way extraordinary, much less a flawless masterpiece. On the contrary, it is intended rather as something representative and so the more instructive. It is merely an example to be analyzed so that you may learn to find and recognize technical devices.

If I knew where to find a flawless piece of work I should not offer it here. For indeed, the technical study of great masterpieces can be dangerous to beginning writers: thus Keats dared not read Milton's poems while meditating his own *Hyperion;* he feared the overwhelming influence of such masterpieces.

In the beginning you will find it easier to learn from the study of contemporary authors. Later the technical beauties and subtleties of the great classics will be more comprehensible and so more useful to you.

Now read *Dakotah Courtship* carefully and follow the instructions for analysis chapter by chapter as they occur in the book.

For your convenience in studying the devices in this story I have numbered the sentences consecutively.

Dakotah Courtship[1]

BY STANLEY VESTAL

1. Joe Lone Bear was a confident young man with a long reach and a steady eye, and plenty proud of his battered, stripped-down car, daubed all over with what Joe believed were the latest collegiate mottoes: MEN AT WORK, CHICKEN COOP, THAT MAN IS HERE AGAIN, SOCKO, SO LONG, EXCUSE MY DUST. 2. But as Joe gradually approached the gate of Chief Hardtack's allotment, his young heart missed almost as often as his chugging engine. 3. Lillie Fineweather lived there.

[1]Copyright, 1939, by W. S. Campbell.

4. That motor trouble in Joe's fighting heart was not entirely due to Lillie's near presence, however. 5. Lillie and Joe had mostly got along fine—at the Indian Boarding School. 6. The pocket of his blue shirt contained a well-thumbed letter in her firm Spencerian hand, assuring him, in a curious mixture of school slang and Indian poetry, that she loved him: "Hurry up, Big Boy. 7. I'm crazy about you. 8. All time you way off in South Dakota, my lips are still on your lips."

9. Lillie was okay. 10. One in a million. 11. But now he had to face old Mrs. Hardtack and her stuffy old man, and hurdle their objections. 12. Dakotah and Crow had been enemies from away back. 13. When a Dakotah boy came courting a Crow girl, there was likely to be trouble.

14. Lillie had warned Joe that her grandma was terrible old-fashioned. 15. Lillie said Joe couldn't wrangle the old lady single-handed. 16. So Joe had brought along his own grandparents to make the match in the old-time way. 17. But now, as he rolled in through Hardtack's gate, Joe began to get cold feet about that.

18. Anxiously, he shouted to caution the aged warrior at his elbow. 19. Chief Lone Bear sat braced against the gale, clutching his splintered stiff straw hat with gnarled fingers, staring fiercely through the windshield. 20. "Grandfather," Joe yelled, "the wars are over. 21. We are friends with these people now. 22. Remember that!"

23. The old Dakotah shifted his moccasins to a firmer position upon the hot floorboards, turned red-rimmed eyes upon his grandson, and showed his yellow teeth in a grin of pleasurable anticipation. 24. "Make your heart strong, my grandson," he quavered. 25. "I know how to handle the Crows. 26. I have killed plenty of them in my day, and made them run like rabbits. 27. *He-han!* 28. Who is this Hardtack? 29. He has seen only seventy-six winters. 30. I have nothing to fear from that boy!"

31. The old man's words upset Joe. 32. Then and there he killed his engine. 33. The car jolted to a stop.

34. It was a good long hundred yards across the blistering prairie to Hardtack's unpainted shack and the brush arbor alongside. 35. But Joe was too disheartened to try to start the car again. 36. Chances were it wouldn't start, anyhow, and he did not want the visit to begin by Lillie's folks having the laugh on him. 37. It would be less humiliating to pretend that he had meant to stop right there, and walk the rest of the way.

38. Joe jumped out, landing on the heels of his tan Oxfords. 39. Chief Lone Bear stepped down, catlike, in the manner of a man who has worn moccasins all his life. 40. Old Mrs. Lone Bear, after a moment's silent dismay at the distance to be covered afoot, heaved her two hundred pounds up from the rumble-seat and slowly clambered to the ground.

41. The spry old man went first, bright-eyed, bow-legged, stooping over his polished cane. 42. Joe nervously hitched up his blue jeans and followed. 43. The old woman pulled her bright new blanket—the price of her participation—over her meaty shoulders, and plodded along behind.

44. Just as they started, Joe saw Lillie leave the arbor and hurry into the shack. 45. It was clear that the Hardtacks knew what was up. 46. Nobody came from the arbor to greet them. 47. The three Dakotahs halted and stood in a row just outside.

48. Joe lowered his head and peered in. 49. Chief Hardtack, hatless and barefoot, lay at his ease in the checkered shadows of the arbor, puffing his long pipe and looking out indifferently through horn-rimmed spectacles. 50. The frames held no glass, but Joe was in no mood to laugh. 51. Hardtack was a big, vital man, and tough as a mule.

52. But when Joe laid eyes on the old woman, he held his breath. 53. Mrs. Hardtack was formidable. 54. She sat upright on the ground—one leg stretched straight out before her. 55. Her flat, uncompromising face was painted red. 56. She had a short hooked nose, like the beak of an owl, and her dark gaze was so searching and hostile that Joe wondered what ailed him. 57. She wore an old-time calico dress with open flaps for sleeves. 58. A regular squaw—even if she was Lillie's grandma.

59. Nobody moved. 60. Nobody spoke. 61. Each party waited for the other to make the first move. 62. Chief Lone Bear would not enter until the Crow had made him welcome. 63. The Hardtacks were ready to sit still forever rather than welcome a Dakotah on such an errand. 64. In the silence, Joe heard the dog scratching himself.

65. Joe couldn't stand it. 66. He broke the ice. 67. *"How!"* he said.

68. At that word, old Mrs. Hardtack drew herself up triumphantly. 69. Her hard face set in lines of scorn. 70. "Dakotah!" she sneered.

71. Hardtack now came suddenly to life. 72. *"Sho-da-gee!"* he cried, in hospitable greeting now that the others had begun the

198

talk. 73. Chief Lone Bear stepped over the pots and firewood, grasped Hardtack's hand quickly, and seated himself on his host's left side—the side nearest his heart. 74. Mrs. Lone Bear, making a purring sound of pleasure, waddled in and found a place beside her hostess. 75. All four of them seemed to be in high good humor, eager to begin the business. 76. All four of them completely ignored Joe.

77. Joe felt like a rank outsider. 78. For a minute he stood still, not knowing what to do. 79. Then he turned hastily and retreated. 80. Nobody wanted him around.

81. Chief Hardtack's allotment was a flat, uncompromising square of short Montana grass surrounded by a sagging fence of rusty barbed wire. 82. The sun beat down on it with all the steady purpose of an August afternoon. 83. Joe decided to wait in the car. 84. It would be hot—but what the hell!

85. To reach the car, Joe had to pass the shack. 86. The door was open, and the aroma of boiling coffee caught his nostrils. 87. Lillie Fineweather stood inside, looking anxiously out towards the arbor through the grimy windowpane. 88. Joe halted in his tracks. 89. "Hey, Lillie. 90. Is that you?"

91. She turned towards him, shamefaced. 92. "Believe it or not," she said defiantly. 93. "Go on and laugh. 94. I know I look awful. 95. Grandma made me do it."

96. She hardly looked the bobbed-haired beauty Joe had dated and dragged to the movies at school. 97. Her hair still had the lustre of a new gun-barrel, but it was parted down the middle now and plaited into two stubby braids made long with strands of colored yarn. 98. Instead of her usual shirt and dungarees, she had on a red calico dress with a yoke and frill—Crow Reservation, fashion 1890—and high button shoes too big for her. 99. Yet somehow, she was pretty in spite of it.

100. Joe could not help laughing. 101. "Are you the kid I come all this way to marry?"

102. "You don't have to," she countered. 103. Relenting, she added, "No kidding, Joe. 104. I thought you were never coming. 105. One more day in this lousy dump, and I'll be coocoo."

106. "Okay. 107. Let's skip," Joe prompted.

108. "Nothing doing, Big Boy. 109. Grandma's got me buffaloed. 110. I'm scared to marry without her okay—supposing you can get it."

199

111. Joe laughed. 112. "Me? 113. What I got to do with it? 114. I'm just a bystander." 115. He moved his pursed lips in the direction ᵣᶠ the old folks. 116. "Well, I guess the war is on." 117. Joe started tᵤ enter.

118. Lillie raised her hand to stop him. 119. "Keep out, Joe. 120. If Grandma catches you alone with me, she'll sure raise hell. 121. She'll call the whole thing off. 122. She's terrible old-fashioned, like I told you. 123. She don't approve of necking."

124. Joe halted. 125. "Who said anything about necking?" he complained.

126. "Nobody. 127. But somebody might think of it. 128. Whyn't you set on the stoop outside? 129. It's shady there. 130. That way we can talk, and watch the old folks at the same time. 131. They can't understand each other's talk. 132. They'll have to use the sign language."

133. "Okay, sweetheart." 134. Joe sat on the stoop, and ran his fingers through his shock of stiff black hair. 135. Looking sideways he could see every movement in the arbor—not a dozen yards away. 136. Lillie was watching through the window.

137. Already Mrs. Lone Bear had begun. 138. Her thick fingers moved in the staccato sequences of the sign talk, in gestures known to all Plains Indians. 139. "My grandson told me he wants to marry your granddaughter. 140. Me and my man come to see this girl. 141. We want a good wife for our grandson."

142. Mrs. Hardtack smiled with marked condescension. 143. "Is that puny boy your grandson? 144. He would be lucky, if she ever looked at him. 145. She could marry any man in the Crow nation."

146. Mrs. Lone Bear settled her weight more comfortably, as if for a long session. 147. Her plump, copper-colored fingers moved with blandly slow precision. 148. "He is strong and brave. 149. His lodge will be full of meat all times. 150. He has many horses."

151. "How many?" Mrs. Hardtack demanded, ticking off the question dubiously on the upraised fingers of her left hand. 152. Her deliberate gesture implied that Joe could not possess more than one, one and a half, or two horses at the outside.

153. Mrs. Lone Bear smiled in a superior way, ignoring the question. 154. "He also has a fast-wagon. 155. Look."

156. Mrs. Hardtack laughed. 157. "I see it. 158. It runs slow and stops quick. 159. I would be afraid to have my granddaughter ride in that."

160. Mrs. Lone Bear's smile turned a little sour. 161. "Moreover, he learned to fight with fists like white men, wearing mittens of leather, in a rope corral. 162. I saw him. 163. He knocked down every young man his size in the school, and four white boys." 164. Mrs. Lone Bear cocked her head on one side, and made a decisive gesture to end her speech: "Cut!"

165. "How many horses has he?" Mrs. Hardtack persisted.

166. "Plenty. 167. Heaps. 168. We come from far to see this girl. 169. Where is she? 170. Why is she hiding? 171. She must be ugly."

172. Then Mrs. Hardtack charged. 173. "My granddaughter does not think of marriage. 174. She would not look at a Dakotah. 175. Your grandson must be crazy to follow her. 176. She is a wife for a chief. 177. She can cook and sew and wash and tan hides. 178. She makes fine beadwork. 179. She is beautiful and modest and strong as a horse. 180. On top of that she belongs to a family of warriors and feastmakers. 181. Her great grandfather was a famous horsethief."

182. Joe looked over his shoulder. 183. "Attagirl, Lillie. 184. Grandma and me think you're tops."

185. Lillie giggled at him. 186. "Tune in, Big Boy. 187. Your time's coming."

188. Mrs. Hardtack never faltered. 189. "Look at my husband. 190. He got his name stealing bread from the soldiers at the fort. 191. He was the meanest boy we ever had. 192. When he was little he used to steal his mother's butcher knife and slash holes in the tent. 193. She could not stop him. 194. He was bad. 195. Heap bad. 196. Always making trouble." 197. She beamed.

198. "Hot dog! 199. What a naughty boy!" Joe jeered.

200. Lillie stiffened. 201. "Lay off my folks," she cautioned.

202. "How about mine?" Joe demanded.

203. "They ain't so hot, I guess," she answered, and kept her face to the window.

204. "Our family is related to Sitting Bull's," Mrs. Lone Bear explained with steady hands. 205. "You Crows all remember him. 206. He stole plenty horses from you—every winter, they say. 207. But he was never mean to women—not even Crow women."

208. Mrs. Hardtack laughed unpleasantly. 209. "He never had a chance to be."

210. Mrs. Lone Bear replied with emphatic gestures. 211. "I was told his warriors gave him a Crow woman. 212. They captured her. 213. Sitting Bull gave her a good horse and sent her home."

214. "No Crow woman would have married him," Mrs. Hardtack snapped back. 215. "She would die first." 216. Her black eyes shone fiercely. 217. "That is the way when Dakotah and Crow marry. 218. They are never happy."

219. Mrs. Lone Bear could not resist that opening. 220. With gusto she signaled, "That was what Sitting Bull said."

221. Joe called to Lillie, in genuine alarm. 222. "Hey, the old girls will be in each other's hair in a minute. 223. Can't you stop 'em?"

224. Lillie scowled at him. 225. Then her face relaxed. 226. "Okay. 227. Coming up. 228. I'll give 'em coffee. 229. But don't pull any fast ones about my folks. 230. I can't take it."

231. "Cross my heart, Lil. 232. Give 'em some eats. 233. They can't swallow and bite at the same time. 234. And put plenty of sugar in the coffee."

235. Hastily, Lillie Fineweather caught up the kettle of stew and the pot of coffee, hurried to the arbor, and placed the food before her grandmother. 236. Then she came back. 237. For a while there was no sound in the arbor but that of resolute mastication. 238. Chewing, for the old folks, was a chore that demanded concentration.

239. The old men, having been served first, finished before the women. 240. Hardtack was host, and had to use both hands to fill and light his pipe. 241. Lone Bear had his chance at last. 242. He smacked his lips, and gestured to catch Hardtack's eye. 243. Then, making sure the women were also watching, he began to make signs.

244. "When I was young, there were many Crow captives among my people. 245. The Crows were always getting killed and captured. 246. They did not know how to take care of themselves. 247. There is a Crow captive now living at Standing Rock Agency. 248. He refused to go back to his people. 249. He was happier with us. 250. It will be so with your granddaughter."

251. Hardtack stopped filling his pipe, and used his hands in talk. 252. "Crows killed plenty Dakotahs. 253. I was not born yesterday." 254. Hardtack went back to work, tamping in the tobacco with his thumb, firmly. 255. Even from the shack, Joe could see how the old man's hands trembled with rage.

256. Lone Bear smacked his lips again and grinned. 257. "The Dakotahs killed Long Hair and hundreds of his soldiers. 258. Their bodies covered the hills like a big blue blanket. 259. I saw it. 260. I was in the fight. 261. You were only a boy then, too young to fight.

262. That was your good luck. 263. But we did not kill many Crows that day. 264. They ran away."

265. Joe groaned. 266. "Zowie! 267. Now Granddad is talking about the Custer Battle."

268. "The Custer Massacre," Lillie corrected him, sharply.

269. Joe bristled. 270. "Massacre nothing. 271. Them soldiers came looking for trouble, and found it. 272. They died fighting— with guns in their hands and cartridges in their belts. 273. That was a fair fight, and no massacre."

274. "That's what *you* think," Lillie snapped. 275. "I know. 276. Some of my relatives were there."

277. Joe swayed with restless irritation. 278. "They did not stay long," he countered. 279. Then, suddenly, he whirled on her. 280. "Hey, Lil. 281. Don't let it get you too. 282. We got to stand together. 283. I'm going to marry you."

284. "Maybe," she said, her eyes brimming with angry tears.

285. "Okay, Lillie, if that's the way you feel." 286. Joe turned his back on her.

287. "Oh, for the love of Mike, shut up," she scolded. 288. "The more we talk, the worse it is. 289. I can't help it, I tell you. 290. I was raised that way."

291. Joe said no more, and watched the old men. 292. Chief Lone Bear was clapping his hands in rapid imitation of rifle-fire. 293. "The soldiers shot fast that day. 294. But we made them run, we killed them. 295. It was a great day. 296. Every little while I picked up a feather for my cap. 297. I cannot remember how many I killed that day."

298. "My relatives told me it was a hard fight to the end," the Crow objected.

299. Lone Bear ignored the interruption. 300. "I was there. 301. I saw. 302. We Dakotahs made the Crows who came with the white men run for their lives. 303. I have heard that they did not stop running for three days. 304. Some of them are running still, maybe." 305. Lone Bear laughed.

306. Hardtack threw up his head. 307. His eyes glittered. 308. "There are too many tongues. 309. That day the Crows fought well. 310. They captured the ponies of your people. 311. Long Hair told them to do that. 312. The Crows charged ahead of the soldiers, and ran off the ponies. 313. But they were not told to stand and die. 314. When they saw that the soldiers could not win, they ran away. 315.

If the soldiers had been smart, they would have run away too. 316. A good warrior knows when to charge and when to retreat. 317. The Crows did both better than the white soldiers."

318. Lone Bear gave a hearty gesture of assent. 319. "The Crows ran well that day." 320. He laughed. 321. "I chased them."

322. Hardtack sucked flame into his pipe-bowl as if he would swallow it. 323. He inhaled two savage puffs. 324. Then he saw that Lone Bear was preparing to make signs again. 325. Quickly, Hardtack handed the pipe to the Dakotah—to keep his hands still.

326. "I have seen Dakotahs running," he signaled. 327. "I will tell you. 328. That was my first warpath. 329. I had seen only sixteen winters. 330. I was too young to be scared. 331. There were eight of us. 332. Big Shoulders was leader. 333. We found a Dakotah camp on the Yellowstone River. 334. It was winter, and the snow was deep.

335. "We kept hidden while Big Shoulders threw dirt on the ice to make a road for the horses. 336. He saw five Dakotahs coming horseback. 337. He ran back to us. 338. Then I ran up to the hilltop and looked over. 339. The Dakotahs sat down to smoke, and their ponies pawed the snow to find something to eat. 340. Then one Dakotah came riding up my hill to look around. 341. I was reckless. 342. I stood up. 343. The four Dakotahs who were smoking saw me. 344. They yelled to warn their friend. 345. Twice they yelled. 346. But it was cold, he had a shawl tied over his ears. 347. He could not hear them.

348. "Then my friend Bear-All-the-Time shot that lone Dakotah's horse. 349. The horse did not fall, but lunged along, and its foreleg swung back and forth, loose—like a rope. 350. The man on that horse jumped off into the snow and tried to get away. 351. The snow was hip-deep there. 352. We all rode after him.

353. "The first Crow hit the Dakotah and took his gun. 354. The other one claimed the horse. 355. The two of them began to wrestle for the gun. 356. I was third. 357. I shot that Dakotah dead. 358. The four Dakotahs who had been smoking got on their horses and ran. 359. They ran well. 360. Maybe they are running yet. 361. But the man I shot did not run. 362. He was dead. 363. I killed him. 364. I have heard that his name was Running Hawk."

365. Lillie turned on Joe, her eyes burning. 366. "Get that, you lousy Dakotah?" she triumphed. 367. "The Crows are not so dumb."

368. Lone Bear sat with hanging head, and sang a sad song.

369. Joe glared at Lillie. 370. He was breathing hard through his nostrils. 371. "Running Hawk was a relative of mine," he said, sternly.

372. "Joe! Is that true?" 373. Lillie turned to him, her face stricken. 374. "Oh, Big Boy, I'm so sorry. 375. Look here, Joe. 376. The old folks know we are watching them. 377. I bet they are trying us out. 378. That's what! 379. If we can't take it, they don't want us to marry."

380. Joe stared at her. 381. He looked quickly at the group in the arbor. 382. "Kid, you're smart. 383. You've said a mouthful. 384. That's it, all right. 385. It's just like them old-time peace treaties Granddad tells about. 386. They got together and insulted each other for all they were worth—to make sure the peace would stick!"

387. Lillie nodded.

388. Joe got up. 389. "Look here, Lil. 390. This has gone far enough. 391. If they keep on, they'll make saps of us. 392. We got to stop it. 393. Come on. 394. I don't give a damn if he was my relative. 395. That was ages ago. 396. It's got nothing to do with us."

397. The old women were weeping. 398. The old men beamed at each other. 399. "A Dakotah and a Crow will always be fighting," Hardtack declared, with satisfaction.

400. "True," Lone Bear assented, with gusto. 401. "They are like two mean dogs. 402. If they fight, you can pull them apart. 403. But if you turn them loose, they will go right back to fighting again."

404. But Joe and Lillie were in the arbor, each talking as fast as possible—the one in Crow, the other in Dakotah, and both in the sign language. 405. "The past is rubbed out. 406. All this talk is no good. 407. We want to get married. 408. We ain't old-time Indians. 409. We got to forget the past, and think about the future."

410. The old folks sat still, astonished at the outburst. 411. One by one they subsided. 412. They sat staring at the ground, with disappointed faces. 413. The women wiped their tears with the corners of their blankets. 414. The old men hung their heads. 415. The happy game of bluff and brag was over.

416. When the young folks stopped talking, they stood there, a little frightened at their own rashness. 417. But after a time, Lone Bear took the floor. 418. He was the oldest man—a man of experience. 419. His face lighted with a smile. 420. He stood up, and began to move his hands in his best oratorical manner.

421. "My grandson is right. 422. The trail behind is lost. 423. The rains and snows of many winters have filled it with mud. 424. It is covered with grass. 425. Here and there it has been plowed under. 426. When I was young, I used to come upon the bones of a man lying on the prairie. 427. Sometimes they were the bones of a Crow, sometimes of a Dakotah. 428. But now I never find bones lying on the prairie. 429. The old trail is lost. 430. The young men cannot find it.

431. "Yet it is good to remember the old ways. 432. Ours was a good trail. 433. Once I had a Crow woman in my lodge. 434. She was my fifth wife. 435. I stole her. 436. She was a fine woman, and we were happy. 437. It is true, I made her very jealous. 438. I never knew when she would whip out her knife and try to stab me. 439. She used to hide my clothes to keep me at home. 440. But now she is dead, and these grandchildren of ours want to get married. 441. That is good. 442. I am willing, we are all willing. 443. It is time to forget the past and think of the days ahead. 444. It is time for us to do something for our grandchildren. 445. They will marry, and set up a lodge of their own, and have a son. 446. That boy must have a good name. 447. What shall we call him?"

448. "Yes. 449. A good name," Mrs. Lone Bear assented.

450. "The name of some friendly animal," Mrs. Hardtack insisted firmly.

451. Chief Hardtack sat up grandly. 452. "Above all, a famous name."

453. "The child will be a Dakotah, like his father. 454. He should be called Sitting Bull," Lone Bear advised.

455. "No," Hardtack objected. 456. "The husband lives with his wife's folks. 457. That is the custom. 458. The child will be Crow. 459. He ought to have a Crow name."

460. "My woman goes with me," Joe gestured, positively. 461. "She does not like it here."

462. Lillie turned on him. 463. "Oh, yeah? 464. That's what *you* think. 465. What's the matter with Crow country, I'd like to know?"

466. "Why, Lil, you told me yourself——"

467. "You're crazy. 468. Anyhow, if we did marry and have a kid, like as not it would be a girl."

469. "My kid a girl?" he protested, grappling with the new idea.

470. "Sure. 471. Why not? 472. What's wrong with a girl? 473. I thought you was modern."

474. "But Lillie——"

475. "I say it's a girl, Joe. 476. That's flat. 477. And you bet I won't have no girl named Sitting Bull!"

478. "Skip it, Lil. 479. Call her Prairie Flower, Milkweed, Sagebrush, Cactus, or Hollers All Night. 480. We got plenty of time to name the kid. 481. Let's get married. 482. Come on. 483. We can find the missionary in town in ten minutes."

484. "Don't get tough, Big Boy. 485. We got to make the old folks like it, or the kid won't have no grandparents to look after it."

486. "Lucky kid," Joe groaned.

487. Lillie's eyes blazed. 488. "You think I'm going to stay home all day with that baby? 489. I ain't no squaw. 490. I want some fun out of life."

491. "Fun!" Joe barked. 492. "They'll be plenty of fun, if you don't take care of my kid. 493. Let's get going. 494. All this fuss makes me sick. 495. Come on." 496. Joe took her by the arm.

497. Stung by the shame of having him touch her in the presence of her relatives, Lillie struggled to wrench herself free. 498. "Let go of me," she raged. 499. "Where do you think you are anyhow?" 500. She slapped him hard across the cheek. 501. Joe let go.

502. Breathless, she stood poised, with open mouth, watching his face. 503. She whirled and ran. 504. The moment she moved, Joe was after her. 505. Two strides brought him close. 506. Lillie heard him coming, stepped to one side quickly, and stuck out her foot. 507. She tripped him. 508. Joe hit the grass on his face.

509. Lillie laughed at him. 510. "Don't you try to boss me, Big Boy. 511. You ain't big enough." 512. She ran into the shack and slammed the door.

513. Joe got up. 514. The old folks were laughing. 515. Joe hitched up his jeans and stalked off to his car. 516. He was still trying to start it when Lillie Fineweather passed by on her way to the gate. 517. She sailed past in her new sneakers, blue dungarees, and a clean white shirt. 518. Her shining bob swung free. 519. Joe thought she looked swell. 520. She was headin' for town, sure. 521. Joe tried to catch her eye. 522. "Where you goin', Lillie?"

523. "Nowhere with you," she replied. 524. "And don't you follow me neither—if you ever do get that thing started. 525. You damn Dakotah, I'm through."

526. Joe stamped on the starter furiously, and held his foot down. 527. Lil went on, and he saw her halt at the gate. 528. A truck was

rolling down the road in a cloud of dust. 529. Lillie raised her thumb and waggled it in the air above her head. 530. Joe saw the truck slow to pick her up.

531. "No you don't," Joe muttered, and jumped from his seat. 532. He sprinted to the gate. 533. The truck had stopped. 534. The driver was a big red-faced bruiser, thick in the neck and wide in the shoulders. 535. Fat, though. 536. Automatically, Joe judged the man outweighed him twenty pounds.

537. The big roughneck looked Lillie up and down. 538. "Goin' to town? 539. Hop in, Sister."

540. Lillie grasped the handbar and set foot on the board. 541. Joe ,erked her back to earth with a single movement, shoved her to one side. 542. He did not hear her protests. 543. "Get going, you big ape," Joe commanded, "or I'll knock you cold."

544. The driver appraised Joe, and laughed. 545. "You and how many more, you damned Indian!"

546. Joe swung himself up, hanging to the truck with one hand, jabbing with the other. 547. The driver raised his feet suddenly, pivoted to face Joe, planted his boots with a violent shove on Joe's middle, then let drive with all his force. 548. As the man's legs straightened, Joe shot backward into the ditch. 549. He did not get up. 550. He lay there, both hands on his belt, gasping for breath.

551. The driver jumped down. 552. "Just a minute, Sister, till I tromp him." 553. He sprang towards Joe.

554. Lillie said nothing. 555. She stuck out her foot. 556. She tripped him. 557. The driver was a heavy man; when he hit the ground, he grunted.

558. But he was soon up, and whirling on the girl to strike her. 559. His first blow barely reached her shoulder, but it sent her staggering.

560. Joe got up then, stumbling across the ruts to slug the big hick scientifically and hard, first on one jaw, then on the other, in spite of the clutching pain at his midriff. 561. The driver put up a fight. 562. But as Joe's wind came back, the other's left him. 563. A final clip on the chin sent the driver back to collapse against the front fender of the truck. 564. He got up blinking, warded off Joe's fists with open hands, and crawled back into his cab.

565. As the engine roared to a start, the driver yelled some words at Lillie Fineweather. 566. She could not make them out, but she saw

his face. 567. She made a gesture, as if she were throwing dirt at it. 568. The truck lurched away.

569. Joe stood panting, looking admiringly at the girl. 570. "Gee, Lil. 571. You sure pack a wicked foot."

572. Lillie's eyes showed fire. 573. "Nobody's going to call you names while I'm around," she declared. 574. "Say, Big Boy, will your old bus start? 575. This dump is getting me. 576. Folks around here do nothing but fight. 577. You got some cash, I guess. 578. Tomorrow the rodeo starts at Sheridan. 579. You promised me we could see it."

580. "Boy howdy. 581. You sure can—after we see the missionary. 582. But what'll I do with my old folks?"

583. "Park them here," Lillie advised sagely. 584. "It's a cinch they can't pull out till you get back. 585. They'll love it; they ain't had a good fight for fifty years. 586. Two-three days here will get it out of their system. 587. Then they'll kiss and make up."

588. Together they walked to the car. 589. Joe got in and fiddled with things on the dash, while Lillie waited to see whether it would go or not. 590. At last, by some method which Joe pretended to understand, but did not, he managed to start the engine.

591. "Hop in, Lillie," he commanded.

592. She stood looking back at the arbor. 593. She seemed troubled. 594. "Hold on, Joe. 595. We forgot the name for the kid. 596. We've got to settle that now, or we'll never have peace in the family."

597. Joe laughed. 598. "That's easy. 599. I already done it. 600. You looked so cute and friendly back there, when you tripped that big bozo, it come to me all at once. 601. I got it."

602. "No soft-soap, Joe. 603. My name won't do. 604. You heard the old folks. 605. All Crow and Dakotah names are out." 606. She remained standing beside the car.

607. "Sure," he answered. 608. "I got it. 609. A good name, a friendly animal's name, above all a famous name. 610. Hop in. 611. We'll call the kid Mickie Mouse!"

612. Lillie Fineweather stood open-mouthed at the dazzling wisdom of his idea. 613. She climbed in obediently, and snuggled close to Joe. 614. "Big Boy," she whispered, "you're wonderful!"

615. Joe Lone Bear made himself look even bigger than he was. 616. He threw in the clutch, the car sailed off, cutting a wide circle through the grass on its way back to the gate. 617. Joe felt like a champion.

618. But by the time that circle was completed, Lillie Fineweather

was herself again. 619. She sat up straight beside Joe, and her face was set. 620. When she spoke, she spoke firmly.

621. "Listen, Joe. 622. We're going to call her *Minnie Mouse!*"

SECTION A-2

We have now to consider a second short story of a different type entitled *A Very Valuable Quality*, by Naomi John White, a former pupil of mine, a graduate of the courses in Professional Writing at the University of Oklahoma. It first appeared in *Collier's*, February 2, 1946, and is reprinted here by the gracious permission of the author.

I have chosen this story for your study, *first*, because it is a good story and admirably suited to one of the so-called "slick" or smooth-paper magazines. It was built around a novel idea, with appealing characters and familiar setting, and written by an author with warm feeling for and clear knowledge of the people of whom she writes; *second*, because it has, in contrast to *Dakotah Courtship*, a feminine viewpoint; *third*, because it is an idea story, a type not too commonly seen; *fourth*, because it is an excellent example of correct viewpoint; *fifth*, because of the skillful handling of scenes; *sixth*, because this story is well adapted to dramatization either for the stage, the screen, or television.

At the time this story appeared the Broadway musical show *Oklahoma!* was a smash hit and as a result the American public had come to regard Oklahoma as a kind of Arcady. This story, though more realistic and contemporary than the show, was nevertheless well adapted to the market at that time.

The author's feeling for Oklahoma is affectionate. She likes her characters, her setting, and has every reason to be pleased with the novel idea through which the heroine solves her problem. By narrating the story from the viewpoint of the heroine's teen-age sister and in the first person, the author not only achieved consistent viewpoint, but a quality of style marked by a somewhat childish repetition, precision, and quaintness that are very appealing, indeed disarming.

Since the narrator, Laurie, greatly admired her elder sister, the heroine, the heroine's intelligence is never mistaken by the reader for guile; the reader remains entirely sympathetic. This was impor-

210

tant, since most readers prefer to have the hero or heroine solve their difficulties by brawn rather than brain. Another advantage of having Laurie narrate the story in the first person is that the reader is not taken directly into the mind of the heroine, so that her plans are discovered only in he process of working them out, through their effects. This, which we may call "the Dr. Watson technique" (used so successfully in the Sherlock Holmes stories), enables the author to unfold her plot gradually and without giving the story away.

A good short story is by definition a tall tale made plausible, and therefore the author's function is *first* to conceive a tall tale and *second* to make it plausible to his reader.

Since all readers are human beings, plausibility is mostly a matter of convincing motivation. For human motives, being more familiar to us all, are more plausible than actions, situations, or settings. The writer must therefore use every means to make the motivation of his characters convincing, and of the various techniques available none is more effective than the scene.

For the first four steps of a good scene (the Meeting, Purpose, Encounter, and Final or Decisive Action) prove, demonstrate, and establish the validity of the state of affairs and resulting *state of mind* in the Sequel. This state of mind is a *motive* which (the plot being in itself so improbable) could not be believed were it not so established and proven. Thus the scene is your best means of making your reader believe that the character actually had the motive or state of mind in the Sequel.

Since a story consists of motives and emotions, not of facts and actions, it follows that unless the motives are convincing, unless they are established, the reader cannot believe in them. Hence the value of the scene.

But the scene serves another very important purpose, because the state of mind (motive) in the sequel in one scene usually provides the purpose (motive) for a scene to follow. Thus all the scenes are bound together by convincing motivation, and the plot (however improbable in itself) is so made plausible.

If you have a good plot, you need good scenes to make it plausible; if your plot is weak, your only hope of keeping the reader happy lies in writing good scenes. Thus, no matter what you do, good scenes are indispensable.

In planning a scenario for his story, the wise author determines in advance just which motives of his characters *must* be accepted

211

and believed by the reader, and then writes a scene which will convince the reader of the truth of each of those important motives. That is to say, each scene is deliberately planned to convince the reader of a given character's motive in each case.

For example, in this story *A Very Valuable Quality* the scenes listed and numbered below prove:

1. Sentences 10–31: that Henry is confused.
2. 34–46: that Suzie is in danger of losing her man.
3. 47–54: that Henry is unhappy and that the Whitsetts like him.
4. 69–72: that Henry is determined to jilt Suzie.
5. 76–130: that Suzie means to hold Henry.
6. 137–50: that Henry is coming, bringing Walters.
7. 165–81: that Suzie is getting rid of Walters to hold Henry.
8. 192–200: that Walters is in love with Janet.

You can readily determine for yourself the writer's purpose in writing each of the other scenes in this story and so learn to make up scenarios of your own.

Now read the story *A Very Valuable Quality,* consider the questions offered regarding it in Work Program 11, and write out your answers. After you have written out your own answers—but not before—you may consult the answers given in the Notes for Chapter 11.

A Very Valuable Quality [1]

BY NAOMI JOHN WHITE

1. Until the day that my sister Suzie was jilted, I didn't know how smart she was. 2. Up until then I had thought of my sister Suzie as being a pretty brunette whose clothes I might be able to wear next year. 3. I, Laurie, am fifteen and large for my age. 4. But the day that Henry Brown jilted Suzie, I learned that she had brains, too. 5. Brains are a very valuable quality for a woman to have.

6. That day all four of us Whitsetts were at home. 7. My mother Bessie and I were on the roof of the back porch seeing if we could

[1]Copyright, 1946, by Naomi John White.

mend the leaky shingles, and my sister Janet, who is eighteen and little and blond like my mother Bessie, was under the porch trying to persuade our cat Violet who had her feelings hurt to come out, and my sister Suzie was painting a porch chair.

8. My sister Suzie is twenty, and she had on blue jeans rolled up above her knees, and a green and blue plaid shirt open at her throat, and her nice curly, dark brown hair piled up on top of her head, and she was painting a porch chair red. 9. She looked cute.

10. My mother Bessie and I were lying flat on our stomachs looking down, and we had just asked Suzie if she was about through with the chair and could she come up and help us, when Henry Brown came around the corner of the house. 11. Henry didn't see my mother Bessie and me on the roof. 12. He just saw Suzie sitting cross-legged on the porch with her tongue in the corner of her mouth, painting a red porch chair.

13. "Hello, Suzie," said Henry. 14. He stood there looking at her with his hat in his hand and even from where my mother Bessie and I were, he looked a little sad. 15. Even the little baldish spot on top of his head, and Henry is only twenty-four, looked sad.

16. "Why, hello, honey," said Suzie. 17. "I thought you had to work this evening."

18. Henry is a clerk in the men's department of the Sunset Department Store, and sometimes of evenings after supper, he goes back and decorates the store windows. 19. Suzie was wearing Henry's engagement ring, and she was planning to marry Henry in June. 20. This was only April.

21. "I did," said Henry. 22. And then because Suzie put her paintbrush down in the fruit jar of turpentine and turned all the way around and looked at him, he said, "I mean I did, but I don't any more."

23. "Well," said Suzie, and she sounded puzzled, "that's nice. 24. Maybe we can go to a movie. 25. Betty Grable is on at the Palace."

26. "No," said Henry. 27. "Not tonight. 28. I mean not any night." 29. He turned his hat over and looked at it carefully.

30. "I thought you liked Betty Grable," said Suzie. 31. And then, when Henry didn't say anything more, she added gently, "Won't you sit down, Henry?"

32. He sat down on the top step, and my mother Bessie and I looked at him with interest. 33. There are not very many unmarried

young men in Sunset, Oklahoma, even with baldish heads, and it is very nice to see one up close.

34. Suzie sat down next to him. 35. Usually Suzie linked her arm with Henry's and they held hands, but now Suzie sat with her hands clasped around her knees, and she said, "What's wrong, Henry?"

36. "I don't know how to tell you," said Henry.

37. "Tell me right out," said Suzie. 38. "Whatever it is, I want to know plainly."

39. Henry ran one hand over his baldish spot and stared at the row of our pink slips and panties hanging on the clothesline. 40. "I would like to break our engagement," he said.

41. My mother Bessie forgot that she was just an onlooker, and she started to say something, but I put my hand over her mouth, and she turned her head and looked at me indignantly over it.

42. "Then," said Suzie, and her voice sounded tight, "you don't love me any more, and there is somebody else. 43. Who is she, Henry?"

44. Henry looked relieved. 45. He looked terribly relieved. 46. "It's Elsie Butterfield," he said.

47. My mother Bessie pushed my hand away from her mouth and leaned her head down over the porch. 48. "Why, Elsie can't even cook, Henry," she said. 49. "And she bleaches her hair."

50. Henry looked startled. 51. He stood up and looked up at my mother Bessie and me on the roof, and his face turned dark red. 52. "I'm awfully sorry, Mrs. Whitsett," he said; "I feel terrible about it."

53. "You poor boy," said my mother Bessie sympathetically, and she clucked her tongue. 54. My mother Bessie could feel sorry for a rattlesnake.

55. My sister Janet backed out from under the porch then with our cat Violet in one hand. 56. She stood up and dusted her knees with the other hand. 57. "Elsie Butterfield has got thirteen pairs of shoes," she said. 58. Janet was wearing a pink playsuit, and even with dirt on her knees, and our brindled cat Violet in her arms, she looked pretty. 59. "Elsie says she has a color of shoes for every mood of her personality."

60. Henry looked at Suzie a little helplessly.

61. My mother Bessie sat up and swung her legs off the edge of the porch roof. 62. She had on a pair of blue slacks and she looked very young. 63. Whenever we all go out together, people say to my

mother, "My goodness, Bessie, I can hardly believe that these three big strapping girls are really yours." 64. And my mother Bessie always looks around at us surprised, too, as if we are three strangers following her.

65. "There's some leftover fish in the icebox," she said. 66. We are used to my mother Bessie's remarks. 67. We knew that she meant for Janet to go inside the house and feed the cat. 68. "And there's some cream there, too," she went on dreamily. 69. "Why, we can make some ice cream and have a party! 70. Henry, you can turn the freezer."

71. Henry twisted his hat some more. 72. "I guess I'd better go now," he said. 73. He looked at Suzie. 74. "Elsie thought—that is, Elsie and I thought—that we ought to tell you how we feel about each other."

75. "That was real nice of you, Henry," said my mother Bessie approvingly, and she swung her blue sandals.

76. Henry turned then and started to go away, but Suzie stopped him. 77. She stopped him by standing up and saying in a clear voice that sounded as if it had icicles in it, "You forgot to ask me what I thought, Henry," she said. 78. "You forgot to ask me if I agreed to breaking our engagement."

79. Henry looked at her surprised. 80. He opened his mouth, and his jaw dropped a little. 81. "Why, I just naturally supposed——" he began, and his voice died away.

82. "Why, my goodness, Suzie," my mother Bessie said, and she leaned over farther to look down at Suzie, "surely you don't want to keep on being engaged to a man who's in love with somebody else!" 83. She looked at Henry encouragingly. 84. "Elsie's really terrific looking," she said. 85. "And I expect maybe she can learn to cook simple things. 86. Like cabbage and cauliflower."

87. "I'm sure it doesn't matter to Henry if Elsie can learn to cook or not," Suzie said to my mother Bessie. 88. She sounded very calm and wise. 89. "At least not now," she added gently.

90. Henry turned dark red again. 91. He looked at his feet and didn't say a thing.

92. "All Elsie's underclothes are colored," said Janet. 93. "Blue and pink and fuchsia and chartreuse. 94. She says that when she feels like a color, she feels like it all the way through."

95. "What do you want me to do, Suzie?" said Henry. 96. He looked very unhappy.

97. Suzie looked at Henry thoughtfully. 98. "Sunset is a very small town," she said. 99. "Isn't it, Henry?"

100. "Why, yes," said Henry. 101. He looked puzzled. 102. "It has a population of five thousand."

103. "And there aren't very many eligible young men here, are there, Henry?" 104. Suzie held her head high and in spite of the jeans and the plaid shirt and the streak of red paint across one cheek, she looked very dignified. 105. "A girl in Sunset has a very small opportunity to meet nice young men, Henry. 106. Even Elsie would admit that."

107. "Yes, I guess so, Suzie," said Henry unhappily.

108. "Then," said Suzie firmly, "I figure that I still have a right to be engaged. 109. For two years, Henry, I have devoted all my time to getting engaged. 110. I bought pretty clothes, and I cooked company dinners, and I filled a hope chest with tea towels and table-cloths and napkins." 111. Delicately, my sister did not mention sheets and pillowcases. 112. "So I think, Henry, that I have a right to be engaged."

113. Henry stared at her.

114. "Not to you, of course," said Suzie, and a pretty pink flush spread up over her face. 115. "I'm not one to hold a man who doesn't want me. 116. But I figure that you have an obligation to me, Henry. 117. I figure that since you are the one who wants to break the engagement, and not I, that you should find me someone else to be engaged to. 118. Someone nice, Henry. 119. Someone as nice as you are."

120. "You mean," said Henry, and his voice sounded startled, "that you want me to find you a—a husband?"

121. "My goodness, Suzie," said my mother Bessie admiringly, "that's a perfectly wonderful idea! 122. And it isn't," she said consolingly to Henry, "as if Suzie were not an attractive girl."

123. "I won't wear your ring any more, Henry," said Suzie, and she took off his ring and held it out to him. 124. "But I don't think you have a right to give it to another girl, until you find someone else to give me another one."

125. Henry let his jaw drop way down.

126. "We have always had a Wednesday night dinner date here at the house, haven't we, Henry?" she said. 127. "So may I expect you for dinner tomorrow night? 128. With a suitable young man for me to meet?"

129. And since Henry just stood there, staring at her, she said gently, "Goodby, Henry," and went inside.

130. Henry stood a moment longer, and then he turned and started around the corner of the house.

131. "Goodby, Henry," called my mother cheerfully. 132. Henry didn't even answer.

133. The next day I had to go to school. 134. All day long, until after I got home from school, I didn't know who was coming to dinner with Henry. 135. It was very hard waiting to find out. 136. It was the first thing I asked.

137. My mother Bessie was in the kitchen making a chocolate cake, and my sister Janet had on a new pink blouse and a new pink skirt and she was standing on a dining-room chair for my sister Suzie to see if the skirt was the proper length all the way around. 138. Our cat Violet was in the window washing her face.

139. I put my books down on the bottom step of the stairway and went into the kitchen to sample the icing. 140. "Who's coming to dinner tonight?" I said.

141. "Why, Henry, of course, darling," said my mother Bessie absently, and she gave an extra swirl to the icing.

142. I ran my finger around the mixing bowl and tasted the icing. 143. "But who's he bringing with him?" I said.

144. "Gordon Somebody," said my mother Bessie, and she tasted the icing, too. 145. "Janet, honey, I think my pearls would look nice with that pink blouse."

146. "Gordon Who?" I asked patiently. 147. Talking with my mother Bessie is like reading the footnotes of a book without reading the book.

148. "Gordon Walters," said my sister Suzie, looking at Janet's skirt critically. 149. "He's the new high-school science teacher who came here day before yesterday. 150. Henry knew him in the Navy."

151. I licked my fingers and went to stand in the dining-room doorway and looked at Suzie. 152. "You've changed your hair-do," I said. 153. "It makes you look very sharp. 154. But older."

155. Suzie stepped back and smiled at Janet approvingly, and then she looked at me thoughtfully. 156. "Does it?" she said. 157. "Bessie, honey, you run upstairs, and put on your pretty blue crepe dress, and I'll finish getting dinner ready."

158. Gordon Walters was a very nice-looking young man. 159. He had brown eyes and brown curly hair, and a nice smile, and all of

us Whitsetts liked him right away. 160. Even our cat Violet, who is a very discriminating cat, came up and rubbed against his ankles.

161. He smiled around at us when Henry introduced him and said how nice it was to be in a real home so soon after coming to town, a stranger.

162. "My goodness, Henry," said my mother Bessie approvingly, "I didn't really suppose you would know such a nice young man."

163. "Mrs. Whitsett is a wonderful hostess," said Henry hurriedly. 164. It would have been quite like my mother Bessie to explain the whole thing to Mr. Walters and tell him why Henry had brought him to see us.

165. "I understand you have your degree from the East," said Suzie when we had all sat down at the table. 166. With the smart black dress and her hair done up on top of her head, Suzie looked very fashionable. 167. "I know little of science, of course, but I am especially interested in psychology and philosophy. 168. I suppose you know a great deal about philosophy, Mr. Walters."

169. We all looked a little surprised, for while my sister Suzie is a very smart girl, she had not ever mentioned before that she was especially interested in psychology or philosophy.

170. "Why, no, I wouldn't say that," said Mr. Walters, and he looked across at my sister Janet who was wearing the new pink blouse and my mother Bessie's pearls. 171. "You know," he said, "I don't think I realized before what a beautiful state Oklahoma is." 172. The way he said it, Janet was Oklahoma.

173. "I read a book on advanced psychology just the other day that I thought was extremely interesting," said Suzie. 174. "I wonder if you have ever read it."

175. Mr. Walters looked at Suzie a little surprised. 176. "Why, no," he said politely. 177. "I haven't."

178. "But I haven't even told you the name of it, yet," said Suzie gently. 179. And even though my mother Bessie tried to say something, Suzie went on discussing the book, which seemed to be a very long and learned one.

180. All through the fried chicken and the hot biscuits and the strawberry preserves and the chocolate cake and ice cream, Suzie told about the book. 181. And Mr. Walters said yes, and no, and he thought so, and looked at my sister Janet in the pink blouse.

182. After dinner, my mother Bessie said that maybe we would all like to sit in the living room and listen to Suzie play the piano.

183. "Oh, but Janet is really the musical one of our family," said Suzie, and she smiled at Mr. Walters. 184. "I think maybe you would rather hear Janet sing and my mother Bessie play her accompaniment. 185. And then we can talk some more about philosophy."

186. And because somehow people always do what my sister Suzie says, we went into the living room and sat and listened to Janet sing and my mother Bessie play the piano. 187. They looked very nice together with their blond hair shining in the light.

188. Then the telephone rang and I went out into the hall to answer it, and it was Mrs. McNalley, one of my mother Bessie's friends, asking for a recipe for icebox cookies.

189. "You know," said Mr. Walters, and he jumped up and smiled around at us, "I used to play the piano a little. 190. Let me try your accompaniment, Miss Janet, while your mother is talking over the telephone."

191. It was like that all evening long, with Mr. Walters playing the piano for Janet to sing, and Suzie and Henry and me just sitting and listening. 192. And finally when they stood up to go, Henry was looking at Mr. Walters very grimly, as if he had been greatly disappointed in the judgment of a friend.

193. But Mr. Walters didn't even seem to notice. 194. "My, I don't know when I've had such an enjoyable evening," he said, and he shook hands all around beginning with my mother Bessie and ending with Janet, and then he just stood there, holding Janet's hand. 195. "It's wonderful to talk again with such a beautiful and charming girl," he said, smiling down at her. 196. "You can't imagine how tired I am of so-called intellectual conversations."

197. Henry looked at him a little coldly. 198. "I shouldn't say that intellect is exactly a handicap to anyone," he said.

199. But Mr. Walters stared back at Henry just as coldly. 200. "It depends on your point of view," he said.

201. And when Henry said goodby, he pressed Suzie's hand, almost as if he were telling her not to feel bad about Mr. Walters' liking Janet more than her. 202. "I'll call you tomorrow, Suzie," he said.

203. After we had closed the door, my sister Janet turned to Suzie and there were tears shining in her blue eyes. 204. "Oh, Suzie," she said, "he asked me for a date, and I didn't know what to say, and he's going to call me tomorrow." 205. Her pretty, soft lips quivered.

206. "You'll say yes, of course," Suzie said, and she went over and hugged Janet's shoulders. 207. "He's just the man for you."

208. "Do you really think so, Suzie?" said Janet, and she looked at Suzie anxiously. 209. "Don't you like him at all?"

210. "I'd love him—for a brother-in-law," said Suzie firmly, and she smiled and kissed Janet and turned out the lights in the living room.

211. The next day was Thursday, and my sister Janet had a date with Mr. Walters. 212. We helped her get ready. 213. She wore her green silk dress and a little green hat with ribbons and with her pretty blond hair she looked like a daffodil shining in the sun.

214. "Why don't you wear my pink blouse tonight, Suzie?" she said. 215. "It would look wonderful on you, and the new man hasn't seen it."

216. The new man was the man Henry was going to bring out. 217. His name was Mr. Tomlison, and he was Henry's uncle from Texas. 218. He was sorry, Henry had told Suzie over the telephone, that Mr. Walters had been so young. 219. His uncle, he said, was older. 220. He was a widower and forty years old, and had some sense in his head, but, of course, he was very young for his age, too.

221. "I believe I will wear it," said Suzie. 222. "The pink will go nicely with my hair." 223. She held the blouse up to her. 224. It did go nicely. 225. With her dark hair shining and loose, she looked about sixteen.

226. At six o'clock Mr. Walters called for Janet to take her out to dinner, and at eight o'clock Henry came with Mr. Tomlison.

227. Mr. Tomlison was very nice. 228. He was little and plump and wore a checked suit and his hair brushed carefully over a bald spot.

229. My mother Bessie opened the door, and at first everything was confused because Mr. Tomlison got mixed up. 230. He thought my mother Bessie was Suzie. 231. And even when Henry explained that she was our mother, and that Suzie was Suzie, Mr. Tomlison still looked mixed up.

232. "I'm so happy you could come, Mr. Tomlison," said my mother Bessie. 233. She had to talk very loud because our radio was playing dance music. 234. "Do come on into the living room."

235. Mr. Tomlison followed my mother Bessie.

236. "This is my favorite dance program," said Suzie. 237. "Do you like to dance, Mr. Tomlison?" 238. She held up her arms gracefully and snapped her fingers.

239. Mr. Tomlison looked startled and backed off a little.

240. "My goodness, Suzie," said my mother Bessie, and she smiled encouragingly at Mr. Tomlison. 241. "Of course Mr. Tomlison dances, but he probably would prefer just sitting and talking."

242. "Yes, indeed," said Mr. Tomlison eagerly and he looked around for a chair. 243. "You know," he went on after we had all sat down, "I can't believe that you are the mother of these two strapping big girls, Mrs. Whitsett."

244. My mother Bessie looked at Suzie and me surprised, the way she always does.

245. "Suzie is a very talented girl," said Henry, looking at Mr. Tomlison. 246. "She is a rare combination of youth and beauty and brains."

247. Suzie smiled at Mr. Tomlison, but he was still looking at my mother Bessie. 248. He hadn't even listened to Henry. 249. "You know," he said, "it's nice to see such a lovely old-fashioned home again after having lived in hotels with furniture that is all angles."

250. "Mother is a wonderful housekeeper," said Suzie. 251. "You must come to dinner sometime, Mr. Tomlison, and eat her fried chicken and hot biscuits."

252. Mr. Tomlison looked at my mother Bessie warmly. 253. "I would love to come to dinner," he said.

254. "Why, of course," said my mother Bessie, and she smiled but looked a little puzzled.

255. "Look, Henry," said Mr. Tomlison briskly, "why don't you two young people go somewhere and dance, and let Mrs. Whitsett and me visit? 256. I know," and he looked at my mother eagerly, "that we must have many things in common."

257. Suzie got up and turned off the radio then, and looked at Henry a little sorrowfully, and Henry put his lips together in a thin line and looked at his uncle disapprovingly.

258. "We can all go to the movies," he said.

259. "But, Henry," said Suzie, and she frowned a little, "do you think Elsie would understand? 260. I mean, if she saw us together again?"

261. So Henry sat back down again, and my mother Bessie said nervously why didn't they all play bridge? 262. Everybody liked

bridge. 263. So she and Mr. Tomlison played partners against Henry and Suzie. 264. From where I sat at the dining-room table working on geometry, I could see them. 265. Mr. Tomlison treated Suzie as if she were just a child; he said he couldn't believe that she was a grown-up young lady. 266. He said that Mrs. Whitsett didn't look old enough to have a grown daughter.

267. And finally when he and Henry left, Mr. Tomlison turned and shook my mother Bessie's hand and told her that this was certainly the happiest evening he had had in a long time, and he was going to be eternally grateful to this young scamp, his nephew.

268. Henry just looked at his uncle, Mr. Tomlison, as if he were seeing him for the first time. 269. As if the checked suit he wore, and the little bald spot he tried to hide, didn't really mean he was young for his age at all.

270. "You know, Suzie," said my mother Bessie when we had closed the door, "I believe Mr. Tomlison likes me."

271. "Of course he does," said Suzie warmly, and she leaned over and kissed my mother Bessie. 272. "I bet he proposes right away."

273. My mother Bessie rounded her eyes and said as if she were shocked, "Oh, no, Suzie, I couldn't."

274. "Of course you can," said Suzie firmly; "you'll be the prettiest bride in Oklahoma. 275. You and Janet." 276. She turned out the light thoughtfully then and went up the stairs without even looking around at us.

277. The next morning Henry telephoned early. 278. I went out into the hall to listen. 279. "Why, that's all right, Henry," Suzie was saying. 280. "That's fine, Henry," and she hung up the receiver very quietly.

281. "Is Henry bringing someone else tonight?" I asked interestedly.

282. Suzie looked at me absently. 283. "We're double-dating tonight," she said. 284. "Henry and Elsie Butterfield, and Howard Burke and me. 285. Howard is from Chicago. 286. Henry knew him in college."

287. It was odd having so many men coming to our house. 288. First, Janet and Mr. Walters going out to dinner, and then my mother Bessie and Mr. Tomlison going to a concert, and now here was Henry bringing out another man.

289. It was exciting.

290. Janet and my mother Bessie had already gone when Henry came. 291. I opened the door, and there was Henry and Elsie, who is a short plump blonde with very light blue eyes, and a tall dark young man with shiny hair.

292. "Is Suzie ready, Laurie?" said Henry. 293. He looked a little unhappy, and he stared around the room and then up the stairs. 294. "We thought we'd go to the club dance." 295. Every Friday night there is a dance at the Sunset Country Club.

296. Elsie had on a fluffy green dress that made her look like a badly wrapped Christmas package, and I wondered if maybe her underclothes were green, too. 297. "Goodness," she said, "but I do believe I could dance the whole night through," and she put one hand on Henry's arm and the other one on the arm of the dark young man and took a couple of steps. 298. She looked silly.

299. "Suzie!" I called up the stairs. 300. "Henry's here!"

301. Suzie came down the stairs. 302. She had on a yellow dress, and her dark hair was very smooth and shining, and she looked beautiful. 303. She looked neat and trim and all of a piece, like a flower. 304. The man with the shiny hair gave a low whistle and took a step toward her. 305. "Hel-lo, Princess!" he said.

306. Suzie smiled at him.

307. "Suzie," said Henry, and he stepped forward between Suzie and the young man, "this is Howard Burke."

308. Howard Burke went around Henry and took Suzie's hand. 309. "Well," he said, and showed his teeth, "I always thought that surely I had some reason for living."

310. Suzie smiled at him again.

311. "Surely," he said, and he pressed her hand, "you don't live in this little jerkwater town!"

312. "Suzie," said Henry firmly, and he moved closer to her, "is a small-town girl."

313. "I don't believe it," said Howard Burke. 314. "New York, maybe, San Francisco, yes. 315. Paris, certainly." 316. The way he said the words, they sounded like poetry.

317. "Now Elsie here has been in all those places," said Henry. 318. "Elsie is really well-traveled. 319. You certainly can't call Elsie a small-town girl."

320. Elsie tossed back her hair and simpered at Mr. Burke, and Henry looked at her as if he were really seeing her for the first time.

321. But Mr. Burke didn't take his eyes off Suzie. 322. "You need a

proper setting," he said softly. 323. "Jewels, limousines, servants
. . ."

324. Henry looked disgusted. 325. "Suzie is the best fisherman in
Sunset," he said. 326. "Suzie won't go out with a man who can't set
a trotline or rope a steer."

327. Suzie looked at Henry and then at Howard Burke and she
let her eyes widen. 328. "I sure do like he-men, mister," she said.
329. "Can you rope a steer?"

330. Howard Burke looked surprised. 331. He also looked suspicious. 332. "If you are being humorous," he said formally, "I'm
afraid I fail to see the humor."

333. "Our friends," said Elsie, and she moved over and put her
hand on Mr. Burke's arm, "have a queer sense of humor. 334. I'm
afraid they are being funny at your expense."

335. "I see," said Mr. Burke.

336. "Look," said Henry quickly, "why don't you two go on to the
dance, and let us come later? 337. Howard is a wonderful dancer,
Elsie. 338. And he's got charm and money and personality, none of
which I have."

339. "Really," said Elsie coldly, "you're being very rude, Henry!"
340. But she tightened her hand on Mr. Burke's arm.

341. "Well," said Henry and he looked at Suzie humbly, "it certainly isn't the first time."

342. Mr. Burke bowed a little formally then to Suzie, and he and
Elsie went out of the room.

343. "Good evening, Henry," said Suzie, and she started to go up
the stairs, but Henry caught her hand pleadingly. 344. "Suzie, please
listen to me. 345. I want to talk with you."

346. Suzie stood and tilted her head politely. 347. "Yes, Henry?"
she said.

348. "No," said Henry miserably, "not here. 349. Come sit down,
Suzie, and I'll explain."

350. Suzie went over to our old wing chair by the fireplace and sat
down and Henry sat down across from her and wiped his forehead
with his handkerchief.

351. "Suzie," he said, "I've been an awful fool."

352. Suzie didn't say anything.

353. Henry cleared his throat. 354. "Can't you possibly forgive me,
Suzie? 355. Just a little bit?"

356. "Why, everything is quite all right, Henry," said Suzie, and

she smiled at him. 357. Henry got up eagerly and then sat down on a footstool at her feet and took her hand.

358. Suzie withdrew her hand gently. 359. "I mean it's all right, you don't have to find someone for me, Henry. 360. I've decided not to marry anyone."

361. "Oh, Suzie," said Henry, and he brought out the ring and held it out to her. 362. "Won't you take it back, Suzie, and be engaged to me all over again? 363. I love you, Suzie."

364. Suzie looked at the ring thoughtfully. 365. "It's a beautiful ring, Henry," she said, and she sighed a little. 366. "But I don't know. 367. I think maybe we might start all over again, though. 368. Would you like to start over, Henry? 369. We could pretend that we've just met again."

370. "Oh, yes," breathed Henry, and he took her hand once more. 371. "Can I have a date tonight, Suzie? 372. And tomorrow night, and the next?"

373. Since they weren't paying any attention to me at all, I went out to the kitchen to see if there was any more angel-food cake. 374. Our cat Violet got up from the window seat in the dining room and yawned and stretched and came out, too. 375. It occurred to me that in two more years I'll be seventeen. 376. By that time no doubt my mother Bessie and my sisters Janet and Suzie will be old married people.

377. I cut myself a piece of cake and gave some to Violet. 378. I decided that I will live with my sister Suzie. 379. When you are seventeen, it is nice to be associated with a woman who has brains.

SECTION A-3

I here offer you for your study a novelette entitled *Eva? Caroline?* by Allan Vaughan Elston, reprinted here by permission of the author. Every writer who has had some success in writing short stories may hope to write and sell a novelette and so receive a bigger check. Elsewhere in this book you will find some discussion of the novelette as a form. Before reading the example offered here, I suggest that you consult this passage—in Chapter 14.

I have chosen this novelette for your study, *first,* because it is a good one, built around an exciting idea with convincing characters, interesting setting, and never-flagging suspense. The problem, though unusual to a degree, nevertheless is skillfully made plausible throughout. The hero, in spite of his somewhat stiff and unyielding character, is made to hold our sympathy, and we wish him well when he sets off to make amends in the last paragraph.

This novelette—so skillfully written as to seem almost a tour de force—deals with one of the most difficult situations to handle sympathetically—that of false suspicion; and also with a problem most difficult to make plausible—that of mistaken identity. The manner in which the author skillfully and gracefully brings off his story to the satisfaction of the reader is worthy of admiration. A less skillful writer could only have made the story seem artificial and contrived.

Much of his story is told in dialogue so well handled that, though it seems quite natural speech and never wrenched from the familiar, it nevertheless advances the story with unbroken continuity. The style is suited to the subject matter. Nobody speaks out of character.

Here, as often in the novelette, the story is in effect one great developing situation or discovery and reversal. Of course this great discovery and reversal is implemented by a goodly number of lesser examples of the same device. Our hero here moves from an absolute No to an absolute Yes. And the curve of his progress from one pole to the other is the pattern of this story. This is one of the most fruitful patterns a novelette can follow.

Now turn to the novelette *Eva? Caroline?*, make a thorough study of it, following the suggestions of Work Program 11, Section A-3.

Eva? Caroline? [1]

BY ALLAN VAUGHAN ELSTON

1. "That," Roger Marsh asserted with a strained effort to speak calmly, "is absurd and impossible. 2. My wife died four years ago."

3. Inspector Whipple, who had just arrived in Baltimore to interview Roger Marsh, gave the photograph a puzzled stare. 4. It was the picture of a woman, one which he had taken himself only day

[1] Copyright, 1949, by Allan Vaughan Elston.

226

before yesterday in Seattle. 5. "Then this," he said, "can't be your wife."

6. Roger tried hard to control himself. 7. "Of course not," he said stiffly.

8. "You admit it looks like her?"

9. "I admit it does. 10. If you'd shown it to me four years ago I might have sworn it was Caroline. 11. But since you took it only this week, it *has* to be someone else."

12. They were in the drawing-room of the old Marsh house. 13. Five generations of Marshes had lived here amid high-ceilinged elegance, the gentlest and richest of the old Maryland culture.

14. And Roger Marsh, severely handsome at thirty-three, looked part of it. 15. A portrait of his great-grandfather over the mantel had the same narrow granite face, the uncompromising gaze of a man who doesn't believe in change. 16. Apparent too was a long-bred restraint which would be instantly revolted by anything sensational.

17. Inspector Whipple studied the man sitting opposite him, then he said, "Who, Mr. Marsh, was with your wife when she died?"

18. Roger reminded himself that this police officer was his guest for the moment and must be treated as such. 19. When he spoke, it was with a carefully disciplined patience. 20. "I was. 21. So was our family doctor. 22. So was a nurse at a local hospital."

23. "Tell me the how, when and where of it, Mr. Marsh. 24. You'd been married how long?"

25. "I was married eight years ago," Roger told him. 26. "Seven years ago I went into the army. 27. Judge Advocate's department, foreign service. 28. In London, three years later, I received a cablegram from Dr. Cawfield, our family physician, saying my wife had pneumonia. 29. So I got an emergency leave and flew home."

30. "Was she still living when you arrived?"

31. "Yes, but failing fast. 32. She lingered on for six more days."

33. "Did she have a twin sister? 34. An identical twin?"

35. "She did not," Roger said. 36. "What are you suggesting, Inspector?"

37. "You're quite certain the woman who died was your wife?"

38. With a stern effort Roger controlled his irritation. 39. "Are you implying I didn't know my own wife? 40. I tell you I was there at her bedside. 41. So was Dr. Cawfield. 42. During those last six days she was occasionally able to talk and receive visitors. 43. Many of her closest friends called to see her."

44. "Was her casket open at the funeral? 45. Did lots of people who knew her well see her then?"

46. "Scores of them," Roger said, his face flushed.

47. "The woman in Seattle," Whipple explained, "is known to the police as Eva Lang. 48. She's a confidence woman and five years ago she killed a man in Detroit. 49. The crime was witnessed. 50. Police had a good description of her but no fingerprints. 51. A week ago we raided a farm near Walla Walla, Washington, where four wanted men were hiding out. 52. Three of them were killed in the fight; the fourth escaped. 53. But we picked up a woman living with them who was identified as Eva Lang. 54. Her defense is: 'I'm not Eva Lang; I'm Mrs. Roger Marsh.'"

55. Roger reclaimed the photograph and gave it a long bitter stare. 56. "This woman just happens to look like Caroline. 57. So now she's using that fact to save her life."

58. "She gave us a list of twenty-eight people in Baltimore who, she claims, will verify that she's Caroline Marsh," Inspector Whipple said. 59. He handed Roger a list of names.

60. Roger saw that his own name headed it. 61. Next came Dr. Cawfield; Effie Foster, who had been Caroline's most intimate friend, was third. 62. Others on the list were neighbors, clubwomen, friends.

63. "This is the most ridiculous hoax I ever heard of," Roger said. 64. "These same people were at her funeral."

65. Whipple nodded in sympathy. 66. "No doubt you're right. 67. But it's something we have to straighten out. 68. Did your wife have any distinguishing scars?"

69. Roger concentrated. 70. "Only one," he said. 71. "Just after we were married, she burned the third knuckle of her right hand with a hot iron. 72. It left a small star-shaped white scar."

73. The statement startled Whipple. 74. "Our prisoner in Seattle," he said, "also has a burn scar on the third knuckle of her right hand."

75. Roger closed his eyes for a moment. 76. This can't be happening, he thought. 77. His mind clung stubbornly to the one certain fact: Caroline's death four years ago. 78. "If Caroline had had a twin sister," he snapped, "she would have told me. 79. I don't want to be brusque, Inspector, but I have no desire to be dragged into this."

80. "The trouble is, you're already in," Whipple argued amiably. 81. "It's like this: the Detroit police want to try Eva Lang for that murder she committed five years ago. 82. But when she claimed she's your wife and named twenty-eight witnesses to prove it, Detroit

got worried. 83. If she really is the wife of a wealthy Maryland lawyer, extraditing her as Eva Lang might get them in hot water. 84. So they tell us to disprove the Marsh angle first, then they'll take her to Detroit for trial. 85. That's why I came here to Baltimore. 86. I want to take the top three persons named on the list back with me to Seattle. 87. They can look at her, talk to her and say whether she's your wife."

88. "You want to take me, Dr. Cawfield and Effie Foster clear across the continent just to say a living impostor isn't a woman who died four years ago? 89. I won't do it. 90. Talk to Dr. Cawfield while you're here and with nurses at the hospital and the mortician if you want to; then go back to Seattle and tell Eva Lang to retract her ridiculous statement."

91. Whipple smiled tolerantly. 92. "I don't blame you for wanting to avoid publicity. 93. But you're heading right into it. 94. Because ultimately she'll go on trial for murder and her defense will be that she's your wife. 95. You yourself will be subpoenaed as a witness to identify her. 96. It'll be a field day for the papers. 97. So why not silence her at once, in the privacy of the Seattle jail? 98. Think it over, Mr. Marsh."

99. Reluctantly Roger realized the inspector was right. 100. "Very well," he agreed. 101. "I'll go. 102. She may look like Caroline, but she isn't. 103. I can trip her up with questions. 104. Small details that no one but Caroline could know."

105. Whipple gave a shrewd nod. 106. "That's the idea. 107. And now about taking along Dr. Cawfield and some close woman friend. 108. We want to keep this hush-hush if we can. 109. So why not call them up and ask them to come over?"

110. An hour later Inspector Whipple sat facing an audience of three. 111. Dr. Elias Cawfield, gray, oldish, testy, was taking Whipple's questions as an insult to his professional integrity. 112. "I issued that death certificate myself," he blazed at Whipple. 113. "I'll have you know, sir, that——"

114. Effie Foster, a plump blonde of Roger's age, put a hand over the doctor's lips. 115. "Now let's not get excited," she soothed. 116. "That woman's just trying to put one over and of course we won't let her get away with it."

117. "Does she presume to give any details as to how she's been spending the last four years?" Roger asked the inspector.

118. "Plenty of them," Whipple said. 119. "'Personally, I don't be-

lieve her, not for a minute. 120. I think she's Eva Lang, a career adventuress guilty of murder and trying to avoid the penalty by claiming another identity."

121. "If she gave details," Roger said, "let's hear them."

122. "She claims that you, her husband, went off to war seven years ago, leaving her in this house with a couple of servants. 123. But as the war went on and the housing and man-power shortages grew, she turned over the lower floor to a society of ladies who made bandages for veterans, laid off the servants and occupied the second floor alone."

124. Roger, Effie and Dr. Cawfield exchanged glances. 125. "That's exactly what Caroline did!" Effie exclaimed.

126. Roger nodded. 127. "Yes, she wrote me about it. 128. For the last year of her life she lived upstairs alone. 129. Everybody knows that. 130. So what?"

131. Whipple resumed: "She says that one night she answered a knock at the door and her own image walked in. 132. The image said, 'You're Caroline, I suppose. 133. I'm Evelyn Blythe.' "

134. Again Roger nodded. "My wife's maiden name was Blythe. 135. But she never mentioned an Evelyn."

136. "What members of the Blythe family did you know?" Whipple asked.

137. "None but Caroline herself. 138. She was twenty-three when I met her, and a salesgirl in a New York department store. 139. When I got to know her better she told me her mother had died when she was fourteen, that she'd been making her own living ever since and that she couldn't remember her father at all. 140. She said her mother would never talk about her father. 141. She knew of no living relatives."

142. "Bear in mind, what I'm telling you is Eva Lang's story, not mine," Whipple cautioned. 143. "It goes on like this: Evelyn told Caroline that they were identical twins; that their father and mother had separated when they were small children, each taking a twin. 144. The father took Evelyn, the mother Caroline. 145. But the father had a photograph of his wife. 146. At his death Evelyn acquired it. 147. She showed it to Caroline and Caroline definitely recognized her own mother. 148. That, plus the testimony of a mirror, convinced Caroline that they were twin sisters. 149. Eva Lang says now, 'I'd always hungered for a blood relative; so I, Caroline Blythe Marsh, took Evelyn to my heart.' "

150. Roger listened, tense and incredulous. 151. Dr. Cawfield snorted: "It's preposterous!"

152. "I can accept the fact of twins," Whipple asserted, "because you all admit that this photograph looks like Caroline. 153. But I don't believe that Eva Lang is Caroline. 154. For my money, she's Evelyn."

155. Roger protested, "It won't stand up, Inspector. 156. Even if we concede that Caroline could have had a twin sister without knowing it, it still won't stand up. 157. Because my wife would have presented this sister to her friends. 158. She would have written me all about it."

159. "According to Eva Lang," Whipple countered, "that was her first and natural impulse. 160. But Evelyn begged her not to. 161. She said she was in trouble. 162. Some men were looking for her and she mustn't let them find her. 163. If Evelyn could just hide here till the men hunting for her gave up and left town——"

164. The pain on Roger's face stopped Whipple. 165. Cawfield and Effie Foster were hardly less shocked. 166. Again Whipple reminded them, "It's Eva Lang's story, not mine."

167. "Go on," Roger said.

168. "It took a lot of pleading by Evelyn. 169. But Caroline, naturally sympathetic and warm-hearted, finally agreed to let her stay in hiding. 170. Evelyn said a few weeks would be long enough; then everything would be safe and she would go away. 171. Actually Evelyn stayed at least two months. 172. She wore Caroline's clothes and fixed her hair like Caroline's. 173. That's why you, Mrs. Foster, were fooled when you popped in unannounced on a day Caroline was out shopping and you chatted ten minutes with Evelyn, thinking she was Caroline."

174. "I?" Effie exclaimed. 175. "Of course I didn't. 176. I'd have known she wasn't Caroline."

177. "You were rounding up some old clothes," Whipple suggested, "for a rummage sale. 178. Eva Lang says Evelyn told her about it when she got home. 179. Evelyn was afraid to turn you down. 180. So she took a few outmoded things from Caroline's closet and gave them to you. 181. You remember the incident, Mrs. Foster?"

182. "I did come here," Effie admitted, "and Caroline gave me a bundle of clothes. 183. But it was Caroline herself."

184. "Take a look at this." 185. Whipple produced a latchkey from

his pocket. 186. "We found it in Eva Lang's purse. 187. See if it fits the front door."

188. Roger took the key to the door and tried it in the lock. 189. The key was a perfect fit.

190. "If you showed me a hundred keys," he muttered, "you still couldn't convince me."

191. "I'm not trying to convince you, Mr. Marsh. 192. I'm just showing you what you're up against with this Lang woman. 193. It's pretty clear the real story is this: After two or three months here, Evelyn made good on her promise and slipped away. 194. No doubt she'd just been hiding out so the police wouldn't grab her for the Detroit murder. 195. When things cooled off she drifted back to the underworld she came from. 196. Then she read in the papers about Caroline's death and got an idea for defense if she was ever picked up. 197. She'd swear she was Caroline and that it was Evelyn who had died in Baltimore. 198. Preparing for it, she took a hot iron and burned the third knuckle of her right hand. 199. But that, of course, isn't the way Eva Lang tells it."

200. "How does Eva Lang tell it?" Roger asked.

201. "She claims that she, Caroline, was wakened one night by coughing. 202. Evelyn had caught a bad cold. 203. So Caroline walked two blocks to a drugstore to get a cough remedy for Evelyn. 204. On the way home two toughies stopped her. 205. 'So it's little Eva,' they said. 206. 'We been lookin' all over for you, Eva. 207. We can't risk lettin' cops pick you up. 208. They'd put on the heat and you might talk. 209. So we're takin' you home.' 210. The next thing she knew she was riding in a closed car."

211. "And she didn't call out to the first passer-by?" Dr. Cawfield scoffed.

212. "She says she was taped up, hands, feet and mouth. 213. The men drove only by night. 214. A week of nights took them to an isolated farm in the State of Washington. 215. Two other men were there, one of them a forger named Duke Smedley. 216. He'd been Evelyn's sweetheart. 217. He walked up to her and took her in his arms. 218. 'Hello, Eva,' he said and kissed her. 219. She slapped him, crying, 'I'm not Eva.' 220. He looked more closely at her. 221. 'Damn it, you're not Eva,' he said. 222. He turned in fury on the two men. 223. 'You stupid fools got the wrong girl.'

224. "Three of them still thought she was Eva; only Duke Smedley

was sure she wasn't. 225. But they had her. 226. They didn't set her free. 227. It meant their necks if they did. 228. So they held her."

229. "For four years?" Cawfield said derisively.

230. "The woman says they didn't mean to. 231. Three of them wanted to kill her right away. 232. But Duke Smedley wouldn't let 'em because she looked so much like Eva. 233. Pretty soon they saw the notice of Mrs. Marsh's death in the Baltimore papers. 234. Smedley got the Baltimore papers to see if Caroline's disappearance would be discovered. 235. His argument then was: 'We don't need to do away with her; she's dead already. 236. Nobody's looking for her.' 237. Too, there was the idea of holding her as a hostage, an ace in the hole if it ever came to a showdown with the police. 238. So the stalemate dragged on, month after month."

239. "I don't believe it," Roger said.

240. "Nor I. 241. The police theory is that Eva Lang went there of her own free will and was part of the mob."

242. Roger rose and crossed the room to stand before the portrait of his great-grandfather. 243. His face, more than ever like pale granite, was brooding and bitter. 244. Nothing like this had ever before happened to the Marshes.

245. "She ought to know that she hasn't a chance in the world to put this over."

246. "I think she does know it," Whipple agreed. 247. "I don't think she has the least idea of being accepted and taken back into your home. 248. But she can get an acquittal if just one juror out of twelve feels a reasonable doubt. 249. Eleven can be as sure as you are that she's an impostor. 250. But if only one juror thinks, well, maybe she *is* Mrs. Marsh, that would be enough. 251. And that, I figure, is all she wants."

252. "The devil it is!" Dr. Cawfield growled. 253. "She'll be after money too, once she's free. 254. She'll pester Roger, parading as his poor disowned wife, till he makes a settlement."

255. "Cheer up," Effie Foster urged breezily. 256. "It's a headache, of course, but it mustn't get us down. 257. We'll go to Seattle and ask her questions. 258. 'If you're Caroline, what did I give you for your birthday five years ago?'"

259. Dr. Cawfield turned to Roger. 260. "Hadn't we better take along your aunt and uncle?"

261. Roger considered for a moment, then shook his head. 262. His Uncle Carey was a fire-eater; he'd want to sue the Seattle police.

263. Aunt Harriet was just the opposite. 264. She was a gullible sentimentalist. 265. Show her an underdog, like Eva Lang, and she'd want to start petting it right away. 266. "No, Doctor. 267. Just the three of us. 268. I'll charter a plane. 269. We'll meet at the airport in the morning."

270. By the time the plane was flying westward Roger Marsh had made a concession. 271. Although the Marsh in him erected an iron wall against any part of Eva Lang's claim, the lawyer in him couldn't deny certain glaring bits of evidence. 272. Evelyn Blythe, alias Eva Lang, was not his wife but she *was* his sister-in-law. 273. And she *had* spent two months visiting his wife.

274. Yes, he thought, reviewing Eva Lang's story once more as he looked out the window of the plane, that much he would concede, but no more. 275. Then he remembered something and beckoned to Inspector Whipple.

276. "I've just thought of something," Roger said when the inspector sat down beside him. 277. "Caroline kept a diary. 278. She made entries every night—all sorts of personal details."

279. "Well, what about it?"

280. "After the funeral four years ago, I happened to think of the diary. 281. It was something too intimate to be left lying around loose in the house. 282. But I couldn't find it. 283. I looked everywhere—it was gone. 284. So I concluded that Caroline had destroyed it herself."

285. Whipple nodded. 286. "I see. 287. And now you're afraid Evelyn took it away with her?"

288. "It's possible," Roger brooded.

289. "If Eva Lang took it," Whipple admitted, "she's had four years to memorize everything in it. 290. She can answer questions like a fox."

291. "You said four men were at the farm with her. 292. Three were killed in the raid and one escaped. 293. Which one?"

294. "Duke Smedley. 295. Smoothest confidence man in the business. 296. The police are after him, coast to coast, on a dozen counts."

297. "He was Eva Lang's sweetheart?"

298. "So our prisoner says. 299. But when he knew she wasn't Eva he gave her a break because she was Eva's sister. 300. It's more logical to assume she was and is Duke Smedley's girl, and that she went back of her own free will to join him at the farm."

301. Roger stoked a pipe nervously. 302. "The point is, Inspector, he's alive. 303. He may be picked up. 304. And he knows the truth about Eva Lang."

305. "He'll be picked up all right. 306. He has a police record. 307. Here's his picture."

308. Whipple opened his suitcase and brought out a photograph. 309. It showed a man of exceptional good looks, well dressed and with an air of sophistication.

310. "He's the tops in his racket," Whipple said. 311. "One time he—but what's the matter, Mr. Marsh?" 312. Roger was staring with a strange intensity at the photograph.

313. "I've a feeling," Roger murmured, "that I've seen this man before. 314. I can't remember when or where. 315. But I'm sure I've seen him."

316. "Then maybe this goes deeper than we think, Mr.Marsh. 317. Maybe he's back of the whole thing."

318. "It's hardly possible," Roger said. 319. "I've a feeling it was years ago when I saw him. 320. Perhaps while I was in the army. 321. He couldn't have schemed this that far ahead."

322. "Well, keep the picture," Whipple insisted. 323. "We have other copies. 324. Look at it every once in a while. 325. Maybe you'll remember where you saw him."

326. A morning later Inspector Whipple led Effie Foster, Dr. Cawfield and Roger Marsh into a reception room at the Seattle jail. 327. Roger stood stiffly, preparing himself for the ordeal of disowning this woman.

328. A police matron came in. 329. Quietly she reported, "I've just brought her to the inspection room. 330. Are these the identifiers?"

331. Whipple nodded. 332. Then he saw the dread on Roger's face and suggested, "Would you rather see her first without her seeing you, Mr. Marsh? 333. You may if you like. 334. Later, of course, you'll have to talk with her for a voice test."

335. "We'd like to see her first," Roger said.

336. "Then step this way." 337. Whipple led him to a far wall of the room and stood him in front of a closed panel. 338. When he opened the panel a circular glass pane was exposed. 339. It was about the size of a porthole in a ship's cabin. 340. Through it Roger could see clearly into the room beyond.

341. Seated in the center of that room, under a bright light, was the prisoner Eva Lang. 342. She was in half profile to Roger. 343.

235

Instantly he felt a surge of relief. 344. For the seated woman didn't look nearly so much like Caroline as he had expected. 345. She seemed much older. 346. There were streaks of gray in her hair. 347. Roger remembered the velvety smoothness of Caroline's skin. 348. The face of this woman was hard. 349. Nothing of Caroline's sweet gentle character was etched there. 350. Instead of Caroline's calm complacent gaze, Roger saw a tense bitter defiance. 351. The eyes were brown, like Caroline's, and the hair was center-parted and fluffed at the sides, like Caroline's. 352. Evidently a hairdresser had worked on Eva Lang in her cell, doing everything possible to make her resemble Caroline. 353. The contours of her face were indeed quite like Caroline's and Roger could understand instantly why a photograph would be more convincing than the woman herself. 354. The photograph didn't show color; it showed only shape and lines. 355. And it failed to reveal character like the flesh itself.

356. Roger stared long and intently through the glass. 357. Then he closed the panel and stepped back to Inspector Whipple. 358. "Before God," he said, "I never saw that woman before."

359. "Your turn, Dr. Cawfield."

360. The doctor went to the panel, opened, peered through it. 361. In a moment he turned back with a snort. 362. "Just as I thought! 363. A masquerade! 364. A monstrous masquerade."

365. "Your turn, Mrs. Foster."

366. Effie Foster took more time than had either of the men. 367. When she closed the panel her face had a clouded disturbed look. 368. "She's not Caroline, of course. 369. But she *does* look like her in a sort of jaded way."

370. The police matron surprised them by speaking up. 371. "Wouldn't you look rather jaded yourself, Mrs. Foster, if you'd been slave and prisoner for four years to a gang of crooks?"

372. Effie flushed. 373. Inspector Whipple cut in quickly, "Well, we'll talk to her, Mrs. Kelly. 374. Right now. 375. That will be more conclusive."

376. Whipple led them through a door into the presence of the woman known as Eva Lang.

377. Roger Marsh breathed deeply in an attempt to slow his pounding heart. 378. This was the moment he'd been dreading.

379. She stood up as they entered, stared for a moment at Roger, her lips parted and her face lighting up. 380. Then she came toward

236

him, eager, confident, her hands outstretched. 381. "Roger! 382. I thought you'd never come!"

383. The uncompromising granite of Roger's face stopped her. 384. "You're not at all convincing, Miss Lang," he said stiffly.

385. The shock on her face was as though he'd struck her. 386. "You don't know me, Roger?"

387. "No," he said. 388. "I do not. 389. You'd know me, of course, if you were Caroline's guest for two months, because there were pictures of me all over the house."

390. Her dazed eyes stared at him a moment longer, then turned to Effie Foster. 391. Then to Dr. Cawfield.

392. Effie didn't speak. 393. Dr. Cawfield's stony face was answer enough.

394. Her eyes went back to Roger. 395. "You mean you're disowning me, Roger?"

396. "Hasn't this gone far enough, Miss Lang?" he parried.

397. For a moment he thought she'd burst into tears. 398. Instead the hardness and defiance came back to her face. 399. "What a fool I've been!" she said bitterly. 400. "To think you'd come and take me home! 401. I might have known you wouldn't! 402. You and your stiff Maryland pride!" 403. She laughed hysterically. 404. "It's so much easier to say you never knew me. 405. Will you take me back to my cell, Inspector? 406. They've seen the rogues' gallery. 407. They've said, yes, she's the rogue, not the wife."

408. Inspector Whipple said crisply, "First, Miss Lang, I've a few questions. 409. Please sit down."

410. She sat down, stiffly facing Whipple, ignoring the others.

411. It had been agreed that Whipple would ask the questions because, as a police officer, he could do so with more authority. 412. Effie had given him a list.

413. "What," Whipple asked, "did Effie Foster give Caroline Marsh for a birthday present five years ago?"

414. "I don't remember."

415. Effie smiled. 416. "You see?" she challenged.

417. "Effie," the accused woman retorted, "won a bridge prize at my house six years ago. 418. What was it?"

419. Effie gaped. 420. "I've forgotten," she admitted.

421. "You see?" 422. The woman's smile mocked her. 423. "That, I suppose, proves she isn't Effie Foster. 424. Go on, Inspector."

425. Whipple read from his list: "Roger Marsh has an aunt and

237

uncle. 426. What are their names, where do they live and what is their telephone number?"

427. "Uncle Carey and Aunt Harriet," the prisoner answered promptly, "live in Edgeton. 428. I've forgotten their phone number."

429. "Roger and Caroline Marsh were in an amateur play one time. 430. What was the play and what parts did they take?"

431. "It was William Tell. 432. Roger was William Tell and I was his son, with an apple on my head. 433. Ask me something hard, Inspector."

434. "Who was the chairman of the Community Chest committee Caroline Marsh once served on?"

435. "I can't remember."

436. Her voice, Roger thought, was a little like Caroline's but definitely bolder. 437. Caroline had been a timid quiet girl. 438. This woman was a fighter.

439. "When Dr. Cawfield was on vacation who was the doctor who substituted for him?"

440. "The name slips my mind, Inspector. 441. Perhaps if I think awhile, I'll remember."

442. Caroline, Roger was sure, would remember instantly. 443. Young and good-looking Dr. Joyce had in fact treated that burn on the third knuckle of Caroline's hand. 444. This woman, he saw, had a burn scar in the same place. 445. She must have inflicted it deliberately.

446. "Caroline and Roger Marsh had one serious quarrel during the first year of their married life. 447. What caused it?"

448. "As if I could forget!" 449. The woman smiled bitterly. 450. "Roger had a too beautiful secretary named Lucile Dutton. 451. I thought he admired her more than he should. 452. One day he went to Annapolis for a trial. 453. He forgot his briefcase. 454. Lucile carried it to him and he took her to lunch. 455. People saw them and told me. 456. I shouldn't have been jealous but I was. 457. And one word led to another."

458. Whipple looked at Roger and Roger, with a grimace, nodded. 459. "I suppose it was all in Caroline's diary," he murmured.

460. "Did Roger ever take Caroline to Honolulu?"

461. "Yes."

462. "What hotel did they stop at?"

463. "I can't remember. 464. It's been eight years."

465. "What was the occasion?"

466. "Our honeymoon."

467. "How long had Roger been married when he went into the army?"

468. "About a year."

469. "That was seven years ago. 470. How many times did Caroline see him after that?"

471. "Not once—until now. 472. Perhaps that's why he doesn't know me."

473. "Who introduced Roger to Caroline?"

474. "No one. 475. He went into a New York store to buy a bottle of perfume. 476. I was the clerk who sold it to him. 477. That's how we met."

478. All that, Roger kept assuring himself, could have been in Caroline's diary. 479. Or Caroline could have confided it during Evelyn's visit. 480. Undoubtedly this was Evelyn Blythe.

481. There were many more questions. 482. To about half of them the woman answered frankly, "I can't remember." 483. But certainly she had briefed herself on Caroline's past with a studied thoroughness. 484. The romantic incidents in it were the ones she knew best. 485. The very ones which Caroline, always a romanticist, would have been most likely to confide.

486. In the end Whipple turned to Roger. 487. "You still say this woman isn't your wife?"

488. "I do," Roger said.

489. Dr. Cawfield echoed him emphatically. 490. "Caroline Marsh died four years ago."

491. Whipple pressed a button and the police matron came in. 492. "We're finished," he said.

493. The prisoner followed Matron Kelly to an exit. 494. Then she turned defiantly to Roger Marsh. 495. "You've asked me a great many questions, Roger. 496. Now let me ask you one. 497. Did you ever read Matthew 19:5?"

498. Without waiting for a response she disappeared with the matron.

499. "The devil," Dr. Cawfield derided, "can cite Scripture for his purpose. 500. Let's get out of here."

501. As they went out Whipple said, "Pretty sharp, wasn't she? 502. Well, now that that's over, the Detroit police will extradite her for trial in Michigan. 503. I'll be glad to get rid of her. 504. Where to now, Mr. Marsh?"

505. "To a hotel," Roger said, "for a night's sleep. 506. Then back to Baltimore."

507. With Effie Foster and the doctor he taxied to a hotel. 508. In his room there Roger saw a Gideon Bible on the dresser. 509. He picked it up and turned to Matthew 19:5.

510. The verse read: "For this cause shall a man leave father and mother, and shall cleave to his wife: and they twain shall be one flesh."

511. When Roger's chartered plane glided to a landing at the Baltimore airport, he saw that the gateway was swarming with reporters.

512. "And look, Roger," Effie exclaimed, "isn't that your Uncle Carey and Aunt Harriet?"

513. "It's the whole town," Roger groaned. 514. "Blast them! 515. Why can't they leave us alone?"

516. Roger fought fiercely through people who waylaid them in the gateway, refusing to answer the questions hurled at him by newsmen. 517. He let Effie and Dr. Cawfield deal with them. 518. He himself broke away, flanked by his uncle and aunt. 519. Reporters, Uncle Carey was complaining, had awakened him at five o'clock this morning.

520. "And what," he demanded furiously, "are you going to do about it?" 521. He was short and bald. 522. His wife, Harriet, was tall and gray.

523. "Nothing," Roger said.

524. "You mean you'll let them drag the name of Marsh through ——"

525. "Oh, fiddlesticks!" Aunt Harriet broke in. 526. "That's all I've heard for forty years. 527. The proud unsullied name of Marsh! 528. For a century you've kept it out of headlines. 529. And now you're in them up to your necks." 530. Her eyes glittered. 531. She herself was a Claypole from the east shore.

532. "Harriet," Uncle Carey rebuked bleakly, "must you be flippant at a time like this? 533. Don't you realize what it means? 534. We're disgraced, all of us. 535. Now look, Roger, I've thought it over. 536. We'll all make a tour of South America till this horrible mess is over. 537. That way they can't drag us in at the trial."

538. "You can run if you want to," Roger said. 539. "I shan't."

540. Just as they reached Uncle Carey's car, Leslie Paxton, Roger's law partner, caught up with them. 541. "Roger," he demanded, "why

didn't you tell me about this? 542. Think of the firm! 543. Have you seen the latest editions?" 544. He had a packet of them under his arm.

545. Uncle Carey herded them into his sedan and took the wheel himself.

546. "No," Roger said. 547. "What about them?"

548. As the car sped away, Uncle Carey trying desperately to elude reporters, Leslie Paxton gave Roger the latest journalistic flashes.

549. "They've traced the background of Jake Lang, alias Jake Blythe. 550. He was a cardsharp who died at Joliet. 551. He came originally from Arizona. 552. A record in an old mine hospital proves that twin girls were born to Jake's wife about thirty years ago. 553. The twins were named Evelyn and Caroline. 554. So that much of it, Roger, can't be denied."

555. "I've already conceded that much," Roger told him. 556. "Eva Lang is my sister-in-law. 557. We have to start from there."

558. "They've taken her to Detroit," Paxton said, "for trial. 559. Don't you see what you're up against? 560. You can't ignore it."

561. "I don't intend to ignore it, Leslie. 562. That's why I want you to go to Detroit."

563. "Me? 564. Why me?"

565. "Because you're a lawyer and my partner. 566. Please tell Eva Lang that you represent me. 567. Tell her that as her brother-in-law, I offer to employ the most competent counsel in Detroit for her defense. 568. Make it clear that I do this not as her husband, but as her brother-in-law."

569. "If she's a criminal," Paxton protested, "why back her at all?"

570. "Criminal or not, she's Caroline's sister. 571. Caroline would want me to do it."

572. Uncle Carey protested loudly. 573. But Aunt Harriet applauded. 574. "That's the most human thing I ever heard a Marsh say. 575. Bravo, Roger."

576. Leslie Paxton reluctantly agreed. 577. He promised to catch a night train for Detroit.

578. The car was passing a pair of tall granite pillars with a grilled gate between them. 579. Roger asked Uncle Carey to stop.

580. "Let me out here, please. 581. I'll take a taxi home."

582. They knew what he wanted. 583. Uncle Carey let him out and the car drove on. 584. Roger passed through the gateway and

took a gravel path through a grove of stately elms. 585. This was St. Cecelia Cemetery. 586. He went directly to the Marsh family plot.

587. Hat in hand, Roger stood beside the newest grave. 588. On its headstone was inscribed:

Caroline Blythe Marsh, 1917–1944

589. Here was a fact, Roger thought. 590. Something to cling to. 591. Here was the one and final answer to Eva Lang. 592. It brought back, vividly, all the incontestable realities. 593. Caroline's last illness, the six days he had sat by her bedside. 594. He remembered her last whispered word, "Good-by, Roger." 595. With her small hand in his, her eyes had closed in death.

596. No fantastic masquerade could possibly gainsay that fact— Caroline's death four years ago. 597. It steadied him now, as he stood by her grave. 598. Confusion, and sometimes whispers of doubt, had taken their toll. 599. There'd been moments when he'd wondered if he was mistaken; brief torturing suspicions that he might be denying his own wife.

600. All that was brushed away now as he stood by Caroline's grave. 601. Dozens of people had seen her lowered here. 602. They'd mourned by her open casket. 603. Every one of them was an unbreachable defense against Eva Lang.

604. For two days Roger dodged reporters and waited morosely for Leslie Paxton's return from Detroit. 605. Paxton dropped in on him late the second evening. 606. "I've seen Eva Lang, Roger. 607. She turned down your offer. 608. What an actress that woman is! 609. She's a scuffed-up imitation of Caroline, but she's not Caroline."

610. "Just what did she say?"

611. "If you want her exact words, she said, 'Tell Roger I'll accept from him the loyalty of a husband; nothing more; nothing less.'"

612. Paxton left a few minutes later. 613. Roger saw him to the door, then went up to his bedroom. 614. As he took off his tie and loosened his collar, he studied the picture of Caroline on his chifforobe. 615. Innocence and pride shone in the loving gaze of her eyes. 616. He thought of Eva Lang's response to Leslie. 617. It seemed more the attitude of innocence and hurt pride.

618. Lucile Dutton, Roger's secretary, was alone in the office when Roger appeared the next morning. 619. With her "Good morning, Mr. Marsh," she flashed him a quick look of sympathy.

620. "Good morning, Lucile." 621. Roger considered her troubled eyes for a moment, then consulted her about the problem that had

kept him from sleep the night before. 622. She warmly reassured him. 623. "Don't let her fool you, Mr. Marsh. 624. Turning down your offer just shows she's smart. 625. She knew you'd react just that way."

626. "But she hasn't a cent. 627. And good attorneys come high."

628. "It'll be worth more, she thinks, to soften you up. 629. And to win public sympathy. 630. The deserted-wife act is her best bet."

631. Roger sat down at his desk and took from his pocket the photograph of Duke Smedley given him by Whipple. 632. He showed it to Lucile Dutton. 633. "Was this man ever in the office? 634. Did we ever have any contact with him?"

635. "I don't recognize him," the girl said. 636. "Who is he?"

637. "He's Eva Lang's boy friend. 638. I've a vague feeling I saw him one time. 639. Keep an eye open for him, Lucile."

640. Later in the day a deputy from the district attorney's office of Detroit called on Roger. 641. He served a summons which required Roger Marsh to testify in the case of the People Against Eva Lang. 642. Roger had been expecting it.

643. "I'm serving a similar summons," the deputy said, "on a dozen or more persons who knew your wife well."

644. "How will you select them?"

645. "We're interviewing all the twenty-eight people named by the accused and will select ten or more who are positive she isn't your wife."

646. "What tests have you made on Eva Lang?" Roger asked.

647. "A blood test and a handwriting test. 648. Her blood type is the same as your wife's, but that would be expected with twin sisters. 649. Her handwriting very closely resembles your wife's. 650. But Eva Lang had four years to practice her sister's handwriting under the coaching of an expert forger, Duke Smedley."

651. "You think he's in on this with her?"

652. "It fits him like a glove. 653. We think their first objective is an acquittal on the murder charge. 654. Probably their second is a raid on your fortune after she's free. 655. She might file suit, for instance, for desertion and humiliating renunciation."

656. "Who'll her lawyer be?"

657. "Young chap assigned by the court. 658. Name of Sprague. 659. He's already put his cards on the table."

660. "What are they?"

661. "That defense concedes the murder of one Rufus Fox by

one Eva Lang in Detroit on a certain day five years ago. 662. But the accused is not, the defense will insist, Eva Lang. 663. She's Caroline Blythe Marsh. 664. That's their case and they'll stick to it."

665. During the weeks that followed, reporters and feature writers dogged Roger. 666. Often, on the way to his office, he heard a camera click at his elbow. 667. Almost hourly the jangle of the telephone brought some friend offering support and sympathy, or perhaps some gossip columnist with an impertinent question. 668. Crank letters, most of them anonymous, cluttered his mail.

669. It seemed to Roger he couldn't pick up a paper without seeing news of the Eva Lang affair. 670. In a metropolitan rotogravure section, on the Sunday before Eva Lang's trial, a full page displayed twenty-nine photographs. 671. The central one was Eva Lang. 672. Surrounding it, each pictured individually, were all of the twenty-eight prominent Marylanders on the list she'd given for identification and vindication.

673. Roger himself was among them; Uncle Carey and Aunt Harriet were there; so were Effie Foster and Leslie Paxton and Dr. Cawfield. 674. The elite of Baltimore were there. 675. The page, in bold letters at the bottom, was titled: "The People Against Eva Lang."

676. When The People Against Eva Lang opened at Superior Court in Detroit, Roger Marsh sullenly absented himself from the preliminary sessions. 677. He barricaded himself in a hotel room near the courthouse all during the selection of a jury. 678. His radio kept him informed and he received all the newspapers. 679. Only when called to testify would he appear in court.

680. It was a week before he was called. 681. By then Eva Lang's murder guilt was clearly established and had not even been disputed by the defense. 682. A hotel clerk had identified the accused as the woman he had seen shoot to death a man named Rufus Fox. 683. It seemed conclusive. 684. But in cross-examination the defense counsel had pointed to a pair of twin girls he had planted in the audience.

685. "Do you remember that one of those young ladies asked you the time on the street this morning?"

686. "Yes," the clerk said.

687. "Which of them was it?"

688. And the witness had been unable to say. 689. Thus the entire case was resolved into an identification of Eva Lang.

690. Roger was called to the stand and sworn in.

691. "Are you a widower?" inquired the prosecutor.

692. "I am."

693. "When did your wife die?"

694. "Four years ago."

695. "State the circumstances of her illness, death and funeral."

696. Roger complied in a cold precise voice.

697. "Look at the accused. 698. Did you ever see her before?"

699. The defendant returned Roger's stare. 700. Her eyes challenged him, bitter and defiant.

701. "Yes," Roger said. 702. "I saw her once."

703. "Only once?"

704. "Yes."

705. "When and where?"

706. "At the Seattle jail two months ago."

707. "That is all. 708. Thank you, Mr. Marsh."

709. In cross-examination the defense counsel asked, "Do you now concede that your wife had a twin sister named Evelyn?"

710. "Recently," Roger answered stiffly, "I've come to that conclusion."

711. "That is all."

712. Roger tried not to hurry as he left the courtroom. 713. He had expected it to be worse. 714. He'd thought the defense counsel would nag him for hours.

715. At his hotel room he picked up the rest of the trial by radio and printed word. 716. Ten other Marylanders were called by the prosecution and all of them, with varying degrees of emphasis, denied that the defendant could be Caroline Marsh. 717. All ten of them had seen Caroline buried. 718. When the state rested, Eva Lang's position seemed untenable.

719. Then the defense opened and the defendant herself took the stand. 720. She told precisely the story she'd told Inspector Whipple from the beginning. 721. Her lawyer produced ten Baltimore witnesses himself, people he'd hand-picked after a series of interviews there. 722. People who were uncertain enough to answer, "I don't know." 723. One was a boy who, during the war, had delivered groceries to the Marsh home. 724. He remembered peering into the kitchen once and seeing two women who looked just alike.

725. "Was the accused one of them?"

726. "I think so."

727. "Is she Mrs. Marsh or the other one?"

728. "I don't know."

729. "I don't know," or, "I can't be certain," was a response given by nine others.

730. A former maid at the Marsh house was asked, "Is there a faint doubt in your mind as to whether the defendant is Mrs. Marsh?"

731. "I'm afraid there is. 732. I don't see how she could be Mrs. Marsh because they say Mrs. Marsh passed away. 733. But she looks like her. 734. I can't be sure."

735. Then came a bombshell. 736. The defense called Mrs. Carey Marsh of Edgeton, Maryland.

737. "Are you Caroline Marsh's Aunt Harriet?"

738. "I am."

739. "You knew your niece quite well?"

740. "Of course."

741. "Can you look at the accused and swear she isn't your niece?"

742. "No," Aunt Harriet said coolly, "because I'm not at all sure she isn't."

743. Later Aunt Harriet herself, marching straight to Roger's room, explained the stand she had taken.

744. "How could you?" he demanded.

745. "How could I say anything else? 746. How can I swear away her life? 747. I'm not sure she's Caroline. 748. But I'm not sure she isn't."

749. He sat on the bed and stared at her balefully. 750. "You're not sure she isn't?"

751. "And deep down in your heart, neither are you, Roger."

752. "Are you crazy? 753. Of course I'm sure."

754. "Your pride's sure," she corrected. 755. "Your stiff-necked Marsh pride made up its mind even before you went to Seattle. 756. You went there to say no. 757. And you said it."

758. Dr. Cawfield and Leslie Paxton came storming in. 759. "And that goes for the rest of you," Aunt Harriet blazed. 760. "You're just like Carey. 761. You don't like scandals. 762. Sensations make you sick. 763. You'll trust a cold gravestone, every time, before you'll trust flesh and blood. 764. Stop glaring at me, Leslie. 765. Has the jury gone out yet?"

766. "It has," Leslie said. 767. He added with a grimace, "And you should have heard the judge charge them! 768. 'If a reasonable doubt exists in your minds,' he said, 'that the defendant is Eva Lang, you will not be justified in a verdict of guilty.'"

769. "Doubt!" snorted Dr. Cawfield. 770. "It's in their minds like a maggot. 771. And you planted it, Harriet Marsh."

772. "Don't you bully me, Elias. 773. They asked my opinion and I gave it. 774. And maybe I'll sleep better than the rest of you." 775. Aunt Harriet flounced out.

776. Roger packed his bags and taxied to the airport. 777. He was in a fever to get out of town before reporters made a mass assault. 778. From now on he didn't want any part of the case. 779. And whatever the verdict, to him Eva Lang would still be Eva Lang.

780. All through the flight to Baltimore the plane's stewardess kept a radio on. 781. A concert, then a newscast. 782. No decision yet in the Detroit case. 783. Passengers whispered, nudged each other, looked covertly at Roger Marsh. 784. He sat there staring frigidly into space.

785. Half an hour before they reached Baltimore the flash came. 786. The jury had reported. 787. The verdict was "not guilty."

788. It wasn't over yet. 789. Roger was dismally sure of it. 790. Eva Lang was free and could never be tried again on this charge. 791. But by trade she was a swindler. 792. So was Duke Smedley. 793. They'd already raided his good name; and now, given time, they'd try to raid his purse.

794. For a month Roger waited, dreading every ring of his phone. 795. Would Eva contact him herself? 796. Or would Duke Smedley do it? 797. Probably not Smedley; being wanted on many old counts, he'd hardly dare come into the open.

798. Eva, Roger learned from the papers, was boldly in the open. 799. She was still a celebrity and every move she made was publicized. 800. The papers said she'd gone to a Florida hotel for a month's rest.

801. But how could she finance a trip like that? 802. A month at a Florida resort would be expensive. 803. Eva Lang, the prisoner, had had no money. 804. The courts had even had to appoint a public defender.

805. Roger saw only one answer. 806. Duke Smedley. 807. While she was in custody he couldn't reach her. 808. Now that she was free, he could and had.

809. This conclusion comforted Roger considerably. 810. No doubt the police were watching Eva in hopes of picking up Smedley. 811. And once Smedley was caught, the truth about Eva Lang would be

known. 812. For Smedley knew everything about her. 813. He'd bridged the gap of those four years with her and so he knew, beyond a shadow of doubt, which of the twins she was.

814. A short time later came a report that the woman once known as Eva Lang was now in New York. 815. She had taken an apartment as Caroline Blythe Marsh and had found herself a job. 816. It was at the perfumery counter of a Fifth Avenue department store, exactly the job held by Caroline Blythe eight years ago when she met Roger Marsh of Baltimore.

817. Roger was alarmed and confused because it seemed out of character. 818. A confidence woman doesn't usually go to work. 819. But Caroline Marsh, thrown on her own resources, would do exactly that. 820. She'd try to get her last job back.

821. Night after night he lay awake, reviewing every step of what had happened, trying to refute the vague uncertainties that had crept into his mind. 822. What if he'd been wrong? 823. What if this woman he had denied were really Caroline, whose love had been the most wonderful thing in his life? 824. He kept telling himself it couldn't be.

825. But he *had* to know. 826. Suddenly he realized that the entire scheme used in identifying Eva Lang had been faulty. 827. They'd taken witnesses from Baltimore to look at her—to say whether she was or wasn't Caroline Marsh. 828. No such scheme could be conclusive, because it was based upon opinion rather than upon incontestable fact.

829. A proper scheme would be the reverse. 830. Instead of people identifying Eva Lang, Eva Lang should be made to identify people. 831. People who'd known Caroline well, and whom Evelyn had never seen, should be paraded before Eva Lang. 832. Recognition should then be demanded, not by the witnesses, but by Eva Lang herself.

833. For instance, Eva Lang had never in her life seen Lucile Dutton. 834. During the war Lucile had left Roger's company to become a Wave. 835. There'd never been a picture of her at the Marsh house. 836. From a diary Evelyn could know about Lucile but definitely she had never seen her. 837. Therefore Evelyn couldn't possibly recognize Lucile.

838. But Caroline, if living, could. 839. And would. 840. No married woman ever forgets a girl of whom she's been jealous—a lovely secretary who'd caused the first marital quarrel.

248

841. So a test, using Lucile as a pawn, should be both simple and conclusive. 842. Roger worked out the details and then rang up a New York client. 843. He made an appointment for eleven the next morning.

844. "It's rather important," he told Lucile. 845. "I'd like you to run up with me and make a transcript of the conference."

846. They caught an early train and were in New York by ten. 847. The conference engaged them till noon, when they had lunch in a restaurant on Fifth Avenue, close to the department store where Eva Lang was working. 848. Roger ordered generously, tried to be gay and they lingered there until almost two.

849. He made it sound casual when, walking to the next corner for a cab, he remarked: "I have a bit of shopping to do, Lucile. 850. I need a new hat. 851. Mind if we stop in here a minute?"

852. They turned into the store. 853. As they threaded through the crowded aisles Roger seemed to have an afterthought. 854. "That reminds me—I'd better pick up something for Ruth Paxton's birthday next week. 855. How would a bottle of perfume do?"

856. Lucile gave him a searching look. 857. "They can always use it," she said.

858. "I tell you: While I get the hat you pick up the perfume. 859. Make any selection you like. 860. Here." 861. He handed her a bill. 862. "Meet me at the Fifth Avenue exit in fifteen minutes."

863. Roger disappeared in the crowd. 864. Circling, he maneuvered to an aisle about ten yards to the right of the perfume counter. 865. He saw Eva Lang, but she, busy with customers, didn't see him.

866. A strange feeling of nostalgia ran through Roger. 867. It was here that he'd first seen Caroline, eight and a half years ago. 868. The woman back of the perfume counter today had gray-streaked hair and looked forty-five. 869. But the hardness was gone from her face. 870. She was gracious, charming. 871. She looked startlingly like Caroline.

872. But she wasn't. 873. Because she was now waiting on Lucile and her smile was entirely impersonal. 874. Not the faintest flicker of recognition came to her eyes. 875. "May I help you? 876. Something for yourself? . . . 877. Oh, a gift——"

878. Unseen himself, Roger missed no detail of it. 879. He saw Lucile master her surprise at seeing Eva Lang. 880. He watched her deliberately take time making her selection. 881. The vital thing, however, was that Eva Lang didn't know her.

882. Roger melted into the crowd, relieved to know that this woman was not Caroline. 883. But mingled with the relief was the unreasonable wish that she might have been.

884. All the uncertainties dissolved, Roger's mind was at ease. 885. It stayed that way till late in May.

886. Then, in the lobby of the Lord Baltimore Hotel one morning, a rough hand clapped his shoulder. 887. A hearty voice boomed, "Roger Marsh! 888. How the devil are you, Roger?"

889. Roger turned to see a big rubicund man in a loose tweed suit. 890. At Roger's blank stare the man's smile broadened. 891. "Don't you know me, Roger? 892. Hell's bells. 893. And I thought I'd made an impression. 894. I must have been too easy on you."

895. With chagrin, Roger finally remembered. 896. "Colonel Cox! 897. How stupid of me! 898. How are you, Colonel?"

899. Cox chuckled, "Imagine a guy not knowing his own commanding officer just because he's out of uniform!"

900. "What about lunch, Colonel?"

901. "Not today. 902. My wife's waiting for me right now. 903. We're stopping here. 904. Give me a ring sometime. 905. See you later, Roger."

906. Roger was thoughtful as he went on to his office. 907. I've shared quarters with Cox in London, he reminded himself. 908. And now, after only three years, I didn't recognize him out of uniform.

909. It was more than seven years since Caroline had seen Lucile. 910. The test at the perfume counter didn't seem conclusive after all.

911. At his office Roger was surprised to find Uncle Carey, who was just back after wintering in California.

912. "Hello, Uncle Carey. 913. How's Aunt Harriet?"

914. "As hard-headed as ever," Carey growled. 915. "You know, Roger, I can't pound any sense into her about that Eva Lang. 916. Just like a woman. 917. They'll never admit they're wrong."

918. Roger's face clouded. 919. "You mean she still isn't sure about her?"

920. "Less sure than ever," Carey said. 921. "Felt sorry for her, she said, right after the trial. 922. That's why she offered to finance her for a month in Florida."

923. Roger stared. 924. "You mean Aunt Harriet paid for that trip?"

925. "Offered to. 926. But Eva Lang wouldn't take it except as a loan. 927. Said she'd pay it back ten dollars a week when she got a job. 928. And blast it, she has. 929. Ten dollars came in the mail

250

every week all winter. 930. Says she has her old job back. 931. So Harriet——"

932. But Roger didn't hear any more. 933. All the certainty of the past month came tumbling down.

934. On the morning of May twenty-fourth, Roger awakened with anticipation. 935. For it was Caroline's birthday and each year he remembered it with flowers for her grave. 936. Today this act would dispel all his doubts, bringing him back to the invincible fact of Caroline's death.

937. At a florist's shop he purchased a wreath and drove with it to the cemetery, parking his car just inside the gate. 938. Elms were in leaf and the grass was green. 939. A clean gravel path took him fifty yards to the Marsh family plot.

940. And there was her headstone. 941. Upright and solid it stood there, a bulwark to his faith. 942. It was his last and final witness. 943. Standing by it steadied him now, as always.

944. Caroline Blythe Marsh, 1917–1944

945. He placed the wreath against the headstone. 946. Then he stood by quietly, his head uncovered. 947. And as the minutes passed, all the nagging doubts left him. 948. Here in this grave, where he had reverently buried her with all his world standing by, lay his wife Caroline.

949. Sustained and reassured, he walked fifty yards back to his car. 950. A sound of footsteps crunching on gravel made him turn. 951. A man, he saw, was approaching the Marsh plot from the opposite direction. 952. The man had a florist's box under his arm.

953. Some old friend of the family, Roger presumed, had remembered the day and Caroline.

954. Getting into his car, Roger waited idly to see who it could be. 955. At fifty yards, through the elms, he saw the man open the box and lay a dozen red roses on Caroline's grave.

956. Then the man removed his hat and stood there with bowed head.

957. He was well dressed, a personable man with brownish wavy hair. 958. His face—with a start, Roger knew it. 959. It was the face in a photograph Inspector Whipple had given him. 960. Duke Smedley!

961. It was the face Roger had vaguely remembered having seen before.

962. He knew now where he'd seen it. 963. The stranger at the

funeral, four and a half years ago. 964. The unobtrusive mourner none of them had known. 965. He'd stood apart from the others and yet had followed them to the grave, this same grave to which he now returned.

966. A tribute for Caroline? 967. It was Evelyn's birthday too. 968. Evelyn was the woman he'd loved, not Caroline.

969. Duke Smedley, all along, had known the truth.

970. And now, with a shock of conviction, Roger Marsh knew too.

971. Roger swerved his car through the gate. 972. It was not yet noon. 973. Driving fast, he could reach New York before the store closed. 974. There, long ago, he had found Caroline. 975. And there, in humble contrition, he must find her again.

SECTION A-4

By this time surely you must be fully aware that the same devices are found and used in all types of fiction, regardless of their length.

Indeed, the various types differ only in their various purposes and lengths and not in the nature of specific technical devices employed therein.

It is true that in a novel, the form best adapted to the display and development of character, most of the devices will be used for purposes of characterization. And of course the novelist will prefer those devices which serve this purpose best. But he is free to use any and all devices found in other forms of fiction, and this is true also of the authors of novelettes, short stories, short short stories, and even anecdotes. The biographer and autobiographer, even the writer of a memoir, also helps himself freely to fictional devices. In short, wherever human relationships form part of the subject matter in hand a writer will feel free to use any and all fictional technical devices.

Yet each kind of subject matter, each special purpose, requires a different emphasis. Moreover, certain writers—somewhat injudiciously—will tend to neglect or favor certain devices merely because they have used such devices successfully before or because some friend or critic has admired these in their work.

Of course every writer should desire to be equally skillful with all devices, but few approach this goal. More would do so if they schooled themselves in writing Finger Exercises on the pattern of all the standard devices.

In the novelette *Eva? Caroline?* we find as many incidents as scenes, and of the scenes not a few are examples of the so-called Messenger Scene in which information is given by one character to others, thus producing an emotional effect upon the others. The high proportion of incidents and messenger scenes in this novelette as compared with a short story is due to the nature of the material, the type of story which the author of the novelette had to tell—the solution of a puzzle through discussion and questioning. Obviously, in such a novelette, encounters between characters are not often needed, since the interest lies not in conflict between the characters but in the working out of the puzzle and in the change in heart of the hero. Of course some scenes are obligatory because they make the motives of the hero plausible.

It is possible to use a twist at the end of a novel, biography, novelette, or short story. But for a short short story such a twist is so usual as to be almost obligatory. The reason for this is that, since so brief a piece offers small opportunity to display character or action, setting or idea, it must depend heavily on surprise instead of recognition—that is, upon the strange or novel rather than on the familiar—to create reader interest.

These examples will suffice to indicate why one finds different devices favored in different types of fiction.

We now offer for your study a short short story entitled *Bargain Hunters,* reprinted here from *Collier's* (June 18, 1949) by the kind permission of the author, W. L. Heath. The story runs to 1,500 words. As you see, it is a "Comes-to-realize" story, with both a twist and a back-twist. Read it carefully. Then make a careful study of it, following the suggestions in Work Program 11, Section A-4. Afterward check your findings by the Notes on Chapter 11, Section A-4.

Bargain Hunters [1]

BY W. L. HEATH

1. We got into a ricksha in front of the Park Hotel. 2. Captain Hedge
gave directions to the coolie, and then settled back beside me and
lighted a cigar. 3. "Now, you leave this to me," he said out of the
corner of his mouth. 4. "I know jade, and I know Chinamen. 5.
They've got some of the finest jade in the world here in Shanghai,
but they'll skin you alive if you don't know how to deal with them. 6.
Just let me know if you see a piece you like, and leave the rest to
me."

7. We jogged along Nanking Road in the brilliant midafternoon
sun. 8. Then we turned into a narrow side street, crowded with
pedestrians and with other rickshas.

9. It was my first trip to Shanghai. 10. The war had been over a
month now, and my squadron had been given the task of flying
Chinese troops up from Luchow to occupy the big port city. 11.
After a year in Burma, I thought Shanghai was paradise. 12. Out-
wardly, the city seemed unravaged by the long years of Japanese
domination.

13. There were night clubs, shiny limousines, pretty girls in Western clothes; there were beefsteaks and even ice cream. 14. I was
feeling exceptionally good, and pleased by my luck in making the
acquaintance of Captain Hedge. 15. He was a liaison officer stationed
temporarily in Shanghai—a big red-faced fellow with a loud,
friendly manner; a little overbearing perhaps, but just the man I
needed. 16. I wanted to buy a piece of jade, and I certainly didn't
want to get skinned.

17. We made two more turns, then Hedge leaned forward and
tapped the coolie on the shoulder, and we stopped. 18. When we
got out, the boy stood by the ricksha, smiling courteously and holding his hat against his chest. 19. He was a very small, thin fellow—
about fifteen years old, I guessed—and he was breathing heavily

[1]Copyright, 1949, by W. L. Heath.

254

from the long pull. 20. When I started to pay him, Captain Hedge stopped my hand.

21. "That's too much," Hedge said. 22. He gave the coolie half the money and handed the rest back to me. 23. As we walked away Hedge took the cigar out of his mouth and inclined his head toward mine. 24. "You want to watch that," he said in a low voice. 25. "If people overpay them, they'll soon be asking higher fares."

26. Shanghai is a strange city. 27. At its center there are tall, modern buildings, with neon lights; but as you go away from the center you move back, street by street, decade by decade, back into old China.

28. The section we were in now belonged to a time many decades in the past. 29. The shops were crowded together under a maze of multi-colored signs, and the people who jammed the narrow street were all dressed in Oriental attire. 30. Hedge paused before a shop, cupped his hands to his eyes and peered in through one of the small glass panes.

31. "Here," Hedge said. 32. "Let's try here." 33. But before we went in, he warned me again: "Remember—if you see something you like, don't let him know that you want it or he'll double the price on you. 34. And no matter what he asks for it, tell him it's too much. 35. He'll come down."

36. It was cool and dark inside, and smelled of teakwood. 37. A tiny bell tinkled above the door as we closed it. 38. After a moment the curtains at the rear of the shop parted, and the proprietor appeared. 39. He was a bent, withered little man, eighty-five at least, with a gray beard that hung down from his chin like a goat's. 40. He wore a shabby green gown and a cap, and in one bony hand he clutched a book. 41. Bowing obsequiously, he shuffled forward and spoke to us in English. 42. "Good evening, gentlemen. 43. How do you do?"

44. Captain Hedge bowed with aloof politeness, and told the old man that we had come to look at some jade.

45. The proprietor scurried about and drew up chairs and a small, low table. 46. Eventually he produced a tray of the most exquisite jade I have ever set my eyes on. 47. Then, with a murmured apology, he disappeared again behind the curtains. 48. I looked at Hedge inquiringly.

49. "Probably going to serve us tea," Hedge whispered. 50. "It's part of the treatment. 51. Now remember, don't appear too anxious

or he'll skin you. 52. Just string him along, and no matter what price he asks, tell him it's too much. 53. We may get something cheap."

54. "I like that one," I said, pointing to a small, beautifully polished piece.

55. "Shhhh!" 56. Hedge held his finger to his lips.

57. The old man brought out the tea and poured it. 58. He pushed the jade aside. 59. And for the next two hours he talked. 60. I have never spent a more monotonous afternoon in my life. 61. I pretended to be interested, of course, because the old fellow seemed to be having a good time, and that meant he'd be easier to deal with when the time came to talk about prices.

62. Captain Hedge did himself proud, listening to every word that fell from the old man's toothless mouth as if it were the wisdom of the ages. 63. It was grueling—but the price of that jade was going down. 64. We listened with reverence as he told us about the Great Wall. 65. We chuckled appreciatively at Chinese anecdotes we did not understand. 66. We bowed our heads with modesty when he praised "the great United States." 67. Two hours passed, and at last the time to bargain arrived. 68. Hedge and I rose stiffly from our chairs. 69. He sent me a final glance of caution, and turned to the old man. 70. "The jade——" said Hedge.

71. "Yes, yes, the jade!" the old fellow cried suddenly, as if he had forgotten what we'd come for. 72. "Do you see a piece that pleases you?"

73. I pointed to the stone I wanted, and pretended to gaze at it skeptically. 74. "This seems to be a *fair* one," I said. 75. I wanted him to make the first move.

76. He looked up at me apologetically with his watery eyes. 77. "I'm sorry I have not a piece that pleases you more." 78. Then he smiled. 79. "You are a very nice young man." 80. He turned to include Hedge in the compliment. 81. "Both of you are—gentlemen."

82. A knowing smile pulled at the corner of Hedge's mouth. 83. The old man said, "I have had the pleasure of meeting only a few Americans, but I have liked them all. 84. They are always kind and generous." 85. He seemed to emphasize the word "generous." 86. Over his shoulder I saw Captain Hedge wink and form the words silently with his lips: *Tell him it's too much.*

87. The old man picked up the stone with his thin, trembling fingers and placed it in my hand. 88. "I want to make you a gift of

256

this little piece of jade," he said, "for listening so patiently to the foolish talk of a lonely old man."

89. Riding back to the hotel in the ricksha, neither Hedge nor I spoke. 90. We didn't even look at each other. 91. I wasn't sure how Hedge felt, but I felt a little sick, myself—sick with shame and humiliation.

92. When we stopped and got out, I paid the coolie—counting the bills in his dirty, calloused hand. 93. Hedge's eyes followed every bill as it left my hand. 94. The coolie already had the amount of the standard fare, but I held one more bill lightly between my thumb and forefinger. 95. The coolie watched it. 96. So did Hedge. 97. "You start overpay——" Hedge began.

98. I turned my head and looked at him, from the visor of his officer's hat to the burnished brown of his shoes. 99. "For the good service," I said to the coolie, and gave him the last bill. 100. Hedge never did finish what he had started to say.

SECTION A-5

Here we have a Practical Article or How-to-do-it Piece. The purpose of the author is to demonstrate a convincing formula for gaining self-control and presence of mind. His method is what one may call the Club Sandwich Pattern—a structure of alternate precept and example. Since the anecdotes and even the precepts involve people, fictional techniques are used.

Read the article carefully. Then turn to Work Program 13 at the end of Chapter 13.

A Formula for Presence of Mind [1]

BY FULTON OURSLER

1. You have been asleep for hours. 2. You open your eyes in the darkness and listen. 3. You hear a footfall on the staircase.

[1]Copyright, 1949, by the *Reader's Digest*.

4. What should you do? 5. Lie quiet and pretend to be asleep? 6. Scream? 7. Shake your spouse awake? 8. Grab the telephone? 9. Turn on the lights?

10. In such a crisis, said my late friend, Deputy Police Commissioner George S. Dougherty, even the most timid persons often show admirable self-control. 11. He added: "After 50 years in detective work, I am convinced that a frantic desire to save his own hide is likely to put any man in a panic, but concern for others often summons up mysterious energies of courage and resourcefulness."

12. There was the case of the housewife and the maniac axe-killer. 13. He had already killed three householders, and newspapers were full of the grisly details. 14. One night she was wakened by the muffled sound of heavy blows. 15. In the dimmish light she beheld a towering figure at the bed beside hers, swinging an axe, blow after blow descending on the bloody head of her husband.

16. Then the killer turned toward her. 17. Again he swung his terrible weapon, but her lifted hands swerved the blow and the edge of the axe only gashed her cheek.

18. "Wait!" she said. 19. "And listen!"

20. For one abysmal hour the woman talked to the madman. 21. With inspired self-possession, she did not weep, nor plead, nor show any symptom of fear. 22. Often her eyes turned to the crib across the room where her one-year-old daughter lay sleeping, while she reasoned like a mother with a misbehaving son:

"You killed a man tonight. 23. If you kill me, too, people will hate you—because our baby needs at least one parent. 24. Someday the police will catch you. 25. If everybody hates you, you won't have a chance. 26. Show me mercy and they may remember it to your credit."

27. Through all 60 minutes, her low forcible tones never faltered, while the man held his axe and remained silent. 28. At last he spoke:

"You gotta come with me."

29. Fur coat over nightgown, bare feet in mules, she preceded her captor out of the house and through dark, empty streets. 30. Reaching open country, he grabbed her by the throat:

"You swear if I ever get caught, you don't know me?"

31. She took the oath and fled wildly home. 32. A year later the prowling axeman was given the death sentence, but not on her evidence. 33. In spite of five hideous blows, her husband had lived to identify the killer in court.

34. "This mother," Dougherty pointed out, "treated the killer like an equal. 35. She reasoned with him, instead of condemning or pleading, and he was flattered. 36. I do not care how vicious a man may be, there is always in him a part of our common humanity. 37. If you can engage the criminal in talk directed toward a definite end, two thirds of your battle is won. 38. All people are reachable somewhere and, if you can learn to subdue your own panic, something in the very danger itself will inspire you how to act."

39. Then the detective told of a lawyer and his wife who, one winter night, were walking home from the theater. 40. As they reached a deserted block, a masked man halted them with a revolver. 41. As he lifted his hands the lawyer said to his wife: "Don't be frightened, Agnes. 42. He won't hurt us," and, to the bandit: "You can take everything, but I must speak with you privately." 43. At the curb he explained: "My wife is soon to become a mother. 44. Please don't do anything to frighten her."

45. The bandit took the lawyer's almost empty pocketbook, leaving untouched the wife who was wearing jewels worth thousands of dollars.

46. Does such self-possession belong only to a superior few?

47. A famous neuropsychologist, who is also a man of deep faith, agrees with Detective Dougherty that the riddle's answer lies in the nature of the soul. 48. The more spiritual the man, the more completely is he ruler of the self and its ignoble emotions, such as fear; his concern being for the larger good, he does not go to pieces when he is in danger. 49. Such was the experience of my friend Blackstone, the illusionist. 50. The prestidigitator was performing before a packed audience in a midwestern theater. 51. Suddenly, in the midst of a trick, he called out to the stage manager: "Ring down the curtain!" 52. Then, seizing a coil of rope, he walked to the footlights.

53. "Friends," he cried, "you have all heard of the Hindu rope trick. 54. A rope is thrown into the air. 55. It stands erect. 56. A boy climbs the rope and disappears. 57. I intend to do that trick for you right now—not here, where you may suspect mirrors, wires or lights, but in the middle of the street! 58. Will you all pass out through the front door, beginning with those in the last row? 59. Thank you."

60. In two minutes the whole crowd was outside. 61. As Blackstone and his troupe marched up the emptying aisle to the lobby, flames were already crackling around the edge of the curtain. 62.

Concern for others had conquered his own almost pathological fear of fire and inspired him to save uncounted lives.

63. Dwell on your own peril and you may be reduced to gibbering panic. 64. Think of others and you may well find yourself doing the precisely correct thing.

65. I remember a story out of my youth, when the Woolworth Building, a pioneer among the great New York skyscrapers, was being erected. 66. One spring noon, three riveters sat on a girder 50 stories above the street, their feet dangling in space. 67. Lunch finished, they were enjoying the warm sun, when the man on the right noticed a dreadful circumstance. 68. The man in the middle had fallen asleep.

69. Obviously, if the sleeper awoke with a start he might plunge below and perhaps drag one or both of his companions to destruction with him. 70. Very quietly, the man on the right explained matters to the man on the left. 71. They knew they had to wake up the sleeping man gradually. 72. So they began discussing, in tranquil tones, his favorite recreation, fishing, until he opened one eye, slowly caught the drift of the conversation and, unstartled and safe, slipped back into full consciousness.

73. Sometimes salvation depends on the wisdom and courage to do nothing. 74. One day a family of three were driving down the Tamiami Trail between Miami and Tampa, a narrow highroad raised out of swamps, with a canal on one side. 75. Suddenly the car skidded, plunged over the side and settled in 12 feet of water.

76. "Don't try to get out," cried the father. 77. Fortunately, with the windows closed, the new four-door sedan was almost watertight. 78. "Now," he added, "don't move. 79. Take little breaths. 80. Make the oxygen last. 81. Lots of people saw what happened. 82. We're going to be rescued."

83. The waiting seemed endless, but the reasoning was correct. 84. Several witnesses sped on to telephone the police. 85. With the emergency squad came a diver. 86. When he lowered himself to the bottom, he found all three passengers sitting quietly. 87. They had remained so for 30 minutes.

88. Do men or women excel in presence of mind? 89. There is an old tale, perhaps apocryphal, that illuminates that question. 90. At a dinner party in India, the talk had turned to poise and self-control, and the old dispute: Which was more reliable in a crisis, man or woman? 91. The males present, army officers and civil ser-

vants, agreed that women were the masterpieces of creation; their one defect was that they went into hysterics in a crisis. 92. That was when you needed men. 93. All the ladies placidly concurred, except the hostess. 94. At the height of the discussion she called a native boy:

"Ali! Kindly fetch a bowl of milk at once and put it on the floor."

95. With a terrified roll of his eyes the boy ran to obey, placing a jade bowl on a flagstone, close to the mistress of the house. 96. Then he stood back, holding a looped whip in his hand, as, from under the white napery of the table, there slithered a long bloated thing, yellowish-brown with white and black marks. 97. The cobra approached the milk and the native boys fell on it and killed it.

98. "Well," puffed a red-faced colonel, "how on earth did you know that snake was under the table?"

99. "It was coiled," replied the hostess, "around my ankle."

SECTION A-6

Here a formal essay is presented for your analysis. Analyze it as instructed in Work Program 13. Then check your findings by the answers given in the Notes on Chapter 13, Section A-6.

Why Medicine Is Not a Science [1]

BY IAN STEVENSON, M.D.

1. Most of us are probably under the impression that the medical profession has arrived at a zenith of scientific achievement, from which it will go on from triumph to triumph. 2. But medicine suffers today from a defect which, unless remedied, may halt its future progress.

3. The defect is that medicine is not now a science, in the sense in which mathematics, chemistry, and physics are sciences. 4. What

[1]Copyright, 1949, by Ian Stevenson.

makes a science is not the collection of facts, but the organization and generalization of those facts and the formulation and understanding of the general laws which govern them. 5. As President Conant of Harvard has pointed out, the great advances in science have come, not from the collection of new data, but from the development of new concepts. 6. Chemistry, for example, gained more impetus from Dalton's atomic theory than Priestley's discovery of oxygen. 7. The discovery of the periodic table by Mendelyeev enabled him not only to organize the available knowledge of the elements, but to predict the behavior and even the existence of others; it freed him from servitude to a host of isolated and apparently unrelated facts. 8. Medicine will not achieve the stature of a science until the basic laws of health and disease have been disclosed. 9. But the search for these laws has hardly begun. 10. No discipline can claim a greater array of equipment by which its research is carried on, yet none is inferior to medicine in organizing its knowledge into coherent principles.

11. That there do exist underlying principles of medicine, if only we could discover and formulate them, has been a haunting thought with great physicians for centuries. 12. Among the Greeks it was particularly common, and the greatest of Greek physicians, Hippocrates, wrote that "in order to cure the human body it is necessary to have a knowledge of the whole of things." 13. Jerome Cardan, the leading Italian physician of the sixteenth century, wrote that he had discovered "how from a comparison of cures of one member and another, some understanding of the causes of disease and methods of treatment may be deduced." 14. And only twenty-five years ago one of the greatest of modern physicians, Sir James Mackenzie, returned to the same theme.

15. "For the intelligent practice of medicine," wrote Mackenzie, "and the understanding of disease, the simplification of medicine is necessary. . . . 16. I hold that the phenomena which are at present so difficult of comprehension, on account of their number and diversity, are all produced in a few simple ways, and that with their recognition what is now so complex and difficult will become simplified and easy to understand. 17. This means a recognition of principles and a knowledge of their application."

18. Yet what is the situation in medicine today? 19. Each bodily system—if not each individual disease—is handled by specialists ignorant of other fields. 20. The leading textbooks of our time are

mere catalogues of disease states; they rarely offer a generalizing statement which might enable a student to apply the experience he has gained in one disease to the management of other diseases. 21. Even such a standard modern textbook as Osler's *Principles and Practice of Medicine* is essentially an inventory of diseases neatly arranged and classified with the skill of a nurseryman's catalogue. 22. More understanding of the general principles of medicine was shown in the works of Hippocrates written two thousand years ago. 23. Teachers of medicine, almost without exception, are innocent of any hint that their subjects might be amenable to broad principles. 24. At medical meetings and among medical editors the presentation of papers dealing with medical theory is frankly discouraged, and hypotheses are often rejected as "unscientific speculation."

25. If the principles of medicine are today unknown, or known to only a slight extent, this is a direct result of the fact that they are no longer sought. 26. Medicine, in short, has succumbed to the twentieth-century habit of concentrating upon techniques rather than upon the quest for understanding; of thinking that when phenomena have been described they have been explained.

27. This defect tends to be self-perpetuating. 28. For the amount of medical knowledge that has been accumulated is so vast as to be far beyond the capacity of any one man to grasp and use. 29. Each year two large and closely-printed volumes of the *Quarterly Cumulative Index Medicus* display to the alarmed and ignorant physician the *titles alone* of medical books and articles published throughout the world. 30. Only the exceptionally talented and indefatigable specialist can "keep abreast of the times" even in his own field, to say nothing of doing any reflective thinking about the facts he has consumed, or of obtaining knowledge of what is happening in other fields. 31. The judgment of Sir Charles Singer, the English medical historian, is apt: "If from the facts no laws emerge, the facts themselves become an obstacle, not an aid, to scientific advance."

32. Most of this vast and unmanageable array of facts has been produced, not through the development of medicine itself, but through the application to medicine of physics and chemistry. 33. Furthermore, most of it has been produced by means of laboratory experiments, many of them upon animals. 34. These experiments have helped physicians to glimpse the intermediate pathways of disease, but have thrown little light upon the true nature of disease. 35. The pancreas of a dog is removed; the dog thereupon shows

symptoms much like those of *diabetes mellitus;* and that fact leads to the isolation of the pancreatic hormone, insulin, which can thereupon be used to control diabetes. 36. Certainly a great discovery; yet few diabetics develop diabetes as a result of having their pancreas removed; and though we are now able to control the disease with considerable effectiveness, we cannot claim to be much closer to understanding the cause of it than we were fifty years ago.

37. Hundreds of other examples could be cited of laboratory experiments which have taught us much about the intermediate mechanisms of the morbid process, but almost nothing about its primary cause. 38. For whenever man, by experimenting, interferes with nature, he removes himself from nature, whose own experiments are delicate and prolonged, revealing themselves only to the most patient observer. 39. It is only by observing the experiments of nature that we shall learn the secrets of biological life—its success in health and its failure in disease and death. 40. "Man who is the servant of nature," wrote Bacon, "can act and understand no further than he has observed, either in operation or contemplation, of the method and order of nature."

41. Not only have we fallen victim to the fallacies involved in artificial experimentation; we have also become so entranced with technical procedures that we have lost sight of the patient himself, the individual person who is subjected to so many of these laboratory tests. 42. He becomes a "case" of a certain disease. 43. We say that we have seen so many "cases" of pneumonia, forgetting that we have merely seen so many superficially similar, but profoundly different, febrile pulmonary reactions in as many different persons. 44. We have come to consider disease not as "life in altered form," but as a mysterious parasitic entity growing on man like mistletoe on an oak. 45. It is fashionable to smile at the seventeenth-century physician who might record in his account book that he had "seen Peter's wife who lay abed of a fever." 46. We are proud that we have broken down the term "fever" into a great number of entities and can distinguish readily between scarlet fever and typhoid fever. 47. Yet we have well nigh lost sight of the most important item in the seventeenth-century physician's diagnosis, which was "Peter's wife." 48. We have forgotten that the actual number of differential diagnoses is no less than the number of people upon this planet.

49. Thus we have neglected both the similarities among different disease states and the differences among patients with apparently

similar diseases. 50. This is because modern medicine, particularly in its research phases, is almost wholly in the hands of specialists, each treating or investigating one organ or system of organs, and necessarily neglecting the others. 51. One may make great progress in studying the liver by restricting one's attention to that organ alone. 52. But in the human body the liver is not alone; and it cannot be studied completely without knowing about the forces which act upon it from other parts of the body. 53. A study of the liver alone eventually becomes no study of the liver at all. 54. Nor is this the only trouble with such specialization. 55. It overlooks also the fact that the person as a whole is something different from a collection of viscera; the wholeness gives some extra, if indefinable, quality to the individual organs. 56. Today we pay for our knowledge of the parts in ignorance of the whole.

57. By this approach, specialism perpetuates itself in medicine. 58. We have different doctors for asthma, diabetes, cancer, and brain tumors because the knowledge of the specialist in one of these diseases has no bearing on another. 59. Had we a grasp of underlying principles in medicine a physician would feel equally at ease with any of these conditions. 60. Yet the specialist studying one organ or one disease is unable to liberate himself by the detection of principles common to all organs and all diseases. 61. Specialism is a necessary evil of modern medicine but is not a necessary accompaniment of the good medicine of the future.

62. How can we return to a study of the patient as a whole? 63. In the first place, our knowledge of patients must be greatly extended in depth. 64. The physician must know them and their environment hardly less thoroughly than he knows himself and his family. 65. Attempts to do this are frequently discouraged as too time-consuming, but for the student of biological medicine they are essential.

66. Our study must also be prolonged. 67. Physicians of a former generation were able to follow their patients for twenty or thirty years, and in rural areas this is still possible. 68. But in the cities it is more unusual; and in the large urban clinics where medical research is mostly conducted today, patients are rarely followed by one physician for more than a few months or a year. 69. A patient may come back later to the same hospital, but even then he will probably be seen by different specialists in different clinics, and his identity will be dissolved in a large "series" of similar cases.

70. There are three states of ill health. 71. The first is a functional

impairment or misuse which is often impossible to detect and may not be noticed by the patient or his physician; the second brings definite symptoms of illness; the third brings structural changes. 72. At present, patients are rarely seen before the second stage has been reached; more often, not before the third stage. 73. To try to learn about an ailment under such circumstances is something like trying to learn about chess by watching only the last moves of a game between two experts, unaware that the outcome is frequently decided in the first moves.

74. Only if individual physicians can study individual patients over a long period of time, and through all the gradations from health to death, observing carefully the similarities between different disease states and also the dissimilarities between different "cases" of the same disease, will we stand a chance of discovering the laws of medicine.

75. Two British experiments point the way. 76. At the zenith of his career as a consulting cardiologist, Sir James Mackenzie gave up his London practice, went to the small university town of St. Andrews in Scotland, and founded an institute for clinical research.

77. He deliberately chose a small town with a relatively stable population, for he wanted to make a long-term study of disease from its beginnings. 78. When Mackenzie died the project withered without his inspiration, but it had already proved the worth of his ideas.

79. The other British enterprise is the Peckham Experiment,[2] a large health center in London which provides facilities for many kinds of sport and recreation. 80. The only stipulations of membership are that entire families join and that every member must submit to annual health examinations. 81. The medical observers have plentiful chances to watch the members under everyday conditions.

82. The success of these and similar studies lies in the fact, common to all, that they have brought the observers to the people and have not awaited the arrival of the latter at large hospitals. 83. Since the large medical centers are manifestly unsuited for such a study by outlook and location, opportunities for its development must be sought elsewhere. 84. It may be that this research can be accomplished only by the one person who sees his patients in their natural habitat, the general practitioner. 85. "People who have spent their lives observing nature," said Aristotle, "are best qualified to make

[2]Described by Mary Palmer in *Harper's*, May 1947.

hypotheses as to the principles that bring great numbers of facts together."

86. But if I point to the general practitioner as the key to our problem, I do not mean the general practitioner as we have usually known him. 87. The public today tends to regard him as the admirable menial of the profession, the genial and beloved drudge who may be roused in the middle of the night to allay some trivial anxiety but is hardly to be trusted with a serious disease. 88. And it is true that he seldom has a chance to be very useful in the study of disease. 89. For even if he has the inclination for research—which in many cases he lacks—he has neither the time nor the money for it. 90. And he is likely to be out of touch with the university centers of research and training. 91. Some way must be found to combine the general practitioner's breadth of experience with the facilities and influence of the medical schools.

92. Why not a system of fellowships and subsidies to enable young physicians to establish themselves in small towns, with sufficient means to combine medical practice with a far more thorough study of their patients than is now possible? 93. Groups of such doctors could in time take over the entire medical practice in certain communities. 94. They should also have appointments on the staffs of neighboring medical schools, in order to keep these schools in touch with the general problems of ill health.

95. Such an experiment would take time. 96. Meanwhile is it too much to hope that our medical schools and medical journals might awake to the need for actively encouraging inductive thought about medicine, and the search for hypotheses? 97. Indeed there is need for a new medical journal dedicated not to the competitive publication of isolated chips of information, but to the broad understanding of disease.

98. Furthermore, the training required of physicians must be broadened and liberalized. 99. In the past thirty years it has become more and more technical, though not necessarily more scientific. 100. Studies which might humanize the students are jostled aside to make room for courses so restricted in content as to make him, frequently, a sort of scientific barbarian, unaware of the truth of Professor Clark Kennedy's dictum: "In medicine we are bound to deal with human life and experience as a whole, and half the art of medicine is to adopt a reasonable and practical attitude to the unknown."

101. In ancient Greece the doctor was primarily a philosopher and secondarily a physician. 102. He was first a student of nature, and secondly a student of nature perverted by disease. 103. Despite the great technical advances of our day, the future of medicine may well depend upon the training of physicians who will be once more humanists and biologists, as well as chemists and physicists.

B. NOTES

CHAPTER 8 · SECTION A-1 · CHARACTERIZATION

1. Joe Lone Bear

ACTION: 16, 32, 38, 42, 47, 48, 66, 78–79, 88, 117, 124, 134, 182, 269, 286, 369–70, 388, 404, 469, 496, 501, 504–05, 508, 515, 521, 526, 541, 546, 550, 560–63, 588.

SPEECH: 18–22, 67, 89–90, 101, 106–07, 111–14, 125, 133, 183–84, 198–99, 202, 231, 265–67, 270–73, 280–83, 285, 371, 405–09, 460, 461, 466, 478–83, 486, 491–95, 522, 531, 543, 598–601, 607–11.

REPORT OF OTHERS: 15, 91, 139, 143–44, 148–50, 154–55, 156–59, 161–63, 166–67, 366.

REACTION OF OTHERS: 4–8, 24, 44, 45–46, 59, 60–63, 69–70, 71–72, 76, 96–100, 118–23, 224–27, 372–74, 421, 462–68, 470–77, 484–85, 487–90, 497–500, 502–03, 509–12, 514, 523–25, 544–45, 552, 572–79, 612–14, 619–22.

REACTION TO OTHERS: 2–3, 9–10, 11, 17, 36, 37, 50, 52–58, 77, 80, 83–84, 87–88, 388–96, 416, 519, 534–36, 569, 571, 580–82, 615–17.

DESCRIPTION: 1, 6, 42, 134.

EXPOSITION: 1, 31, 35, 65.

PSYCHOLOGICAL ANALYSIS: None.

2. Chief Lone Bear

ACTION: 23, 39, 41, 73, 241, 242–43, 256, 292, 299, 305, 417–20, 514.

SPEECH: 24–30, 244–50, 293–97, 300–04, 318–20, 400–03, 417, 421–47, 453.

REPORT OF OTHERS: 576, 582, 583–87, 596, 604.

REACTION OF OTHERS: 16, 17, 18–22, 31–33, 44–46, 49–51, 53–61, 63, 70, 252–53, 254–55, 257–64, 298, 306–17, 322–25, 326–64.

REACTION TO OTHERS: 23–30, 47, 62, 76, 410–15.

DESCRIPTION: 19.

EXPOSITION: 19.

PSYCHOLOGICAL ANALYSIS: None.

CHAPTER 11 · SECTION A-2

Here are the answers to questions given in Chapter 11.

I. A Very Valuable Quality

1. 6,300 words.
2. Idea: that brains are a very valuable quality in a woman.
3. Suzie's story.
4. To hold her man.
5. The main complication in this story is, of course, Suzie's rival, Elsie: 284. The lesser complications are three—Walters: 148; Tomlison: 217; Burke: 284.
6. Love versus pride.
7. Obstacle: Henry's reluctance to find her a husband.
8. Opponent: Henry.
9. Disaster: Henry's pairing off with Elsie, owing to Burke's interest in Suzie.
10. The decision: to double date with Elsie; the sacrifice: Suzie's pride.
11. Burke and Elsie depart. Henry remains.
12. Suzie brings Henry to his senses and refuses to date Burke.
13. Henry's declaration of love.
14. *Suzie*
    Tags:
    SENSORY: beauty
    SPEECH: "Henry"
    GESTURE: smile
    HABIT OF MIND: direct
    Traits:
    HUMAN OR NATURAL: love for Henry
    TYPICAL: pride

MORAL: self-sacrifice
INDIVIDUAL: intelligence
Function: to get Henry
Weapon: brains

Henry
Tags:
SENSORY: baldish
SPEECH: hesitant
GESTURE: twists his hat
HABIT OF MIND: confused
Traits:
NATURAL: likes girls
TYPICAL: unsuspicious
MORAL: fairness
INDIVIDUAL: changeable
Function: to win a mate
Weapon: the ring

Elsie
Tags:
SENSORY: plump, blue eyes, colored underwear, bleached hair,
looks like badly wrapped package
SPEECH: simpers
GESTURE: hanging onto men's arms
HABIT OF MIND: vulgar
Traits:
NATURAL: likes men
TYPICAL: snobbish
MORAL: selfish
INDIVIDUAL: fickle
Function: to rival Suzie
Weapon: fancy clothes

Bessie
Tags:
SENSORY: young-looking
SPEECH: "My goodness"
GESTURE: swings her legs
HABIT OF MIND: vague
Traits:
NATURAL: loves people
TYPICAL: motherly
MORAL: sympathetic
INDIVIDUAL: unimaginative

Function: to be hostess
Weapon: cordiality and food

Tomlison
Tags:
   SENSORY: plump, checked suit, balding, 40 years old
   SPEECH: "Yes"
   GESTURE: looks at Bessie
   HABIT OF MIND: eager
Traits:
   NATURAL: loves food and comfort
   TYPICAL: middle-aged viewpoint
   MORAL: honest
   INDIVIDUAL: frank
Function: to woo Bessie
Weapon: appreciation

Walters
Tags:
   SENSORY: brown eyes and curly hair
   SPEECH: compliments
   GESTURE: smiles and looks at Janet
   HABIT OF MIND: enthusiastic
Traits:
   NATURAL: susceptible
   TYPICAL: enthusiastic
   MORAL: determined
   INDIVIDUAL: independent
Function: to woo Janet
Weapon: dating Janet

Burke
Tags:
   SENSORY: tall, dark, young, shiny hair
   GESTURE: shows teeth
   SPEECH: wolf whistle
   HABIT OF MIND: direct
Traits:
   NATURAL: likes women
   TYPICAL: a fast worker
   MORAL: suspicious
   INDIVIDUAL: fresh
Function: to rival Henry
Weapon: his admiration of Suzie

Janet
Tags:
    SENSORY: fair hair, pretty
    GESTURE: lips quiver
    SPEECH: sings
    HABIT OF MIND: eager
Traits:
    NATURAL: likes Walters
    TYPICAL: trusting
    MORAL: honest
    INDIVIDUAL: frank
Function: to win Walters
Weapon: youth and beauty

Laurie
Tags:
    SENSORY: 15 and large for age
    SPEECH: teen-age idioms
    GESTURE: eating
    HABIT OF MIND: youthful
Traits:
    NATURAL: loves food
    TYPICAL: curious
    MORAL: loyal
    INDIVIDUAL: admiration for brains
Function: to tell the story
Weapon: her tongue
15. Setting:
    Time: April, 20.
    Place: Sunset, Oklahoma, 33.
    Social Atmosphere: home, 7–19.
16. Scenes: 10–31, 34–46, 47–54, 69–72, 76–130, 137–50, 165–81, 192–200, 245–49, 255–69, 312–35, 336–43, 344–60, 361–72.
    Incidents: 42–46, 47–54, 55–60, 183–87, 189–91, 203–13, 214–25, 250–55, 270–76, 277–80, 281–89, 299–303, 304–06, 307–10.
    Happenings: 373–74.
17. Transitions:
    a. place to place: 134, 182, 235, 373.
    b. time to time: 6, 133, 203, 211, 226, 270, 277, 290.
    c. mood to mood: 14, 35, 42, 53.
18. Types of discourse: all. Dialogue, narrative, dramatic action, description, in that order.
19. The title is admirably suited to the mood and theme of this dainty, deft, appealing, and drolly humorous story.

20. Any adult who enjoys a good story of middle-class family life and young love—whether male or female. The reader of smooth-paper fiction.

21. The editor bought this story, one may suppose, because it is amusing, with contrasting, likable characters, a sound theme, a familiar problem, significant form, a novel solution, good scenes, and a regular plot.

II. Devices of the Beginning

22. Bait: 1–5.
23. a. Suzie: 1.
    b. Henry: 4, 10, 16, 19.
    c. Elsie: 46.
    d. Bessie: 7.
    e. Walters: 148–50.
    f. Tomlison: 216–19.
    g. Burke: 284–86.
    h. Janet: 7.
    i. Laurie: 3.
24. See sentences: (a) 4, (b) 40.
25. Solution is hinted at in sentence 119.
26. Emotional Tone: 7, 10, 15, 49, 57.
27. Idea.
28. Plants: 1, 2, 3, 4, 5, 6, 7, 8, 9, 10, 11, 12, 15, 18, 19, 20, 46, 57, 58, 61–62, 63, 75, 92, 98, 103, 122, 133, 137, 144, 148, 154, 158, 163, 165, 183, 189, 216, 219, 228, 291, 296, 317–19, 351.
    Pointers: 4, 11, 19, 26–28, 31, 34, 40, 41, 43, 48, 58, 59, 76, 82, 89, 94, 112, 117, 119, 120, 124, 128, 129, 141, 148, 155, 157, 160, 166, 170–72, 184, 186, 194, 198, 201, 202, 207, 210, 214, 221, 230, 235, 241, 248, 252, 255, 259, 267, 272, 274, 275, 280, 283, 297, 305, 326, 337, 340, 345, 358, 361, 362, 367, 370–72, 375, 376, 378.
29. Flashbacks: 10, 18, 109–10, 126.
30. Infatuation and Love.
31. Promise of Conflict: 1, 4, 28, 35, 40, 46, 77, 89, 117, 124.
32. Characterizations:
    Suzie
    ACTION: 7, 12, 34, 35, 76, 97, 104, 110, 114, 123, 137, 148, 155, 157, 206, 259, 271, 276, 280, 282, 306, 310, 327, 343, 346, 350, 356, 358.
    SPEECH: 16, 23, 37, 42, 77, 78, 88, 89, 108, 112, 115, 124, 126, 127, 128, 131, 167, 168, 206, 250, 272, 274, 275, 279, 280, 328, 343, 347, 356, 359, 360, 367, 368, 369.

REACTION TO OTHERS: 16, 22, 30, 31, 183, 191, 210, 221, 301.

OTHERS' REACTION TO HER: 1, 2, 4, 10, 13, 14, 15, 23, 29, 44, 45, 60, 73, 74, 79, 80, 81, 82, 90, 91, 95, 96, 101, 113, 117, 118, 119, 120, 121, 125, 129, 169, 175, 181, 186, 196, 208, 214, 239, 240, 241, 244, 265, 273, 293, 304, 305, 307, 308, 309, 311, 312, 313, 314, 315, 321, 322, 323, 330, 331, 335, 341, 342, 348, 350, 351, 353, 357, 361, 362, 363, 370, 371, 372, 378, 379.

REPORT OF OTHERS: 122, 152, 153, 154, 215, 243, 245, 246, 325, 326, 332, 333, 334.

DESCRIPTION: 2, 8, 104, 166, 225, 302, 303.

EXPOSITION: 9, 19, 169, 186, 224.

PSYCHOLOGICAL ANALYSIS: 0.

Henry

ACTION: 4, 10, 14, 29, 31, 32, 39, 51, 60, 71, 73, 76, 113, 130, 132, 163, 191, 197, 201, 261, 267, 287, 307, 312, 343, 350, 357, 361, 370.

SPEECH: 13, 21, 22, 26, 27, 28, 40, 46, 69, 72, 74, 81, 95, 120, 202, 245, 246, 258, 294, 336, 341, 344, 345, 348, 351, 353, 354, 355, 362, 363.

REACTION TO OTHERS: 12, 44, 45, 50, 51, 79, 80, 81, 90, 91, 96, 101, 107, 125, 129, 169, 192, 218, 257, 268, 320, 324.

REACTION OF OTHERS: 16, 19, 22, 23, 25, 30, 33, 35, 41, 42, 53, 70, 75, 83, 87, 97, 114, 121, 129, 193, 199, 231, 248, 255, 259, 279, 280, 297, 308, 327, 343, 352, 356, 358, 367.

REPORT OF OTHERS: 11, 77, 78, 116, 117, 119, 123, 162, 165, 168, 267, 312, 325, 326, 333, 339, 346.

DESCRIPTION: 14, 15, 96, 293.

EXPOSITION: 18, 284.

PSYCHOLOGICAL ANALYSIS: 0.

Elsie

ACTION: 297, 320, 333, 340, 342.

SPEECH: 297, 333, 339.

REACTION TO OTHERS: 320.

REACTION OF OTHERS: 124, 280, 282, 284, 320, 335, 337, 338.

REPORT OF OTHERS: 48, 49, 57, 59, 74, 84, 85, 86, 87, 92, 93, 94, 106, 259, 317, 318, 319.

DESCRIPTION: 291, 296.

EXPOSITION: 46, 298.

PSYCHOLOGICAL ANALYSIS: 0.

Bessie:

ACTION: 7, 10, 32, 41, 47, 61, 64, 75, 83, 137, 141, 179, 190, 229, 263, 287, 290.

SPEECH: 48, 49, 65, 68, 69, 70, 82, 85, 86, 121, 122, 131, 141, 144, 145, 162, 182, 232, 254, 262.

REACTION TO OTHERS: 41, 53, 75, 84, 169, 240, 241, 244, 261, 270, 273.

REACTION OF OTHERS: 33, 41, 50, 51, 52, 71, 87, 132, 186, 229, 230, 231, 235, 247, 248, 267, 271, 272, 376.

REPORT OF OTHERS: 63, 163, 184, 243, 249, 250, 251, 252, 253, 266.

DESCRIPTION: 7, 62, 187.

EXPOSITION: 54, 66, 67.

PSYCHOLOGICAL ANALYSIS: 147, 164.

Walters:

ACTION: 161, 211, 226, 290.

SPEECH: 161, 170, 189, 190, 200.

REACTION TO OTHERS: 170, 171, 172, 176, 177, 181, 190, 191, 193, 194, 195, 199.

REACTION OF OTHERS: 159, 160, 183, 192, 197, 203, 204, 205, 206, 208.

REPORT OF OTHERS: 148, 149, 150, 162, 165, 168, 184, 207, 210.

DESCRIPTION: 159.

EXPOSITION: 158.

PSYCHOLOGICAL ANALYSIS: 0.

Tomlison

ACTION: 226, 242, 263, 265, 267, 288.

SPEECH: 249, 253, 255, 256, 267.

REACTION TO OTHERS: 229, 230, 231, 235, 239, 243, 247, 248, 252, 265.

REACTION OF OTHERS: 221, 232, 234, 240, 247, 251, 254, 268, 270, 271, 272, 273.

REPORT OF OTHERS: 219, 220, 241.

DESCRIPTION: 228, 269.

EXPOSITION: 217, 227.

PSYCHOLOGICAL ANALYSIS: 0.

Burke

ACTION: 304, 308, 309, 342.

SPEECH: 305, 309, 322, 323.

REACTION TO OTHERS: 304, 316, 321, 330, 331, 332, 335.

REACTION OF OTHERS: 306, 310, 324, 327.

REPORT OF OTHERS: 311, 312, 313, 314, 315.

DESCRIPTION: 291.

EXPOSITION: 285, 286.

PSYCHOLOGICAL ANALYSIS: 0.

Janet

ACTION: 7, 55, 56, 67, 137, 186, 211, 288, 290.

SPEECH: 57, 59, 92, 93, 94, 204, 214, 215.

REACTION TO OTHERS: 203, 205, 208.

REACTION OF OTHERS: 170, 171, 172, 181, 190, 191, 194, 195, 201, 206, 210, 226.

REPORT OF OTHERS: 63, 145, 183, 207, 274–75.

DESCRIPTION: 7, 58, 187, 213.

EXPOSITION: 376.

PSYCHOLOGICAL ANALYSIS: 0.

Laurie

ACTION: 7, 10, 32, 133, 139, 142, 151, 186, 188, 191, 212, 291, 373, 377.

SPEECH: all through, and 136, 140, 143, 146, 152, 154, 281.

REACTION TO OTHERS: 1, 2, 5, 14, 15, 134, 135, 146, 153, 154, 159, 169, 287, 289, 378, 379.

REACTION OF OTHERS: 63, 373, 376.

REPORT OF OTHERS: 0.

DESCRIPTION: 0.

EXPOSITION: 3, 375.

PSYCHOLOGICAL ANALYSIS: 0.

33. These sentences refer to main Furtherances and Hindrances of the chief sufferer (Suzie):

F.	H.	F.	H.	F.	H.	F.	H.
19	22	117	123	246	247	310	317
23	28	124	131	255	258	326	
34	40	165–83	192	259		328–29	
43	46	196	197	266	268	336	
48–49	53	206–10		274	277	351	
57–59	71–74	213	219		283	361	
77	82	221	226		298	369	
	84–87	230	231	302		370	
96		239		306	307		

34. Repetitions:

"My mother Bessie": 7, 10, 11, 13, 41, 47, 61, 87, 147, 186, 271, 273.

"My sister Suzie": 7, 8.

"My sister Janet": 7, 55, 137, 186.

"Betty Grable": 25, 30.

"Our cat Violet": 7, 44, 45, 138, 160.

"Henry knew him": 150, 286.

"Big strapping girls": 63, 243.

Repetition of Henry bringing the men, trying to make them like Suzie and so convincing himself that she is desirable.

35. Overlapping paragraphs: 7–8, 12–13, 36–37, 70–71, 177–78, 209–10, etc. What others can you find?

36. The Gimmick is the engagement ring: 19, 123, 124, 361, 364, 365.

37. Dialogue at Cross-Purposes: 48, 49, 52–53, 57, 59, 65, 70, 74–75, 78–81, 82–86, 92–94, 95–100, 119–22, 127–31, 143–45, 162–63, 253–54, etc.

38. Device for corroboration: 33, 48, 49, 54, 74, 106, 107, 121, 160.

39. Because the narrator of this story is a child, the methods of indicating the speaker here are few and simple.

    a. Proper name of speaker coupled with verb, as "said Suzie": 13, 16, 21, 22, 23, 26, 30, 36, 37, 52, 65, 72, 87, 92, 95, 98, 100, etc.

    b. Proper name with facial expression, as in 44–46.

    c. Proper name of speaker with gestures (pantomime) added, as in 26–29, 35, 39–40, 57, 80, 82, 123, 148, 165, etc.

    d. Appearance of character only: 58–59.

    e. Personal pronoun with verb, as "she said": 47–48, 126, 141, 144, 171, 173, etc.

    f. Name or personal pronoun with verb and manner of speech added: 42, 53, 68, 75, 77, 104, 107, 108, 121, 146, 162, 163, etc.

40. Discovery and Reversal: 2–4, 40–46, 78–120, 198, 268, 312, 324, 335, 351, 361.

41. The "color" in this story is that of a nice home in a small Oklahoma town. It may be found in sentences 7, 8, 10, 18, 30, 33, 48, 55, 70, 105, 110, 126, 137, 138, 182.

42. Fact Feeling: As each reader must decide for himself which word or phrase best expresses fact or feeling, no absolute check is possible on question 42.

III. Devices of the End

43. Implications are found in these sentences: 25, 49, 59, 65, 85, 89, 111, 119, 162, 171, 184, 267, 280, 338, 343.

Answers to questions concerning the novelette *Eva? Caroline?*

1. 12,000 words.
2. Character.
3. Roger's.
4. To identify Caroline.
5. Mistaken identity.
6. Pride versus loyalty.
7. The tombstone.
8. His family.
9. Loss of his wife.
10. He goes loyally to the grave with wreath. He sacrifices his desire for Caroline, believing her to be Eva.
11. He finds proof that Eva is dead.
12. By recognizing Smedley.
13. Reunion with Caroline (sacrifice of his pride implied).
14. *Roger Marsh*
    Tags:
    SENSORY: narrow, pale, granite face
    SPEECH: direct
    GESTURE: uncompromising gaze
    HABIT OF MIND: stubborn
    Traits:
    NATURAL: love for his wife
    TYPICAL: well-bred
    MORAL: loyalty
    INDIVIDUAL: hates notoriety
    Function: to solve the puzzle
    Weapon: reason

    Inspector Whipple
    Tags:
    SENSORY: 0
    SPEECH: crisp
    GESTURE: puzzled stare
    HABIT OF MIND: searching
    Traits:
    NATURAL: 0
    TYPICAL: curiosity

MORAL: persistence
INDIVIDUAL: amiable
Function: to inform Roger
Weapon: knowledge of case

Caroline
Tags:
  SENSORY: gray hair, hard face, brown eyes, jaded
  SPEECH: bitter
  GESTURE: tense
  HABIT OF MIND: defiant
Traits:
  NATURAL: loves husband
  TYPICAL: competent
  MORAL: honest
  INDIVIDUAL: independent
Function: to win security
Weapon: the truth

Dr. Cawfield
Tags:
  SENSORY: gray, old
  SPEECH: snorts
  GESTURE: 0
  HABIT OF MIND: testy
Traits:
  NATURAL: 0
  TYPICAL: professional man
  MORAL: integrity
  INDIVIDUAL: impatient
Function: to pooh-pooh Caroline's story
Weapon: positive talk

Effie Foster
Tags:
  SENSORY: middle-aged, plump, blond
  SPEECH: she soothes
  GESTURE: gapes, flushes
  HABIT OF MIND: cheerful
Traits:
  NATURAL: 0
  TYPICAL: confident
  MORAL: unfeeling
  INDIVIDUAL: obliging

Function: to waver
Weapon: uncertainty

Aunt Harriet
Tags:
    SENSORY: tall and gray
    SPEECH: flippant; "fiddle-sticks"
    GESTURE: eyes glitter
    HABIT OF MIND: "gullible"
Traits:
    NATURAL: 0
    TYPICAL: outspoken
    MORAL: sympathetic
    INDIVIDUAL: sentimental
Function: to help Caroline
Weapon: her money and her evidence

Evelyn
Tags:
    SENSORY: same as Caroline's
    SPEECH: same as Caroline's
    GESTURE: holds Roger's hand
    HABIT OF MIND: trying to get something for nothing
Traits:
    NATURAL: loves comfort
    TYPICAL: confidence woman
    MORAL: liar
    INDIVIDUAL: weak
Function: to escape the law
Weapon: likeness to Caroline

Duke Smedley
Tags:
    SENSORY: good-looking, well-dressed
    SPEECH: "Hello, Eva"
    GESTURE: hat off
    HABIT OF MIND: sophisticated
Traits:
    NATURAL: loves Eva
    TYPICAL: decisive
    MORAL: swindler
    INDIVIDUAL: sentimental
Function: to identify Caroline
Weapon: flowers on Eva's grave

Lucile Dutton
Tags:
  SENSORY: too beautiful
  SPEECH: reassuring
  GESTURE: lunches with Roger
  HABIT OF MIND: watchful
Traits:
  NATURAL: likes Roger
  TYPICAL: efficient
  MORAL: obedient
  INDIVIDUAL: sympathetic
Function: to help Roger
Weapon: her errands

Police matron
Tags:
  SENSORY: uniform
  SPEECH: quiet
  GESTURE: walks in
  HABIT OF MIND: methodical
Traits:
  NATURAL: motherly
  TYPICAL: firm
  MORAL: sympathetic
  INDIVIDUAL: outspoken
Function: to rebuke Effie
Weapon: her tongue

Uncle Carey
Tags:
  SENSORY: short and bald
  SPEECH: explosive
  GESTURE: running away
  HABIT OF MIND: retiring
Traits:
  NATURAL: 0
  TYPICAL: positiveness
  MORAL: pride
  INDIVIDUAL: fears publicity
Function: to make Roger keep out of it
Weapon: plan to run away

Leslie Paxton
Tags:
  SENSORY: 0

SPEECH: matter-of-fact
GESTURE: carries papers
HABIT OF MIND: legal
Traits:
NATURAL: 0
TYPICAL: reluctant
MORAL: loyal
INDIVIDUAL: efficient
Function: to report to Roger
Weapon: voice

Colonel Cox
Tags:
SENSORY: big, rubicund, loose tweed suit
SPEECH: profane
GESTURE: claps shoulder
HABIT OF MIND: open
Traits:
NATURAL: loves wife
TYPICAL: hearty
MORAL: genial
INDIVIDUAL: memory
Function: to embarrass Roger
Weapon: memory

15. The present time. Places: Maryland, Seattle, and Detroit. Social atmosphere: aristocratic.
16. The number of scenes, incidents, and happenings are as follows:
    a. Scenes: 1–101, 110–90, 191–258, 259–69, 275–325, 279–407, 408–97, 520–39, 540–76, 604–17, 640–64, 684–89, 690–714, 743–57, 758–75, 886–908, 911–33.
    b. Incidents: 105–09, 326–40, 356–58, 360–64, 365–69, 369–72, 498–507, 508–10, 578–603, 618–30, 631–39, 723–29, 730–34, 735–42, 844–48, 849–51, 853–63.
    c. Happenings: 954–71.
17. Transitions:
    a. From place to place: 270, 501, 507, 511, 518, 548, 578, 618, 690, 712, 715, 743, 776, 846, 852, 863, 886, 906, 937, 940.
    b. From time to time: 110, 270, 511, 604, 612, 618, 640, 665, 676, 680, 718, 743, 785, 794, 814, 821, 846, 885, 934.
18. Types of discourse: Dialogue, Narrative, Exposition, Action, Description.
19. Title: It states the problem clearly.
20. Reader of smooth-paper women's magazines.
21. It is entertaining and well written.

282

22. Bait: 1–9.
23. Characters introduced and identified:
    a. Roger Marsh: 1
    b. Inspector Whipple: 3
    c. Caroline: 10
    d. Dr. Cawfield: 28
    e. Effie Foster: 61
    f. Aunt Harriet: 263–64
    g. Evelyn (Eva Lang): 47
    h. Duke Smedley: 215
    i. Lucile Dutton: 450
    j. Police matron: 328
    k. Uncle Carey: 262
    l. Leslie Paxton: 540
    m. Colonel Cox: 889–96
    n. Defense counsel: 721
24. Roger's main problem is to identify Caroline.
    a. 5
    b. 54
25. Solution hinted at: 10.
26. Emotional tone set: 1–6.
27. Omitted here.
28. Principal Plants: 2, 4, 9, 12–13, 15, 18, 25–29, 34, 41, 47, 54, 71, 143–49, 162, 185, 552, 800, 816, 924, 956.
    Principal Pointers: 10, 34, 37, 54, 74, 80, 94, 95, 101, 116, 221, 250, 254, 303, 324, 386, 510, 539, 571, 599, 611, 742, 768, 823, 899, 910, 932, 969, 975.
29. Flashbacks: 20–46, 48–53, 69–72, 111–13, 122–24, 131–33, 137–41, 143–48, 159–82, 193–98, 201–38, 280–84, 299, 431–32, 592–95, 748–50, 753–54, 837–38.
30. Omit.
31. Promise of conflict: 6, 15, 18, 38, 55, 63, 79, 89, 113, 151, 165, 190, 245, 254, 262, 263, 358, 371, 383, 539, 611, 742.
32. Characterization:

a. *Roger Marsh*
ACTION: 6, 40, 242, 327, 356, 509, 516, 567, 586, 620, 843, 848, 937, 971.
SPEECH: 10, 19, 25–28, 239, 335, 358, 389, 396, 488, 513–15, 539, 567, 570, 744, 897.
REACTION OF OTHERS: 17, 332, 617, 619, 856, 895.

REACTION TO OTHERS: 1, 6, 18, 38, 55, 63, 75, 88, 150, 239, 358, 383, 397, 403, 404–07, 458, 642, 669, 677, 713, 870, 883, 890, 970.
REPORT OF OTHERS: 399, 400, 401, 402, 751, 754–57, 838.
EXPOSITION: 12–16.
DESCRIPTION: 15, 16, 243.
PSYCHOLOGICAL ANALYSIS: 99, 270, 275, 589–603, 788–843, 883–85, 906–10, 932, 940–49, 957–70.

b. *Inspector.Whipple*
ACTION: 17, 276, 458.
SPEECH: 191–99, 322.
REACTION OF OTHERS: 0.
REACTION TO OTHERS: 73, 373.
REPORT OF OTHERS: 2.
EXPOSITION: 0.
DESCRIPTION: 0.
PSYCHOLOGICAL ANALYSIS: 0.

c. *Caroline*
ACTION: 58, 203, 219, 379, 380, 410, 449, 494, 498, 699, 719, 800, 816, 873.
SPEECH: 54, 149, 219, 381, 382, 386, 395, 399, 436, 448, 456, 497, 611.
REACTION OF OTHERS: 153, 226, 227, 419, 437–38, 442–45.
REACTION TO OTHERS: 383, 385, 390, 393, 397, 398, 422, 700, 881.
REPORT OF OTHERS: 53, 71–72, 78, 119, 125, 138–41, 205, 218, 246, 254, 358, 362, 369, 384, 503, 553, 607, 630, 647, 649, 701, 728, 926.
EXPOSITION: 241, 446, 484.
DESCRIPTION: 341–55, 868–71.
PSYCHOLOGICAL ANALYSIS: 0.

d. *Dr. Cawfield*
ACTION: 28, 41, 360.
SPEECH: 112, 113, 252, 260, 489, 769.
REACTION OF OTHERS: 0.
REACTION TO OTHERS: 393, 499.
REPORT OF OTHERS: 763.
EXPOSITION: 0.
DESCRIPTION: 111.
PSYCHOLOGICAL ANALYSIS: 0.

e. *Effie Foster*
ACTION: 366.
SPEECH: 115, 255–58.
REACTION OF OTHERS: 0.

REACTION TO OTHERS: 367, 368–69, 372, 392.
REPORT OF OTHERS: 0.
EXPOSITION: 0.
DESCRIPTION: 114.
PSYCHOLOGICAL ANALYSIS: 0.

f. *Aunt Harriet*
ACTION: 573, 775.
SPEECH: 525–29, 574, 742, 745, 774.
REACTION OF OTHERS: 0.
REACTION TO OTHERS: 0.
REPORT OF OTHERS: 532, 771, 914.
EXPOSITION: 0.
DESCRIPTION: 522, 530.
PSYCHOLOGICAL ANALYSIS: 0.

g. *Evelyn (Eva Lang)*
ACTION: 131, 595.
SPEECH: 132, 594.
REACTION OF OTHERS: 173.
REACTION TO OTHERS: 0.
REPORT OF OTHERS: 2, 48, 143–48, 160–63, 168.
EXPOSITION: 0.
DESCRIPTION: 0.
PSYCHOLOGICAL ANALYSIS: 0.

h. *Duke Smedley*
ACTION: 217, 218, 220, 222, 232, 234, 951–52, 955–56.
SPEECH: 218, 221, 223, 235.
REACTION OF OTHERS: 0.
REACTION TO OTHERS: 224.
REPORT OF OTHERS: 52, 294–99, 302–07, 310, 635, 650, 652–55, 812, 957.
EXPOSITION: 215, 216.
DESCRIPTION: 309.
PSYCHOLOGICAL ANALYSIS: 0.

i. *Lucile Dutton*
ACTION: 622.
SPEECH: 0.
REACTION OF OTHERS: 0.
REACTION TO OTHERS: 619, 621, 879.
REPORT OF OTHERS: 0.

EXPOSITION: 0.
DESCRIPTION: 0.
PSYCHOLOGICAL ANALYSIS: 0.

j. *Police matron*
ACTION: 318, 370.
SPEECH: 329–30, 371.
REACTION OF OTHERS: 0.
REACTION TO OTHERS: 0.
REPORT OF OTHERS: 0.
EXPOSITION: 0.
DESCRIPTION: 0.
PSYCHOLOGICAL ANALYSIS: 0.

k. *Uncle Carey*
ACTION: 519, 572.
SPEECH: 520, 524, 532, 534, 536.
REACTION OF OTHERS: 0.
REACTION TO OTHERS: 0.
REPORT OF OTHERS: 0.
EXPOSITION: 0.
DESCRIPTION: 521.
PSYCHOLOGICAL ANALYSIS: 0.

l. *Leslie Paxton*
ACTION: 576.
SPEECH: 542, 577, 767.
REACTION OF OTHERS: 0.
REACTION TO OTHERS: 0.
REPORT OF OTHERS: 763, 764.
EXPOSITION: 0.
DESCRIPTION: 0.
PSYCHOLOGICAL ANALYSIS: 0.

m. *Colonel Cox*
ACTION: 886.
SPEECH: 887, 888, 892.
REACTION OF OTHERS: 0.
REACTION TO OTHERS: 0.
REPORT OF OTHERS: 0.
EXPOSITION: 0.
DESCRIPTION: 889.
PSYCHOLOGICAL ANALYSIS: 0.

33. Furtherances and Hindrances.

H.	F.	H.	F.	H.	F.	H.	F.
1–2	8	190	191–98	395		646	647–49
11–16		201–23		414	420	650	664
20–22	33–37	239			437	677	
43	44	247	254	438	450	682	688
46	54	258	260	458	476	704	710
59–64	68–75	266		480		718	728–42
77	86	271	272	488	497	744	751
88–90	97		280	499	510	753	763
101–04	109	290	298	524	525		787
110–23	124–25	300	315	537	538	800	
128	137	358	369		553		816–20
	146	370	370	555	567		822–24
151–58	163		380	568	575		828
165	173	383	386	589	611	838–39	
	181–82	388		623–30	639	859	866–71
183	189						

34. Repetitions:
Repetitions are not important here. Such as there are, are incremental: the granite in Roger's face, the pride of his family, the scene at the grave, etc.

35. Overlapping paragraphs: 8–9, 43–45, 54–55, 59–60, 72–74, 79–80, 98–99, 189–90, 190–91, 500–01.

36. Gimmick: the tombstone.

37. Dialogue at Cross-Purposes:
The best examples of this are in the passages between Roger and Caroline: 381–84, 385–90, 394–407, 448–58, 494–98, 690–708. Also in 886–99.

38. Corroboration:
This type of story requires constant use of devices for corroboration. 21–22, 41, 46, 74, 124, 134, 188, 241, 362–64, 368, 490, 510, 587, 646–50, 682, 733, 742, 881, 899, 932, 969.

39. Indicating the speaker: no check is required on so easy a question.

40. Discovery and Reversal:
The principal examples here are: 74–75, 79–80, 88–89, 97–101, 123–26, 163–65, 189–90, 251–53, 271–72.

41. Color: This is not a color story. Omitted.

42. Fact Feeling: No check is possible here.

43. Implications: 164, 189, 325, 383, 393, 422, 497, 510, 700, 856, 930, 960.

CHAPTER 11 · SECTION A-4

1. In analyzing the short short story *Bargain Hunters,* you have prepared answers to the twenty-one questions propounded in Work Program 11, Section A-2. Check your answers by the information given below.

2. a. The Twist is found in sentence 88;

   b. The Back-twist is found in sentences 98–100.

3. Main fictional devices found in *Bargain Hunters* are (as indicated by sentence numbers):

   Setting the Stage: 1, 4, 5, 13, 36–37.

   Introduction of Characters: 2, 38.

   Bait: 1–6.

   Promise of Conflict: 15.

   Main Problem Stated: 16.

   Main Complication: 59.

   Hint at Solution: 61.

   Set Emotional Tone: 1, 2.

   Type of Story Indicated: Idea.

   Plants: 1, 2, 3, 5, 6, 7, 12, 13.

   Pointers: 3, 5, 15, 16, 24, 33.

   Hero's Two Conflicting Emotions: 16.

   Characterization:

   BY ACTION: 2, 17, 18, 20, 22, 23, 30, 41, 44, 45, 46, 47, 48, 54, 56, 57–59, 62, 63–69, 73, 76, 78, 80, 82, 86, 87, 89, 90, 92, 93, 94, 95, 96, 98, 99.

   BY SPEECH: 3–6, 21, 24–25, 31–35, 42, 43, 49–53, 55, 70, 71, 72, 74, 77, 83, 88, 97, 98.

   BY REACTION OF OTHERS: 61.

   BY REACTION TO OTHERS: 0.

   BY REPORT OF OTHERS: 25, 33, 35, 49–52, 79, 81, 83, 84.

   BY EXPOSITION: 9–12, 14, 15, 60, 75, 91, 100.

   BY DESCRIPTION: 15, 19, 39–40, 92.

   BY PSYCHOLOGICAL ANALYSIS: 16.

   Flashback: 10–11.

   Color: 7, 8, 13, 26–29, 36, 37, 38, 42, 49.

   Transition:

   FROM PLACE TO PLACE: 7, 8, 27, 30, 36, 89, 92.

   FROM TIME TO TIME: 9–10, 11–12, 92.

   FROM MOOD TO MOOD: 86–89.

I. Answers to Queries in Work Program 12.

1. How to save yourself with presence of mind.
2. Unselfishness.
3. A conflict (1–3) and a query (4–9).
4. The problem is made personal to the reader (1–7).
5. A series of examples, each with its story and moral (12–99).
6. Six.
7. Cases: I (10–33, story; moral, 34–39); II (39–45, story; moral, 47–48); III (49–62, story; moral, 63–64); IV (65–72, story; moral implied); V (various story; moral implied, 73–87); VI (query or puzzle, 88; story, 89–99; moral implied).
8. You, too, may save yourself by unselfishness.
9. 1,750 words.
10. Hey, 21; You, 45; See, 12–99; So implied at end, but suggested in 34–39; 47–48; 63–64.
11. Hey: 21 words.
    You: 45 words.
    See: Case I, 400
    Case II, 200
    Case III, 175
    Case IV, 175
    Case V, 200
    Case VI, 534
    So: Implied.
12. Dialogue in the proportion: 35: 99.
13. Exposition: 20: 99.
14. Description: 10: 99.
15. Narrative: 44: 99.
16. The question is too simple to require a check here. Persons referred to: 22.
17. Four scenes: I (14–33); II (39–45); III (50–62); IV (66–72). Two incidents: I (74–82); II (90–99).
18. Characters: 22.
19. Emotional tone: serious.
20. Yes.
21. Yes.
22. Yes.

23. The editorial policy of the *Reader's Digest* prefers the reassuring note; the author is a skilled professional; the idea is a practical and at the same time a moral one.
24. Short and popular.
25. Practical.

II. a. Corroboration by Conjuring with Great Names.
   b. 1–7.
   c. All of those given in Chapter 12.
   d. All.

CHAPTER 13 · SECTION A-6

I. Answers to questions (found in Work Program 12) on the Article "Why Medicine Is Not a Science."
   1. Medicine.
   2. Critical.
   3. Hey: promise to debunk.
   4. You: danger to health.
   5. See: sad state of medical affairs.
   6. Three main cases; ten sub-cases.
   7. See: Case I: Medicine not science: **1–11.**
      a. Authorities cited: 11–17.
      Case II: Faults of medical science: 18–61.
      a. ignorance: 18–24.
      b. inertia: 25–31.
      c. too many facts: 32–36.
      d. too much lab: 37–40.
      e. patient forgotten: 41–48.
      f. false methods: 49–56.
      g. can't see patient for his organs: 36–61.
      Case III: Difficulty in finding remedy: 62–82.
      a. is remedy possible?: 62–65.
      b. doctors don't know patients: 66–69.
      c. states of disease: 70–73.
      d. doctors must know patients well: 73–75.
      e. examples given: 75–83.
   8. So: Remedy—a streamlined general practitioner: 84–103.
   9. 4,000 words.

10. & 11. Hey: 45 words
         You: 15 words
         See: 3,265 words
         So: 735 words
12. Dialogue (i.e., words in quotation marks): 175.
13. Exposition: 3,825 words.
14. Description: none.
15. Narrative: none.
16. You cannot miss the answer to this.
17. Scenes: none.
18. Characters: none.
19. Emotional tone: serious.
20. Yes.
21. Yes.
22. Yes.
23. Because it offers expert opinion on a controversial subject now much discussed.
24. Formal Essay.
25. Formal Essay.

II. No answers to questions 2 and 4 of Work Program 13 are given here. By this time you should be able to recognize every device we have studied. We repeat, there are no secrets in the craft of writing. Every device ever used is right there under your nose set down on the page in black and white. Once you learn to see them, they are all at your command.

Bibliography

Anderson, Maxwell. *The Bases of Artistic Creation.* Rutgers University Press, 1942.

Bailey, Robeson. *Techniques in Article-Writing.* D. Appleton-Century, New York, 1947.

Brennecke, Ernest, Jr., & Clarke, Donald L. *Magazine Article Writing.* Macmillan, New York, 1930.

Brickell, Herschel. *Writers on Writing.* Doubleday, New York, 1949.

Burack, A. S. *The Writer's Handbook.* The Writer, Inc., Boston, 1947.

Butcher, L. H. (Editor). *Aristotle's Theory of Poetry and Fine Art.* Macmillan, New York, 1923.

Campbell, Walter S. ("Stanley Vestal"). *Professional Writing.* Macmillan, New York, 1938.

——. *Writing Magazine Fiction.* Doubleday, New York, 1940.

——. *Writing Non-Fiction.* The Writer, Inc., Boston, 1944.

Drewry, John E. *Book Reviewing.* The Writer, Inc., Boston, 1945.

Foster-Harris. *The Basic Formulas of Fiction.* University of Oklahoma Press, Norman, Okla., 1944.

Gundell, Glenn. *Writing—From Idea to Printed Page.* Doubleday, New York, 1949.

Hillyer, Robert. *First Principles of Verse.* The Writer, Inc., Boston, 1938.

Hoffman, Arthur Sullivant. *Fundamentals of Fiction Writing.* Bobbs-Merrill, Indianapolis, 1922.

Kamerman, Sylvia E. *Writing the Short Short Story*. The Writer, Inc., Boston, 1946.

Mathieu, Aron M. and Jones, Ruth A. (Editors). *The Writer's Market*. Writer's Digest, Cincinnati, 1949. Reissued annually.

Mirrielees, Edith Ronald. *Story Writing*. The Writer, Inc., Boston, 1947.

Nicholson, Margaret. *A Manual of Copyright Practice*. Oxford University Press, New York, 1945.

Polti, Georges. *The Thirty-six Dramatic Situations*. J. K. Reeve, Franklin, O., 1924.

Quiller-Couch, M. A., Sir Arthur. *On the Art of Writing*. G. P. Putnam's Sons, New York, 1916.

Reynolds, Paul R. *The Writing Trade*. The Writer, Inc., Boston, 1949.

Rinehart, Mary Roberts. *Writing Is Work*. The Writer, Inc., Boston, 1939.

Roberts, Kenneth. *I Wanted to Write*. Doubleday, New York, 1949.

Saintsbury, George. *A History of English Prosody from the 12th Century to the Present Day*. 3 vols. Macmillan, New York, 1923.

Salzman, Maurice. *Plagiarism*. Parker, Stone & Baird, Los Angeles, 1931.

Stevenson, R. L. "On Some Technical Elements of Style in Literature." Chapter I in *Essays in the Art of Writing*, Chatto & Windus, London, 1910.

To Government Writers: How Does Your Writing Read? Superintendent of Documents, U. S. Government Printing Office, Washington, D.C., 1946. (Price 5¢)

Wharton, Mrs. Edith. *The Writing of Fiction*. Scribner, New York, 1925.

Whitney, Phyllis A. *Writing Juvenile Fiction*. The Writer, Inc., Boston, 1947.

Wittenberg, Philip. *The Protection and Marketing of Literary Property*. Messner, New York, 1937.

Young, James N. *101 Plots Used and Abused*. The Writers, Inc., Boston, 1946.

Index

297

299